BEFORE INTELLIGENCE FAILED

MARK WILKINSON

Before Intelligence Failed

*British Secret Intelligence on Chemical
and Biological Weapons in the Soviet Union,
South Africa and Libya*

HURST & COMPANY, LONDON

First published in the United Kingdom in 2018 by
C. Hurst & Co. (Publishers) Ltd.,
41 Great Russell Street, London, WC1B 3PL
© Mark Wilkinson, 2018
All rights reserved.

Printed in India

Distributed in the United States, Canada and Latin America by
Oxford University Press, 198 Madison Avenue, New York,
NY 10016, United States of America.

The right of Mark Wilkinson to be identified as the author
of this publication is asserted by him in accordance with the
Copyright, Designs and Patents Act, 1988.

A Cataloguing-in-Publication data record for this book
is available from the British Library.

ISBN: 9781849043007

This book is printed using paper from registered sustainable
and managed sources.

www.hurstpublishers.com

CONTENTS

INTRODUCTION

OBSESSING ON INTELLIGENCE

Bond, Blair and Iraq

One can only ponder whether the British public would have had the same apparent fascination with secret intelligence were it not for James Bond. Beginning in the early 1950s, over a period of thirteen years, Ian Fleming wrote eleven novels and two short stories detailing the exploits of MI6's most famous agent. Over 100 million copies of these books have been sold around the world and the Bond film franchise has now made 33 films, grossing over $11.5 billion to date.[1] One explanation for this success may well be that these stories offered the average citizen a fictional glimpse into the world of UK secret intelligence. Yet reality often stands a long way from fiction. The true exploits of the UK intelligence agencies largely remain carefully hidden from view to this day.

Although the 1994 UK Intelligence Services Act acknowledged the existence of the Secret Intelligence Service (as did various Intelligence and Security Committee Reports), the absence of any UK government comment or acknowledgement of the actual activities of the Secret Intelligence Service—at least until the Labour government of Tony Blair in 2003—may simply have added to the popularity of Bond.[2] Indeed, within the UK, criminal statutes actively attempted to prevent any intelligence officer from making unauthorised disclosures about the activities of their employers and their agents. Despite this legislation, more intelligence services personnel in the UK have provided public accounts of their activities than anywhere else in the world. Perhaps these revelations simply reflect desires on the part of their authors to mimic the Ian Fleming spy franchise. Numerous disclosures to date have been presented through the publication of biographical memoirs, fictionalised accounts and classic spy fiction.[3] It should therefore be of no surprise that when controversy erupted over the use of secret intelligence by the Blair government to make a case for war against Iraq in 2003, both the public and media appetite in the UK for detailed disclosures was, at times, frenzied. The British interest in all things espionage was once again re-ignited.

The lead-up to the commitment of British troops to play their part in the invasion of Iraq in 2003 is perhaps one of the most controversial and emotive events in recent British political history. Portrayed by some authors as a contemptuous and perverse abuse of both the British democratic system as well as the British people, the after-effects of the invasion continue to be felt around the world to this day.[4] Public demands to be told about the role of intelligence in contributing to the seemingly unstoppable path to war have remained key political issues ever since. One explanation for this interest in the activities of the UK intelligence services lies not in the fact that intelligence was used by policy-makers in the lead-up to war, but that intelligence was publicly released in order to make that case for war. This was a profound and significant act. British Prime Minister Tony Blair therefore not only acknowledged that intelligence had played a key role in his decision to go to war; he also made that intelligence publicly available. Never before had a British Prime Minister felt the need to justify a policy through publishing intelligence in the public domain.

Iraq and beyond: shining bright lights in dark corners

For a long period of time, the UK intelligence agencies had enjoyed a rather comfortable existence. Free from the ties of any kind of legislative framework, they were normally able to ply their trades safe in the knowledge that an almost impenetrable shroud of secrecy would protect them from any demand for explanation or accountability for their actions. Even in the face of significant revelations, such as the exposure of Soviet spies like Kim Philby, public demands for information or explanation rarely managed to penetrate the barriers of secrecy surrounding the agencies. Few people on the outside had any real knowledge of what the intelligence agencies actually did, and even fewer were privy to how they did it. Journalists and academics speculated about what intelligence priorities and targets might be, but once again, in anything other than areas of historical interest, few were probably in a position where they could really relay anything but speculation, which was often more at home with the dramatic plot lines of Ian Fleming than with reality.

Despite a range of legislation coming into force through the 1980s and 1990s, giving at least a degree of parliamentary scrutiny and oversight, the world that the intelligence agencies inhabited appeared to be entirely different from the one in which other governmental departments resided.[5] In 1994, with the passing of the Intelligence Services Act, it was acknowledged that the intelligence agencies did collect information on a range of targets such as terrorism and weapons proliferation. It was also acknowledged that they engaged in a certain amount of disruption, though few details were offered. Certainly, if one considers the core tenets of UK foreign policy, intelligence must obviously have a key role to play in the support of that foreign policy; but once again, the details of what that role was and how it functioned remained a mystery.[6] Indeed, in the context of nuclear, chemical and biological weapons, top of the list of current UK strategic priorities, there was little, if any, public visibility of the role of intelligence in the achievement of this policy goal.[7] By 2003, all this was about to change.

The 2003 Iraq War drew the spotlight of publicity onto the intelligence agencies like never before, making household names of terms such as Weapons of Mass Destruction (WMDs), the Joint Intelligence Committee (JIC) and the Secret Intelligence Service (MI6/SIS). Four inquiries in the space of sixteen months each in turn began to shine their spotlights into some of the darkest and most secretive and sensitive corners of central government. The terms of reference of these inquiries whetted the appetite of even the most cynical observer; for example, by promising to 'investigate the accuracy of intelligence ... and to examine any discrepancies between [that and] the intelligence gathered, evaluated and used by the Government [in the lead-up to the 2003 Iraq War]'.[8] These inquiries also appeared to make unprecedented promises—promises that must surely result in the lifting of the veil of secrecy shrouding the relationship between UK foreign policy and intelligence, even if only in the context of WMD?

Yet any observer sitting patiently waiting for these inquiries to provide details of some of central government's most intimate secrets was soon to be disappointed. The two inquiries that, at least on the face of it, were capable of providing the most fascinating insights into intelligence to the public skilfully sidestepped several key issues. Lord Hutton, investigating the events leading up to the death of the biological weapons expert Dr David Kelly, stated that he had interpreted his terms of reference to mean that intelligence fell squarely outside his area of concern. Given that Dr Kelly apparently committed suicide because of his supposed role in questioning the accuracy of intelligence used by the government in making its case for war, this seems a surprising omission. In his own words, Lord Hutton stated, 'I concluded that such a wide import, which would involve the consideration of a wide range of evidence, is not one which falls within my terms of reference.'[9] Where many commentators considered Hutton's remit to miss the fundamental point—that weapons of mass destruction simply did not exist in Iraq in 2003—for others this inquiry was simply too much.[10] One author described Hutton's approach as akin to that of a DIY bodger applying whitewash: carefully and thinly in order to last years.[11]

Lord Butler, whose focus was entirely on how intelligence had been used by the government in the lead-up to the Iraq War, also managed to avoid looking at what must surely appear to the casual observer to be one of the key issues: the actual interface between intelligence and foreign policy decision-making. Instead he presented an overview of how pre-war intelligence might be seen to have had holes in it, conducting the inquiry entirely in private and hence doing little to expose anything to public scrutiny. At the same time Butler refused to hold any one individual to account—indeed, he even absolved individuals such as John Scarlett, Chairman of the JIC, of any responsibility—a surprising development given the criticisms that Butler levelled at the involvement of Scarlett in the preparation of public dossiers. When one considers that Scarlett went on to become 'C', the Controller of SIS, these issues seem even more surprising—perhaps even whiffing of cronyism. The central point of interest when considering the apparent omissions of the Butler and Hutton Reports therefore appears to relate to what the exact role of intelligence should be in informing foreign policy.

One key aspect of the relationship between intelligence and foreign policy relates to the accuracy of intelligence. For the Blair government, Iraq was a vital issue, and also one on which the Prime Minister was apparently prepared to stake his personal reputation. Though Lord Butler reported at length on the apparently unreliable nature of some intelligence relating to Iraqi WMD (intelligence that the government was apparently only too happy to use through the release of dossiers to the public to convince them of the case for war),[12] nowhere does he discuss whether the willingness of the government to accept low quality intelligence was directly related to an already developed foreign policy course of action, itself centred around a desire to go to war, that the government might have intended to pursue. This is perhaps all the more surprising given that some commentators have observed that at times 'the Butler report found intelligence evidence stretched to the outer limits'.[13] So, in the case of Iraq, did the UK government use intelligence of a 'lower' quality than it would normally consider acceptable? Furthermore, does this suggest that foreign policy decisions relating to the war had already been taken and the available intelligence simply cut to fit?

The issue of what might constitute a 'proper' relationship between intelligence and foreign policy is an important question. Indeed, in 2003, the UK's main accountability and oversight body, the ISC (Intelligence and Security Committee), promised to inquire into precisely this matter. By 2004 these issues had proved to be too complex and taxing, prompting the parliamentarians to back away.[14] One more question would seem fundamental to any investigation into the UK intelligence establishment: did the lead-up to the 2003 Iraq War actually reflect a fundamental shift in the manner in which intelligence interacted with foreign policy in the UK?

Identifying the problems, asking the questions

Despite the fact that British troops left Iraq in 2009, there remains an insatiable appetite on the part of the British public and media to establish 'what really happened' in the run-up to the war. It is perhaps ironic that the publication of intelligence by the government in order to justify the path to war in 2003 has actually served to expose the entire process of policy-making to unprecedented demands for public scrutiny. The Chilcot Inquiry, opened in June 2009, has examined a wide range of intelligence-related evidence specific to a whole plethora of issues linked to the UK involvement in the Iraq War.[15] Throughout its work, the Chilcot Inquiry was regularly paralysed amidst debate and discussion with several government departments relating to requests to obtain currently classified material for use by the Inquiry.[16] When it did finally report, some commentators described it as 'a damning verdict on the decision by former Prime Minister Tony Blair to commit British troops to the US led invasion of Iraq in 2006'.[17] So it is in the morass of the Iraq War that the genesis of this book can be found.

This book will focus on two overarching questions. Firstly, if, as many commentators have stated, the Iraq War represented a failure of intelligence, was this simply reflective of a track record of failure by the UK intelligence agencies in other circumstances? Secondly, was Blair merely following a well-established procedure for considering intelligence when formulating and enacting foreign policy, or had something more fundamental changed? In short, this book aims to establish exactly what happened before intelligence failed, by offering the reader a narrow but detailed glimpse into the activities of the UK intelligence agencies.

In order to assist the reader, it is important to identify clearly at the outset exactly what this book is and is not. It must be stressed that this book is entirely concerned with UK intelligence. Whilst it is acknowledged that foreign intelligence services may at times have had significant roles in aspects of the case studies presented in this book, their roles will not be examined in any detail. Next, the reader should note that this book is focused entirely on the intelligence relating to chemical and biological weapons (CBW). Whilst it is acknowledged that these weapons are in many cases extremely complex and technical, this book will not attempt to engage with the science behind them or their delivery systems. Finally, this book will not offer comparative case studies. The case studies contained within this book aim to deliver an account of the role of UK intelligence in very specific circumstances. Drawn largely from interviews with individuals central to UK CBW-related intelligence, this book makes full use of personal viewpoints, opinions and experiences in constructing its narrative. It is fully acknowledged that research of this type exposes itself to methodological criticism, but these debates should not detract from the detailed and extensive first-person accounts of the key individuals central to the UK intelligence and foreign policy nexus. At the very least, the personal views of senior individuals at the heart of the UK intelligence establishment represent crucial accounts of significant foreign policy matters. There are significant benefits to using a study of other cases prior to the Iraq War to gain a better understanding of how the UK intelligence agencies work in support of foreign policy: in the first instance, they could be used to provide an assessment of whether the Blair government's use of intelligence in the lead-up to the Iraq War reflected a departure from how policy-makers had previously used intelligence. Perhaps more significantly, a detailed assessment of the role of intelligence in the formulation and enactment of UK foreign policy is much needed by those interested in the study of intelligence, foreign policy and political decision-making.

Drawing commentary and opinion from a range of senior figures—from former chairs of the JIC to senior intelligence officers—this book will provide information never before recorded in open literature relating to intelligence and foreign policy interaction. The results of this research allow this book to deliver a candid and forthright analysis of CBW intelligence and foreign policy decision-making in the UK from 1970 to 2004. It is perhaps not surprising that a research project of this type, drawing from interviews of senior persons directly involved in CBW intelligence, has not been conducted before. The secrecy so central to protecting the activities of the UK intelligence agencies has previously shielded the individuals representing a range of organisations that would need to be interviewed in order to complete a study of this type. However, the aftermath of the Iraq War and the exposure of the apparent politicisation of intelligence in the lead-up to it appear to have encouraged many senior civil servants, perhaps at the end of their careers, to be more willing to comment and share their views on matters that, in the past, they might not have been prepared to divulge.[18]

Selecting the case studies: what and how

The Butler Report is an important document for the purposes of this book because it identifies candidate countries for case studies. Specifically, Butler names several states that have in the past been the focus of UK intelligence efforts: there are three pages on the A. Q. Khan network and nuclear weapons proliferation, two pages on Libya and its WMD programmes, and an additional two pages on Iran and North Korea—largely relating to nuclear weapons.[19] Butler also more subtly acknowledges another case of intelligence successfully informing foreign policy—that of the Soviet Union.[20] It might be considered surprising, however, that in a document that heralds the success of intelligence in countering WMD proliferation, solid detail on any case (with the exception of Iraq) is almost entirely lacking. This might suggest that specific examples of intelligence activities in this field were either limited, or there was no desire for a formal acknowledgment of the role of intelligence in those other cases.

Whilst most information relating to the role of UK intelligence in countering WMD proliferation relates to nuclear weapons, it is known from many other sources that there is more detailed information available relating to examples of states that, like Iraq, have attempted to develop (and have indeed developed) chemical and biological weapons.[21] The majority of this information is specific to the chemical and biological weapons programmes of the Soviet Union, followed some way behind by those of South Africa. Furthermore, there is a limited amount of information available relating to the Libyan chemical weapons programme. In the context of this book, these three cases, with the exception of Iraq (of which ample information and controversy already exists), therefore represent useful examples of cases where accessible evidence exists in both public and private domains relating to UK intelligence involvement in chemical and biological weapon counter-proliferation efforts in support of UK foreign policy. In addition, the Soviet Union, South Africa and Libya also represent examples of state-run chemical and/or biological weapons programmes where UK intelligence involvement might be considered to have been successful. Within this context, an intelligence success might be seen to be these states either admitting to having cheated on arms control treaties, or giving up those same weapons in order to be bound by the terms of arms control treaties in the future. Either way, these actions would ultimately meet long-standing UK weapon counter-proliferation objectives and might therefore be considered successes.

A broad framework can therefore be used to examine three examples of state-based weapons programmes as cases that are broadly similar: each is framed within the context of chemical and biological weapon proliferation; each was the focus of UK intelligence efforts; and each has a demonstrable UK foreign policy linkage. This book will therefore present these three cases studies, spanning a thirty-year period before the 2003 Iraq War, in order to establish the role of the UK intelligence agencies within them, and how that intelligence interacted with UK foreign policy to achieve an end state that could be judged as either a success or failure. When the results of this analysis are subsequently placed against what is known about the role of UK intelligence and its relationship with foreign policy relating to the 2003 Iraq War, this book will deliver the answers to the two overarching questions posed earlier.

This book will be presented in eight chapters. This first chapter has provided an introduction to the research to be presented in this book. The second chapter will consider broader issues in order to equip the reader with a clearer understanding of intelligence within a UK context. Specifically, this chapter will ask what intelligence is, what it means, how it works and what the relationship between intelligence (the producer) and the policy-maker (the consumer) might look like. The third chapter will move on to put intelligence into a context specific to chemical and biological weapons: first it will examine the apparatus of UK intelligence, then it will look at the intelligence impact on UK foreign policy, before examining UK policies towards chemical and biological weapon proliferation. This chapter will also analyse the controversy surrounding the use of intelligence by the Blair government in the lead-up to the 2003 Iraq War, identifying the common features of this interaction, drawing from the Chilcot Inquiry Report. The fourth and fifth chapters will present the Soviet case study; the sixth chapter will present the South African case study; and the seventh chapter will present the Libyan case study. The eighth and final chapter will then return to Iraq, asking whether the results of the case studies suggest that the 2003 Iraq War marked a change in the way that intelligence was used to support foreign policy decision-making. This chapter will also link to theoretical discussions, in particular relating to wider contemporary debates concerning the conceptualisation of intelligence. The book will then deliver its concluding remarks.

2

INSIGHTS INTO INTELLIGENCE

Given that this book will focus entirely on the UK intelligence establishment, it is appropriate to establish at the outset an understanding of intelligence based upon UK perspectives. The seemingly simple process of defining intelligence has in the past proved to be challenging; indeed, many believe that definitions of intelligence are, at best, ambiguous.[1] Definitional issues are further compounded by the application of cultural and contextual resonances. There is therefore a danger that resulting definitions may be 'a Mercator Projection of intelligence; one that looks at the problem primarily within the context of East–West confrontations centred in Europe'.[2]

The only UK government (and therefore official) publication to deal specifically with intelligence structures and organisation, *National Intelligence Machinery*, rather surprisingly saves for its annex a definition of only secret intelligence. Secret intelligence is described as 'information acquired against the wishes and (generally) without the knowledge of the originators or possessors'.[3] The official UK definition of intelligence therefore specifies one defining feature: covert action.[4] Yet this seems problematic, as many other definitions of intelligence activities reflect a range of activities. From a UK perspective, what intelligence means, how it works and where it has its effect are key questions if one is to understand how it might ultimately succeed, or else indeed fail its masters.

What it means: defining intelligence

It could be argued that the UK government definition of intelligence is surprisingly narrow and restrictive—in particular for seeing the entire realm of intelligence activities as something that is, by definition, secret. There are, however, several far broader definitions. Some see intelligence as being 'about information: who needs or wants certain information, where that information is to come from, the manner in which it is to be handled, who will learn about it, and how it is going to be used are all central to a discussion of intelligence'.[5] This view is clearly very broad, and unlike the UK definition, it does not explicitly state that intelligence is necessarily secret. But *National Intelligence Machinery* is rather clearer about what intelligence is for: to 'inform policy-making' in support of national security policies.[6] Implicit in this relationship, it would seem that there must be a direct link between UK secret intelligence and foreign policy. It would also seem reasonable to expect this link to be intended to further the likelihood of the success of intelligence supporting the delivery of foreign policy objectives. But, and here lies the rub, if 'intelligence must take into account the nature of a country's foreign policy priorities and perceived threats, the problem is, these are frequently unclear'.[7]

The UK government definition of intelligence also raises other issues. Perhaps most significantly, it omits to mention that intelligence by definition is not secret. Furthermore, it implies that intelligence obtained about a state will always be against that state's wishes. This may perhaps be indicative of the normal manner in which the UK secret intelligence agencies might be expected to operate—through covert action within foreign states. This would also appear to suggest that, at least in a UK view, intelligence is needed primarily in support of the national interest, not necessarily in the interests of the international system as a whole. Is it not possible that UK intelligence could support, for example, internal political changes within a state, encouraging transparency and openness? Certainly, in the context of weapons counter-proliferation, stopping the attempts of a state such as Iraq to attain a WMD capability (or indeed detecting them breaching arms control treaty obligations), intelligence could be considered to be representative of activities primarily for the good of the entire international system, and only secondly—if at all—in the purely selfish interests of that state. This view of intelligence—as a 'force for good'—is one that perhaps suggests the great potential of intelligence spreading beyond the military:

> Like the benefactions of knowledge, of which it is a form, the benefactions of intelligence touch all humankind. In war, intelligence shortens the struggle, sparing gold and blood. In peace, it reduces uncertainty and so relaxes tensions among states, helping to stabilize the international system. These are the ultimate human goods of intelligence; these are the ways this servant of war brings peace to man.[8]

There is perhaps some value in briefly examining other definitions of intelligence; after all, the definition of intelligence seemingly favoured by the UK government is not necessarily a universally accepted one. Some see intelligence as 'a kind of knowledge', 'the type of organisation which produces the knowledge', and 'the activity pursued by the intelligence organisation'—in other words, product, institution and process.[9] With this view, intelligence might therefore be based upon a set of organisations with that name (the intelligence services): intelligence is what they do, and intelligence knowledge what they produce.[10] Others develop definitions of intelligence by considering what intelligence is for: its primary function being to give warning of the hostile plans, military or political, of other nations, but also to supply the information on which policy can be based.[11]

Intelligence might also refer to 'information relevant to a government's formulating and implementing policy to further its national security interests and to deal with threats to those interests'.[12] Perhaps this view also begins to match the previously stated view of the UK government, aside from the fact that the UK government provides its view within a secret context. Some definitions of intelligence even break away from politico-military considerations, suggesting that the characteristics of society have radically changed due to the processes associated with globalisation. Particularly in the West, 'intelligence remains a quintessentially modern institution, albeit one that is operating at the cutting edge of postmodernity in seeking to understand contemporary societal, political, economic and technological change'.[13]

In the context of purpose, intelligence is not only about information for the sake of information. Intelligence can be considered to be 'information that has been processed, evaluated and distilled into a form that fulfils some useful purpose ... to inform policy'.[14] This suggests that intelligence is a kind of knowledge obtained for the purpose of assisting action. The role of intelligence agencies can therefore be seen to be central to a fundamentally simple sequence of actions: to gather information from secret (or open) sources from which to draw knowledge (i.e. process in some way), in order to pass it to the government in order to inform policy-making processes. This clearly suggests that intelligence could be seen to be a tool of foreign policy-making. Quite simply then, the product resulting from the processing of information is intelligence.[15] And it is intelligence that, when provided to policy-makers, can inform and support decisions being made.

How it works: the cycle of intelligence activities

Whilst it might be considered that the intelligence process is pragmatic, not doctrinal, if there is one process within the field of intelligence that might be considered to have a doctrinal element, it is the intelligence cycle.[16] This cycle represents a process through which user requirements and priorities can be applied by the intelligence agencies in order to meet a stated policy-maker's requirement.[17] Furthermore, it assists in the understanding of the intelligence processes taking place, from an initial requirement being identified and tasking being made, through to a fully analysed product being delivered.[18]

The intelligence cycle has been described as a 'traditional model', showing how a question posed by a customer (as a requirement) is defined as an intelligence problem.[19] Implicit in this cycle is the fact that policy-makers, as intelligence customers, provide some sort of guidance (in the form of questions) to intelligence agencies in order for them to begin their work.[20] This does rather assume a relationship whereby policy-makers are already focused, for whatever reason, on an issue or problem, and furthermore that they have already identified the requirement for additional and specific information. Yet this relationship could be problematic: it suggests that the role of the intelligence agencies in drawing the attention of policy-makers to previously unknown problems is potentially of lesser importance than supporting them by providing information relating to problems on which, for whatever reason, they are already focused.

The assumptions presented thus far suggest that intelligence agencies normally carry out work that has been clearly articulated to them. This also implies that policy-makers will generally want information in support of decisions they are about to make, or in order to prove the validity of decisions or policies that have already been made. However, if this describes the relationship between intelligence agencies and policy-makers, it also raises questions over the independence of the intelligence process. Perhaps most significantly, one must consider whether and why a policy-maker would task intelligence agencies to gather information that might ultimately either prove them wrong, or prevent them from carrying out a particular desired course of action. This type of relationship would also suggest that there was no place for proactive intelligence activities carried out on the initiative of individual officers, because the cycle would seem to be, by definition, reactive to the wishes of policy-makers. One must consider whether the first step of the intelligence cycle should relate to attempts to fill specific knowledge gaps, not carry out work generated by policy-makers simply to support their individual desires.[21]

Any conceptual model of intelligence that requires initiation by a customer therefore seems to be at least in part flawed: intelligence processes seem to be entirely reactive to the needs of the policy-maker. This is a problem, because most of the time an effective intelligence capability simply cannot be directed by policy. By the time policy knows what it actually needs to know, it is usually too late for intelligence to respond by developing new sources or cranking up its analytic capacity. As a result, the essence of intelligence should surely be in anticipating what policy will want in the future: building collection and understanding for what it thinks will top the agenda, based on what hints it can glean from policy.[22] So, because intelligence must observe an unlimited range of sources, the initiative for tasking simply cannot lie entirely with the customer. Yet here lies another problem with the traditional intelligence cycle: whilst 'questions that go unasked by policy are not likely to be answered by intelligence ... if intelligence does provide the answers without being asked, those answers are not likely to be heard by policy'.[23] Additionally, the 'points in the policy process when policy is interested in intelligence or information are [therefore] out of phase with the points where intelligence has something to offer'.[24]

It is perhaps for these reasons that Sir David Omand has proposed a 'new' intelligence cycle. This cycle is characterised by networked user interaction allowing for anticipation at strategic, operational and tactical levels.[25] Omand's proposed model appears to address many of the problems that might be considered inherent in the traditional cycle: as has been strongly argued by other authors, in many contemporary examples of intelligence failure, the fault lies not with the analysts but directly with the model they are asked to follow. Surely intelligence in the twenty-first century must be aggressive and intuitive, yet policy-relevant?[26] Asking the right question at the right time must be a key part of intelligence success—something that may be very difficult under the traditional, customer-driven, cyclical model of intelligence. As the rest of this book will show, this simple observation is a highly significant factor when attempting to address criticisms of the relationship between policy-makers and the UK intelligence agencies in the lead-up to the 2003 Iraq War.

The next two steps in the intelligence cycle reflect the processes of collecting and collating data, then evaluating its credibility and reliability. This part of the intelligence cycle would seem to be a reactive process, entirely dependent on the correct and timely tasking by the customer (or policy-maker) to begin the process of gathering intelligence. Understanding the intelligence cycle in this way once more raises several issues. Firstly, and perhaps most significantly, is the fact that intelligence on a specific subject—especially within the realm of WMD proliferation—may take years to collect. To suggest that intelligence agencies can simply produce information at the request, and perhaps whim, of policy-makers would seem entirely unrealistic. Intelligence networks and contacts may take years to cultivate through the lengthy development of analytical projects that might take years to produce—analysis that policy-makers are actually able to act upon confidently.

Traditionally, analysis has been the sole responsibility of the specialist intelligence analyst: material that has been gathered is turned from information into finished intelligence that can be passed to the policy-maker in order to satisfy their requirements.[27] Analysis does not necessarily require the collection of new information, as in most intelligence agencies there will already be large volumes of intelligence material from a variety of sources that might be usable in meeting new requirements.[28] It has been argued that for this reason intelligence managers may be considered the real drivers of the intelligence collection process, as only they are able to identify what information is actually required in order to answer specific questions.[29] Yet structural and managerial issues associated with intelligence agencies may also impact on this process. Information that does not fit the 'party line', or reliance on politically influenced and motivated intelligence managers might prevent or affect the passage of untarnished intelligence product to policy-makers.

An examination of the intelligence cycle as applied within the UK might therefore be considered to present a rather curious example of how the analytical process may actually lie outside the intelligence process. 'Assessment is viewed in the UK as a government function and not specifically as an intelligence function.'[30] As a result, analysis (or assessment) might be seen to be the 'least appreciated and least addressed aspect of the intelligence process'.[31] The implications of this—a situation where a separate agency or department might analyse product collected by another department—are potentially quite serious. One key risk might be the politicisation of intelligence products. The manner in which a political case was constructed to commit UK forces to fight in the 2003 Iraq War would, at least when taken at face value, seem to be a striking example of a range of issues associated with political influences on the intelligence cycle. It has been observed that 'what one person regards as sharpening analysis can easily be seen by another as politicising it'.[32] Related to this is perhaps the problem of analysis being selective, providing product purely to support a particular policy change or course of action. The extent to which governmental IT has enabled policy-makers to reach down into multi-level secure databases of intelligence has, in effect, allowed them to become their own DIY analysts. This trend might continue to be accentuated in the future.

When analysis is complete, the finished intelligence is distributed to the customer. This does not reflect the end of the intelligence process: as a cycle, it is implicit that one rotation of the cycle will feed back into the next. This may be through input from either the customer or the intelligence manager in the form of statements of new needs, definition of new requirements, or through making amendments to existing intelligence programmes in order to improve effectiveness or efficiency.[33] The feedback process is therefore an important part of the intelligence cycle. After all, the product given to customers may be incomplete or unreliable, in particular if analysis is based upon single or limited sources. Feedback may force the subsequent development of both HUMINT (human intelligence) networks as well as the development of technical equipment for SIGINT (signals intelligence), and as a result it should perhaps be considered to be a driver of the entire intelligence cycle.

There are other issues arising from an evaluation of the intelligence cycle besides those considered above. The first and most general observation of the intelligence cycle is that it creates a conceptual gap between the participants—in particular the customer and the intelligence officer. It has been argued that intelligence is a non-linear process; yet, in particular within large organisations, the separation of participants often forces intelligence to be seen as a linear one.[34] Where the intelligence cycle might be seen to be representative of the structure and function of the intelligence community, it does not necessarily describe the intelligence processes at play within it.[35] In particular, when one considers the issues related to examining how intelligence might impact on foreign policy, there is no apparent process through which the intelligence cycle can be assessed in terms of its functional value. Indeed, separation between the customer and the intelligence community—in particular when considered within the context of secrecy—suggests that compartmentalisation and differing governmental departmental agendas are a major obstacle to the integration of intelligence within the normal apparatus of policy-making. The traditional intelligence cycle certainly does not seem to allow for, or consider, wider informal networks, the impact of individuals or organisations (agency and structure) or, in cases of intelligence failures, the identification of where and why failure might have occurred.[36] As a result, it has been argued that intelligence should be seen as a target-centric process. Here, all stakeholders in the intelligence community as well as in the customer organisation should create a shared view of the target in order that participants can extract the elements they need, identify resources and make appropriate taskings in order to create a more accurate process through which the intelligence process can operate.[37] This view enjoys something of a consensus within academic literature. Intelligence 'pushing' could be seen to be vital in large-scale intelligence production processes in order to optimise demand and approval from customers.[38]

If the intelligence cycle is considered to separate and limit interaction between producers and consumers, the reasons that might explain this are significant. Most often cited in explaining this separation is that separation helps to promote objectivity.[39] Whilst it may assist objectivity within an intelligence organisation if work is carried out separated from those responsible for decision-making, one cannot simply assume that intelligence will be used to assist decision-making in the manner an analyst might have intended. As has already been discussed, policy-makers may want intelligence to support a decision that has already been made, or they may not agree with what it tells them. This point seems to raise a whole host of potential problems in considering the producer and consumer relationship. Significantly, it assumes that there is always an expert present within the intelligence community to obtain the required information and then provide analysis—but this may not be the case. Even if an appropriately skilled individual does exist, they may not be senior enough or highly regarded enough either within their own organisation or by others involved in the decision-making process to have the credibility required to drive their product effectively into the decision-making process. Even factors such as inter-personal disputes within departments could therefore conceivably be responsible for product not being submitted upwards to individuals with the power to influence decision-making and thus 'good' intelligence being neglected or ignored.

There are a number of issues that have been considered so far which appear to suggest the need to conceptualise a 'new' intelligence cycle: firstly, organisations must have processes in place that allow resources to flow freely, drawing on appropriately skilled individuals regardless of where they work; secondly, individuals should be automatically allocated to taskings that demand specific specialisms and skill sets; thirdly, organisations must encourage new and novel approaches; and finally, there must be a process through which the producer and consumer are linked up.[40] Through a consideration of these issues it is possible to conceptualise an alternative model for the relationship between consumers, producers, analysts and collection assets. Key to this model is the removal of separation between all elements found in the traditional intelligence cycle. The work of Omand relating to the 'new' intelligence cycle certainly appears to address some of the problems and issues raised here.[41]

Although this section is aimed at a brief consideration of the traditional intelligence cycle, it does also perhaps go some way to proposing the development of an alternative model of intelligence. This new model might be considered to differ from the traditional intelligence cycle in several key ways. First, the separation between customer and producer might be removed. Through this, the intelligence community could perhaps improve its understanding of the actual requirements of the customer. Next, organisational changes within both the government and the intelligence machinery could be made to ensure that both the correct and appropriately knowledgeable individuals are employed on the most suitable taskings—at an extreme, the traditional model could be seen at present to be structurally flawed because of the way in which product is filtered through layers of bureaucracy. Finally, the problems related to agency and structure within intelligence organisations and their customers might be considered and addressed, for it is here that key explanations for intelligence being ignored or wrongly interpreted might be found.

Intelligence effect: the consumer and producer relationship

There are two main theories of intelligence relating to the relationship between producers and consumers: those of Sherman Kent and those of William Casey. Both theories go some way towards providing a more intellectual basis to the issues raised thus far. Whilst both these theories describe the processes leading to intelligence effect, each has its own peculiarities that will now be considered.

The theory of the intelligence consumer and producer relationship proposed by Sherman Kent is based on the underpinning premise that effective intelligence must be independent. For Kent, recognised as one of the founding fathers of the contemporary intelligence community within the US, analysis was the most critical component of finished product.[42] For Kent, centralised intelligence analysis was a defining feature of any conceptualisations of intelligence. This feature was all-important because in general terms intelligence organisations found that gathering scarce information was very expensive. As a result, that information was often considered authoritative when analysed by organisations with recognised credentials.[43] Kent often expressed his concern that analysis must be carefully segregated from policy-making processes: 'too much mixing it up in policy-making circles would cause intelligence officers to become policy advocates, and hence lose their credibility as objective judges of world trends'.[44] For Kent, the producer and consumer relationship essentially represented the producer as a kind of pseudo-academic, focusing his efforts purely on research and subsequent analysis. This view probably reflected his own background in later life as a university academic. For Kent, the 'truth' could, with enough effort, normally be obtained through research guided by a systematic method—intelligence, for this very reason, did not have to be secret.[45]

Kent also believed that intelligence managers and analysts should be entirely free to set intelligence requirements, deciding on their own which projects would best suit the needs of the consumer. He argued that this approach guarded against the politicisation of intelligence, because it created both procedural as well as physical barriers that prevented policy-makers as consumers from influencing both the questions posed as well as the answers provided through finished product.[46] For one who saw intelligence as an almost entirely intellectual exercise, this view of the producer and consumer relationship provided for significant intellectual independence within the intelligence community within any guidelines implicit in the tasks given.

The model proposed by Kent essentially represents 'a grand bargain between policy makers and intelligence professionals ... the intelligence community is master of its own house, but analysts and intelligence managers must avoid becoming embroiled in political decisions or commenting publicly or even privately on current policy or political issues'.[47] This approach is not without associated problems. Firstly, Kent was criticised for neglecting to consider the influence of factors such as economics, variables and other uncertainties in intelligence analysis.[48] This could potentially result in analysis being restricted by the very separation from policy-makers that this model proclaimed was so important. It was also argued that Kent's model could generate suspicion between policy-makers and the intelligence community—in particular where those policy-makers had little knowledge about the intelligence community. The secrecy surrounding many aspects of the intelligence process can only be assumed to increase the potential impact of this issue.[49]

Another potential problem with this model is that it implies that the intelligence community itself is capable of a degree of 'self-regulation'. In this sense, one must assume that for the intelligence community to work effectively, relevant analysis would have to be accepted by senior managers and then fed into the policy-making process. Only if this system functioned effectively could policy-makers base their decisions on all available evidence and information, regardless of whether they chose to act upon that provided by the intelligence agencies or not. If senior managers within an agency did not accept the findings of one analyst, there is clearly a danger that potentially valuable information would not be passed upwards at all. The potential for organisational structures and hierarchies to prevent the consideration of detailed, technical or subtle intelligence findings for a whole plethora of reasons could therefore be a very real concern. Whilst Kent's approach therefore implies benefits from separation and independence, it also risks intelligence being too far separated from policy-makers—it might be received too late, cover the wrong topics, lack detail or not be presented at all. All this may result in intelligence being seen by a policy-maker as being either of little use or useless.[50] A further problem is that a range of other policies enacted by policy-makers may inadvertently impact upon the international landscape that the intelligence analysts are observing. Ironically, without close contact with policy-makers, intelligence officers may not know about important areas of input and influences into the international system, namely that from their own country. It is perhaps in recognition of these issues that it was also in the US intelligence community where an alternative model of the interaction between intelligence producers and consumers was developed.

William Casey was appointed as head of the CIA by the Reagan administration in 1981. Casey believed that the system of analysis he had inherited had serious shortcomings. In particular, he believed that a much more vigorous and activist system was required in order to support policy-makers in their decision-making.[51] The key change that Casey introduced was the removal of the separation between analysts and other areas of government as well as policy-makers themselves. Where specialists were required, for example to deal with highly technical questions, appropriate individuals were located, if necessary from other organisations, to ensure that the best and most appropriate person was always employed in that tasking.[52] This change relied on the assumption that analysts must be entirely aware of the needs of policy-makers, and that intelligence managers were obliged to task the most appropriate analysts in order to produce material of use to their consumers.[53] Certainly, in the US, where policy is a significant factor in any predictive equation used by intelligence agencies, intelligence analysts must be close to those policy-makers if they are to be able to predict events effectively that might relate to that policy. This model thus allows 'policy makers to pull information'.[54]

Whilst the model introduced by Casey brought clear benefits, it also brought its own potential for problems. The great benefit of this type of approach is that product will normally be actionable, as there is a greater chance that it will meet precisely the specific needs of the consumer. The danger, however, is that the consumer and policy-maker may come into office with their own view of how the world works and therefore look to the intelligence community to provide them with intelligence that allows them to implement their policies based on those views.[55] This might, at an extreme, result in policy-makers posing loaded questions to the intelligence community in order to ensure that they gather the intelligence they require to support these views. Alternatively, they might not ask the 'correct question' in order to ensure that intelligence analysis countering their desired policy will not be produced.[56] Particular criticisms of this approach have suggested that intelligence managed in this way becomes the advocate of policy, bending and shaping analysis to fit specific policies.[57] As a result, important intelligence might be ignored, distorted or used to support incorrect positions. An alternate view might suggest that intelligence analysis is often 'based on half buried assumptions. To counter this ... intelligence would need to interrogate policy about its assumptions or mind-sets, then try to validate or discredit these assumptions.'[58]

The theories of Kent and Casey therefore articulate and reflect a range of problems that might be assumed to be also present within the UK. These relate both to demands for intelligence gathering as well as to subsequent collection and analysis. These theories are also of some use in developing an understanding of the structure of the UK intelligence machinery, along with the potential problems that might be considered to be inherent in its establishment and processes. It is to the UK intelligence establishment that attention will now turn.

3

PUTTING IRAQ INTO CONTEXT

UK INTELLIGENCE AND CHEMICAL
AND BIOLOGICAL WEAPONS

According to the UK government, the UK national intelligence machinery comprises: the central intelligence machinery based in the Cabinet Office, the Secret Intelligence Service (SIS, or MI6), GCHQ (Government Communications Headquarters), MI5 (Security Service), Defence Intelligence Staff (DIS) and the Joint Terrorism Analysis Centre (JTAC).[1] Of this group, SIS, MI5 and GCHQ are collectively known as 'the agencies'.[2] There are numerous high quality and detailed accounts tracing the evolution of these agencies, and that detail will not be repeated here.[3] This chapter aims to provide only an overview of the UK intelligence machinery. As discussed previously, this overview will be cited within the context of UK policy towards chemical and biological weapons, though analysis will also return once again to the 2003 Iraq War as well as the case studies that will subsequently be considered in the remainder of this book.

Understanding the apparatus of spying

The UK intelligence agencies generally work as separate entities in fulfilment of their own distinct mission statements. As a result, there has historically been a degree of rivalry between the agencies. In part, this is a direct result of both the structure and management of the agencies as separate bodies. In their day-to-day activities, the agencies operate under the direct control of their respective heads who are in turn responsible to ministers. The Prime Minister has overall responsibility for intelligence and security matters, but is supported by the Secretary of the Cabinet, to whom the Joint Intelligence Committee are responsible. Furthermore, the parliamentary oversight committee, the Intelligence and Security Committee, reports directly to both the Prime Minister and parliament on issues relating to the policy, administration and expenditure issues of SIS, MI5 and GCHQ. The Home Secretary is specifically responsible for the Security Service; the Foreign Secretary for SIS and GCHQ; and the Secretary of State for Defence for the DIS. Intelligence collected as a result of specific requirements is passed directly to 'customer' departments in government where, at least in theory, it assists in decision-making.

The main body for advising on and identifying priorities for intelligence gathering, making tasks, as well as assessing its results, is the Joint Intelligence Committee (JIC). The JIC brings together all UK intelligence agencies to plan and prioritise the gathering of intelligence in order 'to monitor and give early warning of the development of direct or indirect foreign threats to British interests ... [and] to assess events and situations' in order to protect those interests.[4] It is wholly responsible for providing ministers and senior officials with regular intelligence assessments on a range of issues of both immediate and long-term importance to national interests, usually in the fields of security, defence and foreign affairs. The JIC was previously under the control of the Ministry of Defence until in 1957 responsibility for it moved to the Cabinet Office. The official view given for this move was that it would be better able to 'give higher direction to and keep under review the organization and working of intelligence as a whole at home and overseas'.[5] It was within this new mandate that producers and consumers responsible for national intelligence requirements were directed to agree on both intelligence requirements and priorities on an annual basis.[6]

It has been argued that JIC procedures could actually serve as a model to other democratic countries.[7] Because its staff are drawn from the intelligence agencies and policy-forming branches of government (including the Foreign Office, the Treasury and the Home Office) there is perhaps 'a sharper sense of what the real issues are and what information or analysis might be helpful when they come up for decision. Such participation improves the chances that intelligence will be useful when alternative courses of action are debated.'[8] One obvious risk of the JIC model is that of politicisation of the intelligence analysis process. By involving policy-makers in the analysis of intelligence, and the selection of it for passage up to perhaps Prime Ministerial level, there is a risk that information may be selected and used because it supports decisions or policies that a government might wish to pursue. Some authors have been quite critical of this, suggesting that 'the UK intelligence system is notoriously "analysis-lite" ... and indeed lacks a professional analytical service. This lends itself to the stove piping of raw intelligence to specialist consumers.'[9] In the light of the observations made by Lord Butler and discussed earlier (in Chapter 1), these concerns may be well founded.

It should also be noted that the JIC is supported in its work by the Joint Intelligence Organization which comprises a permanent assessments staff, a coordinator's group and a secretariat. This organisation was founded within the Cabinet Office in 2005 as a direct result of the Butler Report after the 2003 Iraq War, and incorporates both the assessments staff and the professional head of intelligence analysis. The assessments staff are responsible for drafting the assessments of situations and issues of current concern, informed by all available information, including the intelligence reports produced by the agencies. All assessments are subject to inter-departmental scrutiny at the drafting stage in sub-committees of the JIC, known as CIGs (Current Intelligence Groups). These bring together experts from a range of government departments and agencies. On CIG approval, reports are submitted to the JIC for further approval before finally being circulated to ministers and senior officials.[10]

The role of the JIC is important in the context of this book: its role is to assess and coordinate all intelligence so that the government can be best informed as to the issues involved.[11] The JIC is entirely independent of political decision-making and hence, at least in theory, ensures that the correct product is submitted to the appropriate political masters to aid in decision-making. One interesting feature of the UK intelligence machinery under the JIC is that other government departments are involved in discussions and decision-making as appropriate. Furthermore, papers drafted (by assessments staff) for the JIC are done so independently of departmental positions.[12] At least in theory, then, UK intelligence machinery ensures that intelligence assessments are formulated independently of the political process.

To use or not to use: intelligence and UK foreign policy

Sir Percy Cradock, a former chair of the UK Joint Intelligence Committee, stated that intelligence and policy are usually kept apart, though he also commented that the divide must be thin if intelligence assessments are to answer the questions uppermost in ministers' minds.[13] In effect, Cradock suggested that intelligence and foreign policy are closely linked. But how exactly does this 'closely separate' relationship between intelligence and policy work within the UK?

As has already been shown, policy-makers might be seen to face three possible options relating to how to use intelligence: they may ignore it altogether; they may consider it but decide it is not significant enough to influence decision-making (leaving that intelligence to be reinforced if it is to be of use in the future); or they may accept it and make decisions based upon its recommendations or suggestions. As Michael Herman, a former UK intelligence practitioner, comments, 'what intelligence produces may well be incomplete, inaccurate or positively misleading in particular cases, but decision-takers that use it regularly are likely to have better track records than those that manage without it'.[14] It might therefore be considered that in the UK 'the shaping of policy is determined much more by the intelligence dimension than the political or ethical dimension'.[15] One assumption underpins this statement: that appropriate, full and relevant intelligence is actually presented to the JIC, and that it is subsequently assessed and found to be sufficiently strong to require forward circulation to the highest echelons of government.[16] In some ways this process could be seen to act as a filter for intelligence, ensuring that the results of analysis actually reaching policy-makers had already been in some way quality-controlled. Yet for this process to work effectively, there is a requirement not only for managers within the intelligence community to identify correctly and pass upwards important and correctly analysed intelligence, but also for the JIC to be absolutely free from political influence in reaching its decisions. Whether these conditions exist or not could therefore have profound influences on the role of intelligence in directing and informing policy.

The UK system for intelligence analysis within the JIC relies on a group of individuals known as the 'assessments staff'. In the past, these individuals have not normally been 'dedicated intelligence professionals [but] people seconded from customer departments'.[17] Whilst this does perhaps introduce a broad range of perspectives into the analysis process, the fact that 'the chief of the Assessments Staff has almost always been a Foreign Office secondee' might perhaps raise concerns over how far departmental bias, agendas and loyalties might influence and ultimately impact on the results of assessments.[18] What might therefore seem at face value to be a robust intelligence process is not without potential and significant flaws.

Another potential flaw in this process might be the willingness of an individual Minister to listen to the advice they are given by the intelligence services via the JIC. By way of example, Jack Straw was a complete contrast to Robin Cook in his use of intelligence: he 'behaved as if he knew it all from day one'.[19] This provides a useful example of what happens if intelligence does not fit with the views that a policy-maker already has, if intelligence is not persuasive enough to alter a predetermined view or position, or if the analyst responsible for the preparation of specific intelligence is not considered credible—in all these cases, the intelligence may not have any effect on policy-making. This could be a potentially dangerous arrangement: if intelligence is correct but does not fit with desired policy objectives, the wrong policy might be adopted. Alternatively, if intelligence is wrong and it influences the making of a wrong decision, grave repercussions may result.

Within the UK, there is also evidence that structural factors within central government affect the ability of intelligence to influence policy-making. In particular, one key issue that has been shown to impact on the relationship between intelligence and foreign policy is the differing interests of separate government departments. The key problem here is that, particularly in the UK, government departments are powerful entities in their own right and also in a strong position to pursue their own organisational self-interests. Indeed, they may concurrently pursue very different, often conflicting agendas.[20] Sometimes, the reactions of different government departments towards intelligence can be quite diverse:

> Foreign Office representatives will tend towards bland interpretations; they have seen it all before; however difficult it is, it is probably negotiable; in any case their business is peace-making rather than conflict. Defence Department representatives will have leanings towards worst-case scenarios, because that is what they fear being called upon to handle in the last resort, and probably with inadequate means. The representatives of secret intelligence departments tend to have an in-built preference for arcane

interpretations or at any rate for subtle and complex ones, further penetration of which would require the acquisition of more secret intelligence.[21]

It might therefore be argued that not only can different government departments have different requirements and uses for intelligence, but intelligence might also be accepted or rejected as an influence on policy-making based purely on whether or not it fits the desired aims of that department at a specific moment in time. In addition, if intelligence is considered as a possible influence on policy amongst an audience of policy-makers from different departments of government, the rivalries between those departments might also affect how and if intelligence is accepted. Clearly this represents another layer of potential problems in the already complicated mechanisms for intelligence and foreign policy interaction discussed earlier. To succeed, not only does intelligence need to be accepted by policy-makers, it also needs to be capable of convincing other departments within the policy-making apparatus. This may be problematic if some sort of 'pecking order' exists within government, reflecting a hierarchy of most to least powerful departments in the context of policy-making.

Another issue that may accentuate the issue of departmental interest selectively accepting intelligence is secrecy. Whilst it may seem obvious, within the UK 'the high classification of [some] intelligence product puts it outside the reach of many of the officials taking part in the interdepartmental committees managed by the Cabinet Office'.[22] One of the reasons why an official might be attracted to certain intelligence material might actually be because of the security classification it carries. It has been convincingly argued that a 'piece of information contained in an ordinary diplomatic service telegram marked "Confidential" and circulated in the ordinary telegram distribution would attract less attention than the same piece of information contained in a report marked "secret" in red letters and conveyed to a top person by a special, exclusive procedure'.[23] The restrictive nature of intelligence and the preventing of widespread access to material due to security classification may also affect the perceived value of that intelligence. After all, why should an individual accept an argument for a particular course of action based on certain information when not all those involved in the decision-making process are actually privy to that information?

Credibility, in particular from the perspective of the recipient, is another important factor when considering the ability of UK intelligence to affect foreign policy.[24] It seems logical to suppose that the respect that generates and sustains a healthy appetite for intelligence must come from intelligence product that is consistently accurate.[25] As a result, the policy-maker who respects intelligence would probably be more inclined to use it in their own decision-making process.[26] Sources of intelligence can also have an effect on credibility. The risks associated with policy-makers trusting intelligence that comes predominantly from single sources has been well documented in the range of inquiries after the 2003 Iraq War.[27] One must assume that, at least in general terms, the respect of a policy-maker for intelligence would normally develop over a period of time and across a range of subjects, not be something that existed immediately a policy-maker assumed their post and that the intelligence agencies could take for granted. In essence, credibility and respect relates to intelligence track records relating to both individual analysts as well as agencies (or departments of agencies)—in effect, this can be seen as reputation.

Given the apparently subjective nature of the perception of intelligence by policy-makers, some authors have been highly critical of both the purpose of intelligence and its role in the intelligence and foreign policy relationship. Mark Curtis has gone so far as to question the very purpose of the UK intelligence agencies. He suggests that 'the role of MI6 is to protect Britain's economic wellbeing by keeping a particular eye on Britain's access to key commodities, like oil or metals [and] the profits of Britain's myriad of international business interests'.[28] In the context of intelligence informing UK foreign policy, he argues that MI6's psychological warfare section is actively attempting to 'massage public opinion into accepting controversial foreign policy decisions'.[29] As a result, for him, the UK intelligence agencies are complicit in the violation of international law and an ally of many repressive regimes: the Blair government's ethical foreign policy, he argues, was quite simply a web of deceit.[30]

The evolution of UK policy towards chemical and biological weapons

The UK has a long history of both chemical and biological weapons (CBW) development.[31] However, since the 1960s the UK government has been adamant that 'we neither develop nor produce bacteriological weapons' and there was 'no stockpile of [these] offensive weapons in the United Kingdom'.[32] To this day the UK therefore remains one of only a few examples of countries that has willingly given up offensive chemical and biological weapons programmes.

It was the Treaty on the Non-Proliferation of Nuclear Weapons (NPT), opening for signature in 1968, that precipitated the start of a search for a global ban on chemical and biological weapons. The UK was a key driver in the ultimate achievement of treaties eliminating both of these types of weapons. Several reasons have been suggested as to why the UK apparently took the lead in pushing for a global ban. Certainly, it appears that economic factors may have played a significant role. Of particular significance in this decision may have been the efforts being made in the UK to attain a nuclear capability at this time and the great costs associated with it.[33] In addition, there were increasing concerns about the viability and effectiveness of chemical and biological weapons within the UK military establishment that further stressed the case for purely defensive programmes—nuclear weapons were, after all, perceived to be the ultimate guarantee of security.[34] There is therefore a strong argument that the motivation of the UK to disarm was at least partly a function of a shrinking defence budget and a growing nuclear weapons programme.

One should not however dismiss as purely economic the attitude of the UK towards chemical and biological weapons disarmament. It appears that there was a very strong view that 'it is almost inconceivable that enemy forces would use chemical weapons against NATO forces except in the circumstances of a mass invasion—in which event more terrible weapons would surely come into play'.[35] The difficulties experienced in developing a viable capability that the UK had faced during the time when an offensive programme was in operation also perhaps led to the conclusion that not only were CBW irrelevant when compared to nuclear weapons on a modern battlefield, but that if the UK could not develop them effectively it would be most unlikely that other, less technically advanced nations would be able to do so.[36]

The UK attempted to encourage the international community to address the problem of biological weapons disarmament first, underpinned by the logic that because these weapons were of relatively little utility on the battlefield, a treaty could probably be concluded relatively quickly. It was presumed that all world governments would share the same view towards these weapons that the UK held. In previous disarmament negotiations, chemical and biological arms control had always been considered together, and the Soviet Union was immediately suspicious of what the motives of the UK government were in suggesting this split in negotiations to tackle the biological weapons problem first.[37] Regardless, the UK persisted with its lobbying for a ban on BW, supported by the US under President Nixon, who had announced on 25 November 1969 the unilateral abolition of biological weapons. It is highly likely that this was, at least in part, due to public controversy relating to the use of herbicides in the Vietnam War.[38]

One interesting aspect of the UK proposals to ban BW was that an international inspectorate should be established to monitor compliance with treaties.[39] Under the auspices of the United Nations, this inspectorate would investigate any alleged use of these weapons on behalf of the Security Council. Any evidence of use could then be considered against a range of possible consequences. The UK also proposed an absolute ban on offensive research into biological agents—something that without the acceptance of an inspection regime would be very difficult to police. This was also an area that, until an abrupt U-turn took place, the Soviet Union found totally unacceptable. It is highly significant to note that it is in this U-turn lay an early but important clue as to the intent of the Soviet Union with regard to BW development—something that was ignored by the UK and other governments with the successful conclusion of the Biological and Toxin Weapons Convention (BTWC) in April 1972. Regardless, the UK had therefore played a key role in pressing for the negotiation and conclusion of this treaty, though arguably at the cost of excluding areas such as a requirement for verification. These mechanisms were to become desperately needed in later years when suspicions of cheating on the treaty by states such as the Soviet Union began to appear. Without in-built verification or other confidence-building measures, the challenge would later fall to the UK intelligence agencies to provide conclusive proof of non-compliance to political leaders.

It is therefore possible to argue that the UK was so focused on successfully concluding a BW treaty that it was prepared to give up on any requirement for verification in order to achieve its aim. This omission may have been at least in part due to the attitude of the UK government centred around a perceived lack of utility of these weapons in the nuclear age. Ironically, this attitude was to go on to be reflected in a stubborn refusal of the UK government to acknowledge or respond to early indications of violations of the treaty in the Soviet Union. Whilst the benefit of hindsight may tell us that this omission was grave, it also perhaps goes some way towards explaining how intelligence agencies became so central to arms control verification. In the absence of verification mechanisms within treaties, information relating to non-compliance would need to come from covert sources, both technical and human. The role of the intelligence agencies here is obvious.

Once the BTWC was concluded, the UK government next turned its attention to chemical weapons. This area was far more difficult than it had been for BW—not least because of the large stockpiles of these weapons held by both the US and USSR. Once again, the UK saw an inspection regime as central to the potential treaty, and now the USSR was far less resistant to this suggestion than they had been in the past. Some evidence suggests that this apparent change in position was due to the fact that the Soviet Union had already successfully developed binary chemical agents that, as separate compounds, would fall outside the remit of a future CWC (Chemical Weapons Convention).[40] As a result, as long as Western nations remained ignorant as to the extent of their technical abilities relating to CW, the Soviet Union would have nothing to fear from the inspection of Soviet sites that had been involved in the production of now obsolete agents.

The UK was very active in lobbying for the establishment of an inspection regime for CW. Over a period of fifteen years, numerous papers were submitted to the United Nations Committee on Disarmament arguing for the inclusion of an intrusive 'challenge' inspection regime. At the same time the UK government worked hard to encourage all NATO members to lobby for progress towards the same goal.[41] By the time both the Soviet Union and the UK had opened up the previously secret chemical warfare research establishments at Shikhany and Porton Down, it appeared that verification measures would be universally accepted and included in the future treaty. In 1997 the CWC entered into force, owing a large part of its text relating to inspection and verification to the hard work of the UK.[42]

From the mid to late 1990s to the present day, the UK FCO (Foreign and Commonwealth Office) has continued to consider the countering of proliferation of Weapons of Mass Destruction to be one of its top priorities.[43] UK policy clearly articulates that the spread of weapons, including chemical and biological:

> and their possible use, including by terrorists, remains a major threat in its own right. Preventing terrorist groups from obtaining nuclear, radiologi-

cal, biological or chemical weapons will be a key task. Strengthening efforts to combat the spread of these weapons will be critical in the next decade ... preventing states, in particular Iran and North Korea, from acquiring or spreading WMD, and ensuring more effective global non-proliferation mechanisms, will be a top priority.[44]

This position appears to assume that treaties such as the BTWC and CWC have been largely successful in transforming a predominantly state-centric threat into one of proliferation, although it still accepts that 'multilateral arms and export controls [must] evolve to reflect techno-logical change, agree more effective verification, and negotiate stronger compliance measures for biological arms control'.[45]

In terms of situations where firmer action might be required to coun-ter the proliferation of chemical and biological weapons, Prime Minister Tony Blair was clear about the lengths he was prepared to go in order to prevent proliferation of these weapons. Speaking in 2001, Blair stated:

> I sometimes think that there is a kind of word fatigue about chemical and biological weapons. We're not talking about some mild variants of every-day chemicals, but anthrax, sarin and mustard gas—weapons that can cause hurt and agony on a mass scale beyond the comprehension of most decent people ... The question is: how to proceed ... Diplomacy is vital ... but ... diplomacy has to be backed by the certain knowledge ... that behind the diplomacy is the possibility of force being used.[46]

This goes some way perhaps towards explaining the position of the UK government in the lead-up to the Iraq War in 2003, a war that might be considered to be the first 'war of counter-proliferation'.

The UK government has also publicly identified other methods through which it intends to attempt to counter the threat of prolifera-tion: in particular, through national and multilateral export controls, including support to the Australia Group, the Nuclear Suppliers Group and the Missile Technology Control Regime, along with financial com-mitments to cooperative threat reduction programmes, and the Global Partnership launched in 2002 by G8.[47] Support of the Proliferation Security Initiative also potentially gives the UK an ability to intercept shipments of illegal weapons en route.[48] Finally, the Global Threat Reduction Programme brings together ministers from the FCO, MoD and BERR (Business, Enterprise and Regulatory Reform) to monitor and review the performance of UK attempts to counter proliferation.[49]

Central to the effective enactment of these initiatives is accurate and timely intelligence.

The importance of intelligence, in particular from secret sources, therefore has a significant role in supporting UK policy towards CBW arms control. The overview of UK policy provided so far also suggests very clear means by which that support has been provided: intelligence agencies have acted as gatherers of information, observing the international landscape through the lens of counter-proliferation, attempting to observe and record occurrences when treaties were not being adhered to. But this implied process of gathering information also suggests potential problems: how can intelligence persuade policy-makers that a threat might exist when they may not wish to accept that one does? Furthermore, what might be considered to be effective evidence and proof of a threat existing, and how does this relate to the willingness of those policy-makers to challenge foreign policy towards states suspected of breaching their treaty requirements? The lead-up to the 2003 Iraq War usefully illustrates many aspects of this complex relationship.

Unpicking the web: the 2003 Iraq War

In the lead-up to the Iraq War, intelligence played a central role in the formulation, development and enactment of UK foreign policy. As Chilcot reported:

> the ingrained belief that Saddam Hussein's regime retained chemical and biological warfare capabilities, was determined to preserve and if possible enhance its capabilities, including at some point in the future a nuclear capability, and was pursuing an active policy of deception and concealment, had underpinned the UK Government's policy towards Iraq since the Gulf Conflict of 1991.[50]

Controversy regarding the real motivation for the 2003 Iraq War aside, at least in the short term, intelligence allowed the government to build a case through which it could argue for its publicly stated desired objective: the need to take stronger action against Iraq (with the credible threat of force). In effect, intelligence is something on which policy-makers might draw in order to support their formulation and enactment of foreign policy. This would seem to sit comfortably alongside the discussion of the possible roles of intelligence presented earlier in this chapter. It is however important to bear in mind that there is no 'rule' that intelligence must represent a part of the normal foreign policy decision-making process, nor that foreign policy will be unsuccessful without intelligence input. It is equally important to recognise that intelligence success must be clearly related to the successful achievement of foreign policy goals—albeit from the perspective of intelligence. The link between successful intelligence and successful foreign policy would therefore seem to be a strong one.

In the case of Iraq, the actual processes through which intelligence interacted with foreign policy appear on the face of things to be relatively straightforward. The UK government had a foreign policy towards Iraq that had developed over a considerable period of time, with antecedents dating from the aftermath of the 1991 Gulf War. Specifically, UK foreign policy aimed to see Iraq complying with the requirements of the United Nations Security Council Resolution 687 and the later Resolution 1441.[51] This policy relied strongly upon intelligence input, in particular to support a range of diplomatic and military activities—not least those associated with the destruction of suspected WMD stockpiles as authorised after the 1991 Gulf War by UNSC Resolution 687. Intelligence contributed 'a steady flow of intelligence covering Iraqi procurement activities, attempts to break United Nations sanctions, concealment of prohibited programmes and plans for handling UNSCOM and IAEA inspections'.[52] Essentially, via the JIC, the UK intelligence agencies were able to provide 'Ministers and senior officials with co-ordinated intelligence assessments on a range of issues of immediate and long term importance to national interests', specifically relating to counter-proliferation policy. It might certainly therefore be argued that there were direct influences on the course of foreign policy relating to Iraq due to this intelligence input.[53]

The Butler Report also provides useful commentary on the nature of the intelligence and foreign policy interface. Within the report, whilst Butler recognised that the mechanics of the intelligence and foreign policy interface were relatively simple, he also acknowledged that the relationship itself was dynamic. Certainly, his report suggests that over a period of time from the end of the 1991 Gulf War onwards, as foreign policy objectives were either toughened or changed, intelligence requirements were also adapted. Possibly of most significance here, specifically in the context of understanding the intelligence and foreign policy relationship, is the period from September 2001 onwards. From this period of time the rhetoric being used by the UK relating to the perceived threat from Iraq's WMD appears to have been significantly strengthened. Chilcot also refers to the evolution of a JIC view moving from 'inspectors [being] unable to account for some ... chemical and biological weapons material' towards one that was perceived to be entirely 'intended to underpin a decision on military action against Iraq'.[54] It is in this change of language that a clear indication rests of how the intelligence and foreign policy interface might actually function.

By the spring of 2002, the UK government apparently believed that 'stronger action (though not necessarily military action) needed to be taken to enforce Iraqi disarmament'.[55] This change can be partly explained by the fact that after the 9/11 attacks, the JIC believed that 'Usama bin Laden's philosophy, combined with suicide attacks, had changed the calculus of the [WMD] threat'.[56] In addition, the JIC assessed that 'from the early 1990s, Usama bin Laden has sought to obtain nuclear and chemical materials for use as weapons of terror'.[57] Chilcot stated that from February 2002 'Mr Blair and Mr Straw began ... publicly to argue that Iraq was a threat which had to be dealt with'.[58] But there were also other less obvious influences on this development of policy:

> The government, as well as being influenced by the concerns of the US government, saw a need for immediate action on Iraq because of the wider historical and international context, especially Iraq's perceived continuing challenge to the authority of the United Nations. The government also saw in the United Nations, and a decade of Security Council Resolutions, a basis for action through the United Nations to enforce Iraqi compliance with its disarmament negotiations.[59]

It was therefore apparent that any change in government policy towards Iraq, particularly if that policy was to be toughened, also required an accompanying change in what intelligence had been doing until then to support foreign policy. This change was to prove problematic for the government: if the government were to stand a chance of persuading the UN Security Council to take the view that Iraq was sufficiently in breach of previous UNSC Resolutions to warrant the use of force, it would have to provide incontrovertible proof of large-scale violations of Iraq's obligations. That proof would most likely have to come from intelligence sources—the problem though was that, as Lord Butler acknowledges, 'the intelligence then available was insufficiently robust to meet that criterion'.[60] The question was 'whether in doing so, they conveyed more certainty and knowledge than was justified'.[61] Chilcot certainly appeared clear that this 'was likely to have created the impression that Iraq posed a greater threat than the detailed JIC assessments would have supported'.[62]

The analysis offered thus far suggests a very definite dynamic at play in the intelligence and foreign policy interface: intelligence does not simply provide information to allow the formulation or support of foreign policy, it should actively seek to provide information to support a foreign policy that has already been decided upon. This is significant: intelligence could now be seen to be a tool through which the government could provide retrospective evidence to support an already established position: the problem though, in this case, is that whilst policy had now changed, the intelligence being obtained to support that policy had not. To return to the theoretical models of intelligence and foreign policy interaction described earlier in this chapter, in the lead-up to the Iraq War it would seem that Casey offers the best explanation for what is seen here. Where Casey argued that intelligence and policy-makers must be fused together, he was actually suggesting that intelligence must support decision-making. To do this effectively, intelligence agencies must be fully aware of the needs of the policy-makers. In the case of Iraq, it would seem that UK policy-makers knew exactly what was needed to support their own decision-making and they used intelligence agencies to support that need. Whilst this explanation does not take into account the rights and wrongs of using intelligence in this way, it does provide a useful explanation of the possible dynamics of intelligence and foreign policy interaction.

In many ways, concluding that the use of intelligence by the Blair government in the lead-up to the Iraq War simply reflected the theories of Casey neglects giving attention to many issues which might also be seen to affect the intelligence and foreign policy interface. One key problem here is if assessed intelligence product is passed to policy-makers simply on the basis of its ability to support an already made decision, as opposed to its relevance or importance generally. Another issue relates to the methods available to an intelligence agency to obtain information: dictating the information that is required might severely restrict the means available to obtain it.

A growing reliance on HUMINT also becomes a significant characteristic of the role of intelligence in the Butler Report. From 1991 to 1998, 'the bulk of information used in assessing the status of Iraq's biological, chemical and ballistic missile programmes was derived from UNSCOM reports'; but when UNSCOM left Iraq in 1998, this source of information obviously disappeared.[63] As a result, the UK had relatively few primary sources of intelligence, and those it did have often did not corroborate the information received from other sources. Even worse, some of those sources were later found to be passing on information that was hearsay, of doubtful accuracy, or simply downright unreliable.[64] That said, Butler is adamant that in the case of Iraq, human sources of intelligence were vital to the overall picture being obtained of Iraqi WMD programmes.[65] His report therefore suggests that whilst a change in foreign policy may have required far more robust and detailed intelligence, the intelligence agencies were not in a position to provide this: certainly not to the standards of reliability that one might expect. Chilcot is rather more damning; 'the deliberate selection of a formulation which [reflected] what Mr Blair believed, rather than in the judgements which the JIC had actually reached in its assessment of the intelligence, indicates a distinction between his beliefs and the JIC's actual judgements'.[66]

It is important to note that whilst Butler is critical of the apparent weaknesses in the selection and validation of sources and information received, in particular by SIS, he appears to be content that 'in general ... the intelligence material was correctly reported in JIC assessments'.[67] Once again, Chilcot takes a harder line: 'The assessed intelligence had not established beyond doubt [the existence of WMD and the] JIC should have made that clear to Mr Blair.'[68] If intelligence was generally correctly reported, it perhaps reduces some of the impact of arguments that Blair blatantly lied to the public in order to give his support to the US—perhaps one of the most controversial explanations for the UK's part in the Iraq War. It has been argued that the general subservience of the UK to the US is actually representative of 'poodleism'—a term first used by the Liberal Democrat leader Charles Kennedy.[69] In effect, 'poodleism' represents a description of an unthinking Prime Minister, unwilling to act counter to the views of its master—in this case the US President George Bush.

When one considers the profound impact of the terrorist attacks of 11 September 2001 in the US, it is clear that Bush explicitly linked 9/11, al-Qaeda and Saddam Hussein's Iraq. Accordingly, as US foreign policy began to focus on 'regime change' in Iraq, the 'poodle' theory suggests that Blair would naturally be inclined to align UK foreign policy and follow down the same road to war. What is seen by some as the deliberate misleading of the British people in constructing a case for war against Iraq could actually be seen to be a means by which Blair could provide the US with a 'political fig leaf' as a coalition partner bringing legitimacy to what might have otherwise been unilateral US military action.[70] The views of the former UK ambassador to Washington, Sir Christopher Meyer, appear to bring further support here. Meyer commented that he believed Bush had decided to pursue a policy of regime change in Iraq on or about 20 September 2001.[71] Indeed, by 7 April 2002, Blair himself was articulating support to that US policy through the alignment of British foreign policy objectives. In a speech at the George Bush Senior Presidential Library on that same date, Blair said:

> ... when America is fighting for those values, then, however tough, we fight with her. No grandstanding, no offering implausible but impractical advice from the comfort of the touchline, no wishing away the hard not the easy choices on terrorism and WMD, or making peace in the Middle East, but working together, side by side. [...] If the world makes the right choices now—at this time of destiny—we will get there. And Britain will be at America's side in doing it.[72]

If one follows this explanation right through to the invasion of Iraq in 2003, it might seem that UK involvement in the war alongside the US was something of a 'done deal'. In effect one could argue that UK foreign policy would have always been led by and then aligned to US foreign policy. That said, one must still question the use of intelligence subsequent to the 2002 hardening of position towards Iraq.

Through the release of the September 2002 dossier, the government appeared to break into new territory in the way it used intelligence:

> The dossier broke new ground in three ways: the JIC had never previously produced a public document; no government case for any international action had previously been made to the British public by explicitly drawing on a JIC publication; and the authority of the British intelligence community, and the JIC in particular, had never been used in such a public way.[73]

When one considers the acknowledged general weakness of intelligence supporting a case for war, this seems particularly strange. It is perhaps true that 'intelligence is shaped and influenced by policy and bad policy sets the stage for bad intelligence'.[74]

There is not only evidence of intelligence collection being driven by policy here. One must also consider that there may have been a relationship between the apparent need of the government for intelligence proving the existence of Iraqi WMD programmes to support their stronger position, and the lack of rigour in assessing intelligence by the JIC. This observation does however need to be considered alongside both the shortening timescale available to the government for action and the increasing currency of Iraq as a political issue. The government was and remained adamant that intelligence was never presented to the public in order to 'make a case for a particular course of action ... it was intended by the government to inform domestic and international understanding of the need for stronger action'.[75] This comment does, however, seem curious in the light of observations from analysis considered so far. As a result, one might remain in a position whereby it can be argued that foreign policy appeared to be being informed by intelligence that was actually being filtered to suit the intended foreign policy position—a position that had already been established—regardless of what intelligence had informed those policy-makers until then. Whilst it could be argued that it does not necessarily matter if policy-makers drive intelligence processes, it seems equally valid to argue that it certainly does matter if policy-makers are demanding specific intelligence to justify and support policies that have already been decided upon. This is perhaps an intricacy of intelligence and foreign policy interaction that is not adequately discussed, or indeed warned against, by Casey.

To summarise the discussion here so far: in terms of foreign policy it appears that in the case of Iraq, before 2001 intelligence had been collected for a clear foreign policy objective of counter-proliferation. After 2002, it seems that intelligence was demanded by policy-makers to support an already established change in foreign policy aims. Central to this apparent shift lies the fact that the government had a pressing short-term need for intelligence in order to make a case for stronger action to the international community. This suggests that whilst the Casey theory might explain intelligence and foreign policy interaction in the UK immediately prior to 2003, the theory of Kent perhaps better explains that interaction prior to 2001, when intelligence was separate from policy-making, but offered to assist and support decision-making.

Viewed from the perspective of the Butler Report, it would therefore seem that when the UK government position towards Iraq was changed to become tougher, time became a key factor. As the time available for action to be taken reduced, specific intelligence was directly sought by the

UK government to support that new position. As a result, intelligence was used to support a policy change that had already taken place, in the process sacrificing some of the high requirements for robust and correctly validated information normally demanded by the JIC in making recommendations to policy-makers. This actually suggests that when policy-makers require intelligence to support a change in foreign policy that has already been made, they will accept the lowest quality of intelligence by way of evidence in order to support that change. It is perhaps for this reason that Sir Percy Cradock, a former Chair of the JIC, warned:

> ideally intelligence and policy should be close but distinct. Too distinct and assessments become an in-growing, self-regarding activity, producing little or no work of interest to the decision makers ... Too close a link and policy begins to play back on estimates, producing the answers the policy makers would like ... The analysts become couriers, whereas their proper function is to report their findings ... without fear or favour. The best arrangement is intelligence and policy in separate but adjoining rooms, with communicating doors and thin partition walls...[76]

Attention will now turn to examine the cases of the Soviet Union, South Africa and Libya in order to establish whether the relationship between intelligence and foreign policy during the period of the 2003 Iraq War simply reflected established practices and procedures in the intelligence and foreign policy communities, or whether it marked a departure from this.

4

FROM REFUSAL TO DISBELIEF

THE SOVIET UNION

In July 1992 the Russian Federation, under the leadership of Boris Yeltsin, submitted to the UN Department of Disarmament a document acknowledging that the Soviet Union had conducted activities that were in clear breach of its obligations under the BTWC (Biological and Toxin Weapons Convention). Through this seemingly innocuous act, Yeltsin admitted that the Soviet Union had systematically and comprehensively deceived the international community for almost twenty years by developing weapons and technologies that were subject to an absolute ban. Put simply, the Soviet Union, a state that had signed the BTWC in April 1972, had deliberately and intentionally cheated on this treaty from its inception. Chillingly, this had given the Soviet Union an absolute strategic advantage in an entire class of weapons, simply through cheating on an arms control treaty—a treaty with no built-in verification system and therefore little risk of being caught. It is in this stark fact that the roots of the case study presented in this chapter lie. But just what effect, if any, did UK intelligence ultimately have on the Yeltsin decision to admit cheating on the BTWC?

Hands up: the admission of cheating

On the face of it, admitting to cheating on an arms control treaty might seem a surprising course of action for a newly elected Russian president to take. The collapse of the Soviet Union and election of Yeltsin, a president keen to forge closer links and secure investment from Western nations, might perhaps go some way to explaining these actions. Yet the facts surrounding the admission are far more complicated than this straightforward explanation might suggest. The exact events around the submission documents to the UN by the Russians detailing non-compliance are complicated, but for the purposes of this chapter it is clearly important to investigate how it came to be that this admission was made. In particular, to what extent did UK foreign policy facilitate this admission, and how was that decision-making supported by intelligence?

It is possible to identify two factors from the very outset that may assist in understanding why the Russian admission was made. Firstly, existing literature appears to be in agreement that there was significant political pressure placed upon Yeltsin by the UK government to terminate the former Soviet BW programme.[1] Secondly, it also seems apparent that UK intelligence held extremely detailed information on the Soviet BW programme and that this may have played a key role in forcing the Russian admission.[2] Before an examination of these factors can be made, it is first necessary to consider how the Russian admission of Soviet breaches of the BTWC came about.

The 1992 Russian submission to the UN, known as 'Form F', represented a fulfilment by the Russian Federation of its requirements under agreements made at the third BTWC review conference in 1991. The basis for this requirement had been a declaration made by the Second BTWC Review Conference in 1986:

> The Conference, mindful of the provisions of Article V and Article X, and determined to strengthen the authority of the Convention and to enhance confidence in the implementation of its provisions, agrees that the States Parties are to implement, on the basis on mutual co-operation, [specific] measures, in order to prevent or reduce the occurrence of ambiguities, doubts and suspicions, and in order to improve international co-operation in the field of peaceful bacteriological (biological) activities.[3]

This declaration was followed up by a further declaration made by the Third BTWC Review Conference at which the requirement for the submission of Form F by states parties originated:

> In accordance with the decision of the Second Review Conference, and taking into account views expressed concerning the need to strengthen the

implementation of the provisions of Article V, the Conference reviewed the effectiveness of the provisions in Article V for consultation and cooperation and of the cooperative measures agreed in the Final Declaration of the Second Review Conference...The Conference notes the importance of the confidence-building measures agreed upon at the Second Review Conference, as well as the modalities elaborated by the Ad Hoc Meeting of the Scientific and Technical Experts from States parties to the Convention held in 1987 ...The Conference urges all States parties to submit information to future rounds of information exchange.[4]

The submission of Form F documents to the UN Department of Disarmament represents inter-governmental exchanges of information. Official holders of completed forms include the governments of states parties, the UN DDA (Department for Disarmament Affairs) and the WHO (World Health Organisation). These forms are therefore official documents and, from a UK perspective, there is no desire to make their contents public.[5] Copies of Form F documents are, however, available from academic sources where translations of the original document made by the UN, WHO and University of Georgia have been obtained for the purposes of this research, and it is these that have been drawn upon for the purposes of this case study.[6]

Whilst different translated versions of the original Form F document contain some disparity, each version essentially details the same basic information: in essence, that offensive biological research and development programmes were run by the Soviet Union between 1946 and March 1992.[7] These programmes focused on 'prevention, pathology and virulence studies, diagnostic methods, aerobiology, detection, treatment, toxicology, physical protection, decontamination, as well as other related studies'.[8] In addition, the Soviet Union developed dispersion systems and facilities to 'investigate the feasibility of mass producing biological agents'.[9] The document is however insistent that 'no biological stockpiles were created' during the period that the programme officially ran.[10] This may perhaps suggest more about how these weapons were to be deployed, rather than a lack of intent to develop offensive capabilities. Regardless of this point, these activities were clearly counter to the obligations assumed when ratifying the BTWC—most significantly because that treaty forbids any of these activities for offensive purposes, activities that by their own admission in the Form F submission the Soviet Union had been conducting.

The submission of the Russian Form F was the culmination of several years of diplomatic effort by the UK, as well as other governments, to bring an end to the Soviet BW programme. This was an objective pursued in accordance with UK foreign policy objectives relating to the non-proliferation of WMD and their associated technologies. In particular, since 1989 and the defection of a senior scientist from Russia, the UK had apparently held detailed and incontrovertible proof of the existence of the Soviet BW programme.[11] Since then there had been political engagement at the highest level in an attempt to persuade the Soviet Union to end this programme. Curiously, it was only with the change in Soviet/Russian leadership from Gorbachev to Yeltsin in June 1991 that developments that could be considered by the UK to be positive, at least in the context of foreign policy objectives, began to be observed. Again, this raises interesting questions relating to the interaction of intelligence and foreign policy in the UK, and in particular, how intelligence can be successfully used in the support and enactment of foreign policy.

The Russian Form F submission was actually only one of several events that signalled a change in Russian attitude towards the importance of complying with the BTWC. Prior to the Form F submission, in an address to his domestic audience in a televised speech, on 29 January 1992, President Boris Yeltsin had stated:

> Russia favours the rigorous implementation of the 1972 convention banning biological weapons, and the creation of appropriate mechanisms on a multilateral basis for monitoring the implementation of measures for building confidence and openness. Considering that there is a lag in implementing the convention, I can state that Russia is renouncing that section of provisos concerning the possibility of the retaliatory use of biological weapons—they were made by the USSR under the Geneva Protocol of 1925 banning the use of chemical and bacteriological weapons in war.[12]

Whilst this speech did not represent an outright admission of breaches of international treaty obligations, it did indicate that a 'lag in implementation' was an acknowledgment that programmes existed in the Soviet Union contrary to the terms of the BTWC. This is not the same thing as an outright admission that offensive programmes were run in direct breach of the BTWC, yet, given the fact that it was made within six months of Yeltsin coming to power, it did suggest that BW was an important issue on his political agenda. This perhaps also hints that the UK was beginning to have some success in the fulfilment of its foreign policy objectives, given that it had already been established that considerable diplomatic effort had been expended in pursuit of this. It is perhaps as a result of this effort that Yeltsin had felt under pressure from Western leaders pursuing their desire to bring an end to these weapons programmes. This might perhaps account for Yeltsin's preparedness to act where Gorbachev had not. Regardless, this speech does suggest that following twenty years of cheating on the BTWC by the Soviet Union, the UK was finally in a position where it could apparently affect change in another state related to its foreign policy objectives through the use of its diplomatic instruments.

President Yeltsin also took steps to consolidate his overall intent towards biological weapons programmes through domestic law within the Russian Federation. On 11 April 1992, three months prior to the Form F submission, President Yeltsin signed Presidential Decree number 390. This decree, entitled 'on ensuring the fulfilment of international obligations in the area of biological weapons', resolved to:

> ... establish that development and implementation of biological programs in violation of the Convention on Prohibition of Development, Production and Stockpiling of Bacteriological (Biological) and Toxin Weapons and on their Destruction is not permitted on the territory of the Russian Federation.

> To make surveillance over fulfilment of the requirements of this Convention the responsibility of the Committee on Conventional Problems of Chemical and Biological Weapons under the President of the Russian Federation.

> That the Committee on Conventional Problems of Chemical and Biological Weapons under the President of the Russian Federation is to submit, within a month's time, proposals for amplifying measures of openness and trust and expanding international cooperation within the framework of the indicated Convention.[13]

This decree, whilst appearing to be directed at the domestic audience, also communicated to the international community that clear and concrete steps were being taken by the Russian leadership to encourage openness and transparency of the (former) BW establishment in accordance with the BTWC. Once again, this may be a response to pressure being placed upon Yeltsin by Western leaders. One must assume that the Form F submission, made in July 1992, had been sanctioned at the highest political level, especially given the significance of the content of the document. The Russian decision to admit cheating on an arms control treaty would not have been taken lightly, if for no other reason than that it called into question the compliance by the Soviet Union with a whole range of other arms control treaties. This could have brought with it the potential for a wide range of politically and economically damaging consequences for a country that, during a period of deep political transition, was heavily reliant on good relations with other states, in particular for desperately needed investment and trade.

Following the submission of the Form F, the Russian deputy Foreign Minister, Berdennikov, reiterated the desire of the Russian government to acknowledge the non-compliance of the Soviet Union with the BTWC when he stated during a press conference on 14 September 1992:

> You know that since 1972 the Convention has been in existence. This is the Convention on the Ban on Bacteriological Weapons. But, regrettably, it has happened so—and we made an official statement to this effect this year in the UN—that the Soviet Union was violating this convention and was running a programme in the sphere of offensive biological researches and developments, which has been declared unlawful by the Convention. These activities were in progress since 1946 until March of 1992. They were discontinued at the decree of 1992.[14]

This statement not only suggested a desire to send a clear signal to the international community relating to the Russian Federation policy on biological weapons over and above the requirements of the Form F, but it also demonstrated a joined up and united policy within the administration of Yeltsin, along with an indication of the assumed effectiveness of newly passed legislation relating to BW activities. These comments represented the final public statement to date made by Russia relating to BW.

To summarise the discussion thus far, when analysing events at the simplest level, they represent an apparently plain and forthright acknowledgement by the Russian government that the Soviet Union had cheated on the BTWC from its inception. Furthermore, for whatever reason, the new Russian government did not wish to be associated with these actions and, indeed, wished to ensure that the BTWC was now to be fully applied. Yet these events also suggest the presence of more complicated issues. Firstly, why did the UK government feel it had managed to exact such concessions from the Yeltsin government when they had apparently failed with previous administrations? In particular, one might have expected Prime Minister Thatcher to have had some success in addressing these issues with President Gorbachev, especially given the apparently warm relationship between the two leaders. Secondly, was the apparent UK foreign policy success directly related to the accuracy and completeness of intelligence held? If so why was this success not achieved earlier, given that one could reasonably have expected that the collection of intelligence on Soviet BW would have been a high priority for the UK throughout the Cold War? Can one really attribute this simply to the end of the Cold War? Finally, is a more acceptable explanation apparent from a consideration of the currency of the Russian admission as a political issue: put simply, were UK policy-makers not willing to act upon intelligence earlier because it did not suit a particular political agenda? By the time of the admission, was the intelligence picture so overwhelming and powerful that it was impossible to ignore? Or else was there merely a perceived political gain to be had by the UK government in pushing Yeltsin into making an admission of cheating? These questions will be the focus of attention for the remainder of this chapter.

A long time in the making: the Soviet biological weapons programme

As it has already been established that Russia admitted conducting activities that were in direct breach of the BTWC from the date that it was ratified by the Soviet Union, the signature of the BTWC by the Soviet Union in 1972 provides the baseline from which any analysis of UK intelligence relating to Soviet BW activities must begin. One important question to ask is whether there was evidence available during this time that could have alerted UK intelligence agencies to this deception? Perhaps more fundamentally though, why did it take so long for policy-makers to take action with regard to an issue of such importance?

Russia and the Soviet Union have a long association with both the research of biological weapons and related technologies and the development of the sciences related to them. This history has been well documented elsewhere, yet some points are worth reiterating briefly here, particularly as this section aims to consider whether information might have been available to UK intelligence warning of possible Soviet intentions when signing the BTWC.[15]

It is important to note that Russian scientists were at the very forefront of biological research as early as 1897. By the end of the nineteenth century, Russia had become a world leader in the export of vaccines—in particular, plague vaccine was mass-produced at a laboratory near St Petersburg in greater quantities than even at the Pasteur Institute in Paris.[16] Military interest in the potential for use of biotechnology on the battlefield can be traced to the early 1900s, though following the Russian Revolution, when diseases like typhoid ravaged the population of Russia, some senior officers within the Red Army began to realise 'that disease had served as a more potent weapon than bullets or artillery shells'.[17] By 1925, Yakob Moiseevich Fishman, Director of the Red Army's Military–Chemical Directorate (VOKhIMU), was reported to have initiated the first Soviet biological warfare research at a laboratory based in Moscow.[18] Fishman also initiated the use of both civilian and military facilities for biological warfare research. Whilst it is likely that this was due to a desire to make maximum use of scientists and facilities, the Soviet Union continued offensive research in civilian facilities up to the 1990s. It was also in the 1920s that intelligence relating to Soviet biological weapons development began to reach the West. In one case a report from 1927 was produced by the British Secret Intelligence Service detailing Soviet tests of air-dropped bacteriological bombs on a test range.[19]

Following the signing of the Geneva Protocols on the use of asphyxiating, poisonous or other gases in war by the Soviet Union in 1927, information relating to biological weapons continued to reach the West. For example, in 1928 the Revolutionary Military Council signed a decree ordering the transformation of typhus into a battlefield weapon. The February 1928 Decree was made by Kliment Voroshilov, the People's Commissar for Defence.[20] As a result, Yakob Moiseevich Fishman wrote a document asserting that 'the bacterial option could be successfully used in war'.[21] Interest in the military application of biotechnology continued to grow in Russia during the approach of the Second World War. There were extensive efforts to study 'the possibility of using aircraft and artillery to carry Biological Weapons' as well as to design 'a special reconnaissance tank ... to diagnose Biological Weapons dispersed by an enemy'.[22] There was also extensive cooperation between Germany and the Soviet Union during this period.[23]

After the end of the Second World War, UK intelligence obtained extensive information from German scientists relating to Soviet BW capabilities. One captured senior scientist wrote that by 1939 the Russians were under 'the conviction that the BW preparations were pushed to such a degree of development in the imperialistic and fascistic

countries as to make their use, in case of an emergency, a foregone conclusion'.[24] As a result, Stalin made an order 'to accelerate BW preparations'.[25] At the same time as research and development were being carried out, the Soviet military were also putting in place a doctrine for the
operational use of biological weapons. For example, courses at the
Moscow General Staff Academy in 1940 identified potential uses for
Soviet biological weapons in offensive operations.[26]

There was therefore clear evidence showing how far the Soviets had
gone to ensure full integration of offensive biological warfare operations
into military operations following the Second World War. Some evidence even suggests that biological weapons were used by the Soviet
Union against German forces during the Second World War.
Information contained in one UK intelligence report from this period
stated that the German army had received 'information from prisoners
that the Russian army in front of Stalingrad had all recently been immunized against plague. This is not normally a focus of plague infection.' It
was therefore considered likely 'that the Russians might be contemplating the dissemination of plague ... As a result [it was decided to] dispatch
to the front of enough vaccine for one million men.'[27] Ken Alibek, a key
defector from the Soviet biological weapons programme in the 1980s,
remains convinced that the Soviet forces did use biological weapons,
most significantly in the battle for Stalingrad. In his book, as well as
before a US Joint Economic Committee meeting in May 1998, he stated
that in his opinion the Red Army had used biological weapons against
German troops in 1942.[28]

After the Second World War, information relating to Soviet BW
capabilities became much scarcer in the West. As the CIA observed, 'a
dearth of information continues to keep open the Soviet germ warfare
intelligence gap'.[29] In a detailed 156-page report on the Soviet BW programme, the CIA reported in 1961 that:

> There is insufficient direct evidence on which to base a firm assessment of
> Soviet BW offensive activities ... [but] we estimate that a BW research and
> development program is under way ... which probably encompasses both
> offensive and defensive aspects ... available evidence does not permit us to
> determine with certainty which BW agents are under investigation ... No
> BW production facilities have been identified in the USSR.[30]

Evidence available in the UK at the same time also suggests that the
Soviet biological weapons establishment was significantly reorganised

after the Second World War. Many universities and technical institutes were believed to have had secret laboratories to carry out government research established within them, for the explicit purpose of commandeering any new scientific idea for military purposes.[31] By 1957, the use of new types of weapons began to be actively discussed by the Soviet Communist Party Central Committee, where the term 'Problem Number 5', which persisted through to the 1990s, was first applied to issues related to biological weapons.[32]

The 1960s probably provided the strongest indications of how important the Soviet Union considered BW to be. Concern expressed within the Soviet scientific community suggested that new developments in biotechnology in the West were responsible for an apparent backwardness of Soviet science. Military personnel used these arguments to gather support for militarily significant biotechnology, recognising that civilian scientists had to be involved in development projects. The admission of civilian scientists into military institutes was unprecedented; 'fundamental problems in microbiology' were quickly identified and the government set towards 'catching up and leaving behind [any] potential enemies'.[33] By 1966 the Soviet Council of Ministers took the decision to establish the Main Directorate of the Microbiology Industry (Glavmikrobioprom or Biopreperat). This structure was expanded in the 1970s to integrate civilian and military biological research more closely.[34] By 1975, when the Soviet Union had ratified the BTWC, a proposal by the 15th Directorate in the Ministry of Defence to expand biological weapons research was accepted by the Politburo. By the beginning of the 1970s, the Soviet biological weapons establishment essentially comprised military, political and civilian components, controlled by the 15th Directorate. This allowed the Soviets to make maximum use of scientific talent for military purposes in the design and development of biological weapons, largely hidden within an ostensibly civilian organisation. The BTWC therefore provided a real opportunity for the Soviet Union to gain outright superiority in a strategic weapon.[35]

Soviet BW and the BTWC negotiations

So far it has been argued that not only did the Soviet Union have a long and successful history of research into biological materials for offensive military use, but that there was also a considerable amount of information available to the West that indicated these capabilities. But if specific intelligence was held by the UK government relating to the Soviet BW programme in the lead-up to the BTWC negotiations, why was it not used to challenge the Soviet Union before the BTWC was signed?

During the negotiations leading up to the agreement of the text for the BTWC in 1972, the British position with regard to Soviet interest and capabilities in biological weapons is of considerable interest. Throughout the 1960s, intelligence assessments published by the Joint Intelligence Committee Scientific and Technical Intelligence Sub-committee had presented detailed overviews of Soviet biological weapons capabilities and intentions. The fact that these reports were written clearly indicates that somewhere within the Defence or Foreign Office establishments, there was enough knowledge of Soviet BW to indicate that it was important to attempt to gather further information relating to their programme. In a report entitled 'Soviet Biological Warfare', the following observations relating to Soviet offensive biological warfare preparedness were made:

> ... statements from time to time by various leaders have indicated that weapons suitable for waging this type of warfare [biological] would be included in the Soviet armoury in the event of a future World War ... The Soviet Union possesses a large number of institutes and experimental stations, many of which could conduct biological warfare research ... some give cause for concern ... Quantities of pathogens sufficient for use in covert BW could be produced in the Soviet Union at any time ... Soviet microbiologists have paid great attention to the reduction and enhancement of virulence, and to the production of antibiotic strains ... the Soviet authorities are in a favourable position to conduct BW research and development unknown to the rest of the world ... The Soviet Union is capable of developing and using various means of disseminating liquid suspensions of BW agents on a large scale such as cluster bombs delivered from aircraft, rockets or cruise type missiles and spraying directly from such vehicles at low level.[36]

This report was notably confident about the perceived value of biological warfare within the Soviet Union. It also appears to mark the start of a pattern of events relating to the impact of intelligence on UK foreign policy regarding biological warfare and the Soviet Union, where assessments were providing full and clear warnings and indicators of Soviet capabilities, but were being ignored by policy-makers. The concerns of some officers in the DIS (Defence Intelligence Staff) were present in official correspondence from early on, though the attitude of the FCO was equally clear:

> ... the UK took the lead in submitting a draft Convention to the UN in 1969, despite misgivings in some quarters on the dangers of the UK becoming a party to an agreement devoid of any verification provisions. The precedent thus set was a further cause for concern but it was stressed that a BW agreement would facilitate a later agreement on CW. Further, there were strong diplomatic and political forces for control of BW and some unwarranted scepticism about its utility as a method of warfare.[37]

Evidence illustrating these differing agendas can be found in many letters exchanged between the UK FCO and other government departments and agencies. In a letter from the UK FCO Disarmament Department to the Cabinet Office Assessments Staff, the FCO state:

> It seems unlikely that Soviet leaders expect biological weapons to play a part in any future large-scale war ... as the Soviet Government has now agreed to work for the prohibition of biological methods of warfare, it seems unlikely that they envisage such methods of warfare being used in any future large-scale war in which they are involved.[38]

These comments, directed to the assessments staff in the Cabinet Office—a part of central government responsible not only for considering intelligence, but also for defining and delivering the objectives of the government, seem even more surprising when one considers that they appear once again to fly in the face of several other documents detailing the assessed position of the Soviet government relating to biological weapons. For example, in February 1971, the Soviet Section Research Department of the UK FCO had been tasked with collecting statements by senior Soviet government officials 'which might indicate whether the Soviet Union maintains stocks of chemical and/or biological weapons'.[39] They reported that 'we know of no Soviet official statement saying this in so many words. However, we have compiled a few statements by Soviet military leaders, which make it pretty clear that the Soviet Union expects C and B weapons to be used in a future war.' These quotes, all from the time period 1956–66, included the following:

> Marshal Zhukov, 1956: 'A future war, if unleashed, will be characterised by ... different means of mass destruction, such as atomic, thermonuclear, chemical and bacteriological weapons.'

Lt. Gen. Med. Service Molchanov, 1962: 'Not only atomic, but chemical and bacteriological weapons as well as combinations of them are utilised in modern combat operations.'

Marshal Sokolovsky, 1963: 'It can be expected that chemical and biological weapons ... will be used in future wars.'

Col. Gen. N. A. Lomov, 1966: 'Bacteriological weapons are very effective.'[40]

The response to this information from the UK FCO Disarmament Department was 'it would, of course, help us if we could provide hard evidence of Soviet possession and deployment of C and B weapons. Unfortunately, such evidence does not seem to be available.'[41] Further correspondence from the UK FCO Disarmament Department echoed this apparent refusal to accept the credibility of intelligence information. For example, comments by the UK FCO on DIS documents provided analysis identifying 'the apparently unthreatening nature of Soviet CBW preparations ... [and] the apparently rigid and unimaginative state of Soviet Military planning on CBW'.[42]

The US position relating to Soviet biological warfare capabilities was similar to the British, in that it was reluctant to accept that the Soviets would use biological weapons; yet, unlike the FCO, it remained open-minded and stated a need for further intelligence. In the US, a report to the National Security Council stated: 'the Soviets have all the necessary means for developing an offensive [biological] capability [but] we believe that Soviet vulnerabilities would weigh heavily against Soviet initiation of BW ... We believe it unlikely that the Soviets would employ BW as a primary means of initial strategic attack.'[43] This report went on to state a requirement 'for more definitive intelligence on other nations' CBW capabilities', something that one might have expected to see in the UK.[44]

The British position immediately prior to the negotiations for the BTWC in the early 1970s was therefore paradoxical. On the one hand, intelligence information did suggest that the Soviet Union had at least an ability to produce and deliver biological warfare agent. Yet at the same time, elements of the FCO and Cabinet Office staff were of the opinion that the Soviet BW threat was negligible and should certainly not stand in the way of the negotiation of the BTWC. This difference in opinion between elements of the intelligence community and the Foreign Office was to be significant, as it became apparent that the Foreign Office believed that the BTWC could be successfully concluded.

The Soviet Union made it clear in the early phases of the BTWC negotiations that they felt the 1925 Geneva Protocols provided adequate prohibition of biological warfare. From the Soviet position, the Protocols essentially prohibit the use of biological weapons only in relation to other states bound by it. Furthermore, they cease to be binding if an enemy fails to respect those prohibitions.[45] Documents produced by UK FCO staff reported that the Soviet Ambassador to disarmament negotiations at Geneva stated at a press conference 'that the Soviet draft CBW Convention admitted the right of reprisal in kind', going on to comment that 'the Soviet Union will never agree to give up the right of retaliation in kind'.[46]

The implication of the Soviet position in the negotiations for the BTWC was that if they refused to give up a right to retaliation in kind for a biological weapons attack, then it could be assumed that they might be likely to have a capability through which this response in kind could be generated. What makes this position even more curious is the fact that Western intelligence reports stated that 'the USSR expects NATO to deploy BW in the event of war'.[47] Those same reports go on to state that 'we believe it is highly unlikely that the Soviets would employ BW in an initial strategic attack'.[48] Given the previously considered UK intelligence assessments detailing Soviet preparedness for biological warfare, one would logically assume that this capability did in fact exist or at least could be achieved very quickly. However, the Foreign Office appeared to be so set on pursuing a successful conclusion to the BTWC negotiations that a lack of intelligence on Soviet BW was increasingly interpreted to be a lack of the existence of a programme.

Another initial stumbling block to the BTWC negotiations was the refusal of the Soviet Union to separate biological arms control from chemical arms control. The British position relating to this matter was that the distinction between chemical and biological weapons lay in the fact that chemical weapons had already been used in war, whilst biological weapons had not and might therefore be easier to ban.[49] The US position on this matter was identical to the British, indeed Nixon had announced on 25 November 1969 the unilateral abolition of biological weapons.[50] It was therefore of some surprise when, in August 1970, the Soviet Union suddenly announced that it would accept the differentiation between chemical and biological weapons and so make the BTWC possible.[51] UK FCO representatives in Geneva were told by London that 'we shall not, repeat not, try to score debating points out of the fact that the Russians, for whatever reason, have done an about turn and broadly speaking come round to our point of view'.[52] In the light of the argument presented so far, this attitude seems extraordinary: did the FCO really believe that almost overnight the Soviet Union had fundamentally changed its attitude to these weapons?

Opinions as to why the Soviet about-turn took place are varied. Some academic explanations tie the Soviet view of arms control and disarmament to the political philosophy of communism: in particular, the communist belief that militarism and the accumulation of arms is a direct product of capitalism.[53] Other explanations consider that the Soviet leadership considered military parity with the United States and other NATO members as the main means of strengthening national security.[54] Soviet arms control negotiation strategy can therefore be considered to be a simple case of 'obtaining unilateral American concessions, exchange the least for the most, and reduce the impact of Soviet concessions'.[55] Essentially, it has been argued that the Soviet motivations for engagement in the negotiations for the BTWC were simply 'because they gave promise for certain advantages'.[56] In this case, as has previously been stated, unilateral biological disarmament by the United States in a treaty with no requirement for verification handed a strategic advantage and initiative to the Soviet Union by denying the enemy an entire class of weapon.[57] Given the efforts that the Soviet Union then put into developing biological weapons, this desire for a clear strategic advantage over the West seems a compelling explanation for the Soviet about-turn.

Western explanations as to the apparent change in position by the Soviet Union in their acceptance of the BTWC are significantly different. Ambassador James Leonard, Assistant Director of the US Arms Control and Disarmament Agency, believed that 'they wanted to do business with the Nixon Administration, this was high politics at a major level and a minor move in a bigger game plan on arms control, involving mainly nuclear issues'.[58] This view would appear to be borne out by the fact that within a month of signing the BTWC, the US and Soviet Union began the Strategic Arms Limitation Talks (SALT) which eventually resulted in the agreement to limit deployed strategic nuclear weapons as well as to facilitate the negotiation of the 1972 Antiballistic Missile Treaty (ABM).[59] The dominance of nuclear weapons in strategic military thinking is well articulated by President Nixon, who commented 'we'll never use the damn germs ... if someone used germs on us, we'll nuke 'em'.[60] In addition, documents from the US National Archives show Henry Kissinger stating 'we do not need BW for deterrence when we have nuclears'.[61]

Alternative views from the actual time period explaining Soviet motivations are difficult to locate. Whilst many authors now (writing with the benefit of hindsight) cite the Soviet change in position as a deliberate decision to launch a covert biological weapons programme, other accounts are generally confined to those of defectors from the Soviet Union.[62] Perhaps the most significant alternative explanation for the Soviet change in position is that of Arkady Shevchenko, a Soviet diplomat at the United Nations at the time of his defection:

> at a meeting in the spring of 1972, it was decided to sign the convention on the liquidation of biological weapons. But General Aleksei A Gryzlov told me that Defence Minister Andrei Grechko had instructed the military not to abandon its program to produce these weapons. It is not possible that the Politburo was unaware of this order.[63]

There is in fact additional evidence that supports this argument. In 1974, Ovchinnikov, a senior figure in the Soviet biological warfare establishment, summoned a group of biologists to a meeting where he stated that 'they were confronted by a major political challenge. The Americans had stopped work on a super-powerful bacteriological weapon, and it was for the Soviet scientists to make the most of this opportunity ... who would volunteer? It would be a storm troop, a force of marines, a biological commando.'[64] Once again, the implication of this evidence is, therefore, that the senior leadership of the Soviet Union had decided to sign the BTWC whilst at the same time deciding to continue a covert biological weapons programme. This perhaps sits comfortably alongside arguments previously stated that suggest the Soviet Union wanted nothing but a clear military advantage through the treaty. The BTWC was easily exploitable and had the potential to give the Soviet Union a weapon with no equivalent in Western armouries.

The subject of the motivations behind Soviet breaches of arms control treaties has been covered in detail elsewhere.[65] It is, however, perhaps worth reiterating here the view generally held in the West, in particular during the 1980s, that 'cheating and deception, when used in support of Soviet strategy, are entirely moral activities from the Soviet perspective

... Cheating is a serious activity that is in the main reserved for tasks that advance state interests.'[66] A former DIS officer commented on the possible Soviet motivation for signing the BTWC: 'in the Russian view Conventions are great. You sign Conventions to cheat because you deny the enemy a weapon which suddenly becomes important because they've stopped doing any work on it.'[67] Once again though, this view, common among members of the intelligence communities, seems to be at odds with that held by policy-makers.

In summary, it therefore seems ironic that the BTWC actually went some way towards providing a framework to facilitate Soviet deception. The lack of measures for compliance, applied to a country with the potential for the 'Soviet authorities ... to conduct BW research and development unknown to the rest of the world' had already been identified by British intelligence, but was almost entirely ignored by FCO officials involved in the negotiation of the treaty.[68] The BTWC seemed to allow the Soviets free rein to interpret or ignore the treaty at their own will, safe in the knowledge that the renunciation of biological weapons by the US, the UK and other countries gave them the potential for overwhelming advantage in an entire class of weapons, and probably also indicated to them that Western intelligence agencies would not be particularly focused on gathering information on a threat which they probably did not believe existed. In addition, the attitude of the UK Foreign Office during the BTWC negotiations seemed to be characterised by a desire to put a successful conclusion to the treaty, above all else. It appears that intelligence officers' individual concerns about Soviet BW research were allowed no opportunity to influence those negotiations. The view of the Foreign Office towards Soviet BW was therefore a simple one: it recognised no threat. This view is an important one, as it appears to define the position of UK government that was to persist for many years. It also marks the adoption of a position by the UK government that the intelligence agencies would struggle for many years to challenge.

Reconstructing UK CBW intelligence: re-recognising the threat

For the UK government, in particular the FCO, the BTWC appeared to signal the demise of any threat that might previously have existed from BW. With the FCO satisfied that for whatever reason the Soviets had now given up on any attempts to develop BW, the government next began to consider whether or not it actually needed the establishment that had evolved over the years since the end of the Second World War to counter the threat from BW. This section will therefore analyse the relationship between the intelligence gathered by UK agencies relating to Soviet BW in the period immediately after the signing of the BTWC and how foreign policy reacted to that intelligence.

The apparent confidence of the UK government in the disappearance of any BW threat from the Soviet Union, or indeed any other state, is most strongly reflected in the fact that within the UK there was no unit within any intelligence agency with responsibilities for monitoring treaty compliance. This does not seem entirely surprising given that this chapter has already shown how confident the FCO was that the BTWC marked the end of a BW threat. Furthermore, for those in the FCO concerned with arms control, it was simply not believed that any state that had signed the BTWC would deliberately breach it. One explanation for this position might lie in the fact that the UK simply perceived that other governments would act in the same way that UK did with regard to treaty compliance. However, this attitude was described by one intelligence officer as reflecting 'national un-receptiveness' in the face of 'intimations that the USSR had not reduced its considerable interest in BW since satisfying the BWC'.[69] The implication here is clear: that policy-makers were once again simply not willing to accept the information passed to them from the intelligence agencies. Yet despite this significant challenge, it is perhaps worth remembering that as Vice Admiral Sir Louis Le Bailly records, intelligence must 'tell those who won't listen all the things they don't want to know'. It is to the credit of a small number of intelligence officers that a motivation to do this persisted.[70]

Yet for those working within the fields of CBW in the intelligence agencies, other views relating more to economic factors than military threats also prevailed:

> ... there wasn't any unit for assessing compliance [with the BTWC]. The reason we signed the convention was basically political ... It was a way to save money because they were looking to close down the Microbiological Research Establishment without bothering to have a threat assessment because they had made the decision that they [the Soviets] were out of the business. And the long-term aim was having got the BTWC, without even bothering to find out whether there was actually a threat ... was purely political. And they also made the decision that once the convention had

bedded down then they would have a CWC basically along the same lines so then they could close down Porton Down.[71]

Official documents echoed these comments:

Inevitably, the emergence of the BWC led to some political clamour for the closure of the Microbiological Research Establishment (MRE) at Porton, which under several titles had been the focus of the UK's R&D in this field since the early years of WWII. The 1969 abandonment by President Nixon of the US offensive capability and restriction of the US R&D to solely defence needs was a further factor. Probably however, the major factor was the UK need for economies in the defence sector [along with] considerable competition for funds and resources in the major defence fields in the early 1970's.[72]

These views seem to suggest two issues relating to intelligence on CBW. Firstly, they suggest that the intelligence establishment was at a structural disadvantage in terms of its resources, capabilities and ability to influence policy. As a result, if it were to be capable of directly challenging policy-makers, it would probably require evidence of non-compliance amounting to nothing less than absolute proof. Secondly, it would appear that there was no relationship between perceived threats from CBW and spending on defence against them. Here, evidence suggests that there were clear economic drivers behind desires to cut BW research in order to divert funding elsewhere. Indeed, these pressures were felt across the intelligence establishment in the early 1970s. One former director general of intelligence in the Ministry of Defence described how he was forced by Treasury officials to 'define the purpose of [his] expenditure and ... expected results', which he argued it was 'impossible to do'.[73]

However, these decisions to make cuts could only be justified if there remained a situation whereby it was perceived that no BW threat existed. If one had confidence in the BTWC achieving its aim of banning offensive BW, then these decisions appeared to be sound. The danger of this line of thought however is obvious: if economics dominated the decision rather than the reality of the threat, any attempt by the intelligence agencies to provide information detailing that a threat did indeed exist would probably be ignored, purely because it did not sit comfortably with a political decision that had already been made. Furthermore, that decision was not unrelated to pressures to drive down government spending, a perennial issue in the 1970s. As a result, it was likely that the rationale underpinning that decision would prevail—unless, of course, any intelligence reporting was so powerful that it was impossible to ignore.

Events within the UK from the period immediately after the signing of the BTWC can therefore be characterised by an apparent struggle between intelligence agencies on the one hand, trying to prove that the Soviets were conducting activities counter to the BTWC, and policymakers on the other hand, ignoring the intelligence agencies and trying to proceed with cuts in funding to the UK BW (and CW) defence establishment. Economic factors appear to have been a key tenet of the policymakers' agenda, despite the views of the intelligence agencies. One official document presenting an overview of the 'Effects of the 1972 BW Convention in the UK' stated:

> In the mid-1970's the possibility that the UK's BW defence R&D at MRE might be reduced was increasingly discussed. Eventually, it was decided that this R&D should be continued on a much-reduced scale at CDE [Chemical Defence Establishment Porton Down] and that the MRE should be taken over by PHLS [Public Health Laboratory Service] to pursue R&D outside the Defence Sector. To this end MRE were transferred to CDE to become the nucleus of the new Defence Microbiological Division ... Inevitably, whilst the MRE building had been designed specifically for microbiological research, no buildings in CDE had been designed with such purposes in mind. This, the smaller numbers of staff and loss of special facilities all combined to change the R&D programme in practice but not in its long term aims ... a 'watch-tower' role in the surveillance of microbiological and allied advances likely to increase the hazard of BW.[74]

One former DIS officer was extremely critical of these decisions, stating that although in an attempt to preserve some BW expertise 'someone had this wonderful idea that 10 people would be transferred from MRE when it closed, into CDE to maintain this ... watchtower in case new developments posed any problems for the convention ... but the people that transferred over weren't BW experts, so it was a farce'.[75]

This appears to reflect the argument already stated above: that as long as no BW threat was seen to exist, it became a common-sense decision to save money by cutting the UK BW defence establishment. The establishment of a unit as a 'watch-tower' is however an interesting move. In essence, this gives responsibility to a department within a defence research establishment for monitoring intelligence on offensive BW. It appears ironic that intelligence on a possible Soviet BW threat was ignored in order to justify cuts in the BW defence establishment, only then to give back responsibility for the monitoring of BW to a much reduced part of that establishment. One might even go so far as to argue that this was a somewhat notional responsibility: if intelligence could not persuade officials that a threat existed before, how would a much smaller establishment be capable of succeeding in its place? Equally, if the FCO was so sure that the BTWC had eliminated the BW threat, why was there a need for this 'watch-tower' in the first place and what intelligence would that 'watch-tower' need to obtain to give a warning sufficient to generate action?

Whilst the evidence considered so far portrays a situation where central government was ignoring evidence provided by the intelligence agencies, further research has provided an even more vivid picture of the reality of how this relationship was managed by policy-makers. Two separate interviews have provided information stating that intelligence officers were actually prevented from passing intelligence relating to the Soviet threat through their reporting chain. The first individual painted a picture whereby the apparent small-minded careerism of his superior manager resulted in analysts being essentially forbidden to do their jobs properly:

Well, if I can go back to DI 53, when I joined DI 53 I succeeded a chap called X—I don't know whether you've met him ... he was DI 53 B and the previous DI 53 B was a chap called Y ... Now Y had been made redundant in a distillers company and his brother-in-law who was DI 53 A, a chap whose name was Z, his brother-in-law got him this job in DI 53. And Y was so reluctant to be, well reluctant is not the right word, so afraid of being declared redundant again, although redundancy wasn't a possibility in the civil service at that time, that he thought he would be very, very careful with the result that neither he, nor X, or myself, was allowed to make any startling deductions based on intelligence ... [so] for many years [this] meant that the BW threat was obscured due to this reluctance of Y.[76]

The second individual was also critical when reflecting on the problems in UK BW intelligence at this time:

... in 1978 there was one guy, X, in the DIS who was responsible for sort of keeping an eye on what was going on in the world. Nobody would listen to a word he said because nobody believed anything. Plus, the guy who was AD [Assistant Director] in those days, Y, he ... wouldn't tell anybody if he knew anything. So you had this wonderful ingredient of a guy who actually knew quite a lot but was not pushy and didn't sort of say too much, Y, who would classify the time of day and wouldn't tell anyone as a matter of principle ... although the basic story that the Russians had a programme was there ... nobody would take any notice of it. In 1978 the actual BW intelligence desk was abolished to save money so you had nobody other than X on one day a week coming up just to sort of keep the desk ticking over, that's how bad it was.[77]

It is however worth pausing in light of these comments to consider what intelligence was actually held at this time relating to Soviet BW. Once again, for the two individuals whose comments are transcribed above, there seem to be four strands to this issue. Firstly, that whilst intelligence may have been 'circumstantial',[78] it nonetheless suggested that a threat existed. Secondly, there appeared to be a concerted effort on the part of the government to 'explain away' this intelligence. Thirdly, an examination of these first two strands suggests that signals intelligence (or SIGINT) appeared to be held in such high regard that it alone could validate or reject intelligence on BW from other sources. Finally, that acknowledging a Soviet threat from BW did not fit the UK government (and in particular FCO) view of Soviet capabilities, and so evidence of any BW threat from intelligence sources must therefore, by definition, be wrong.

To turn our attention first to the fact that intelligence on Soviet BW did exist, there appeared to be evidence available provided by other sources. For example:

... at that time [mid to late 1970s] DI7 [satellite imagery] material from the US and in UK hands covered all the major BW sites in the USSR, so I think at that time at least five out of the seven or five out of the six [suspected facilities] were identified and studied and had been for years by JARIC, but nobody was interested ... these [photographs] indicated the bringing together of a microbiological programme and explosives, and there was no other alternative role other than BW.[79]

Another intelligence officer made similar comments relating to intelligence on Soviet BW held at this time:

... there was enough low level intelligence to suggest that something was going on ... What you are talking about are people like Jewish émigrés or Russians who managed to get out on a trip who would be interviewed in Germany by the refugee resettlement agency. But these were people who were low level who were saying, you know, 'I went in this place and there was this funny general' or 'I'd heard that'. So it wasn't that the guy had been in the programme telling you, it was lots and lots of little bits, you know the jigsaw puzzle, that you'd painstakingly try and put together, all of which sort of said, 'Hey, there's something bloody funny going on here,' and then, you know, particularly because of the availability of aerial photography, the guy would describe this place with six fences, you'd look at the picture and sure enough there was six fences, you know it's supposed to be a biological vaccine factory, bloody hell.[80]

But not all intelligence available was taken from 'low level' sources. Other imagery provided photographs 'where you could see 20 ton fermenters going into the Biopreparat [Soviet BW programme] places'.[81]

The official response to this intelligence, and the second strand alluded to above, appears to remain remarkably consistent over a considerable period of time. That response is characterised by the views of one intelligence officer: 'nobody was interested ... [it] was essentially just ignored [and] wasn't considered to be proof that a threat might exist ... having made [a decision to close MRE] ... they didn't want to hear anything which ran counter to that'.[82] Another officer stated:

... overall there was this sort of [view] we don't like the subject so it can't be true, we've signed the convention, you really telling us the Russians are cheating? And we'd say yes probably, you can't say that, you can't just go and accuse them of cheating unless you've got absolutely the holy grail. What was the holy grail? ... And these photographs, well they could be anything, just because they've got six fences around there and bunkers, nuclear hardened, environmental control, low temperature bunker, well it could be for storing anything. So there was this positive attempt to explain away anything that looked nasty.[83]

The apparent power of SIGINT to validate threats is another interesting consideration here. One intelligence officer explained the official view that, at best, intelligence on Soviet BW was circumstantial when he commented on the fact that 'because there was no SIGINT it [Soviet BW] didn't exist. So there was a tradition, obviously coming from Cheltenham, that if there is no SIGINT, we're OK.' He went on to state that 'another big bar to perceptions of the BW threat was ... that the atomic threat from the USSR manifested plenty of SIGINT but the BW threat didn't, therefore there wasn't a BW threat'.[84] Once again these comments are reiterated elsewhere: 'if [GCHQ] listened to people

[Soviets] saying BW we might actually take it seriously, [but] because we never heard anybody say BW, it's all a load of crap'.[85] That same officer added to his answer:

> But what they forgot of course was who was active during this whole period ... Geoffrey Prime at GCHQ ... worked in the branch and was telling the Russians exactly what we were reading ... So they knew what we were reading and they made sure we read what they wanted us to read ... I had this big row once at the CIG where somebody said 'well we don't hear it' and I said 'just because we don't hear it doesn't mean it's not there'... but [the response was] 'we're the Soviet experts ... we've been reading and listening in for years, we know what they're doing'. And that arrogance, in terms of the attempt to produce a decent JIC assessment, that's what screwed us.[86]

These comments make interesting observations about the apparent power of SIGINT in the late 1970s, not least in its ability to provide hard evidence—if not fact—to policy-makers, at the same time dismissing intelligence from other sources if it did not match.

The final strand to this issue is the attitude of the UK establishment towards any intelligence relating to Soviet BW that was taken forward. The Western view of Soviet capabilities, in particular in science, appears to be a key piece of what allowed that attitude to form. Recounting a meeting with a senior manager in one intelligence agency, one officer recalled the view that 'if it had been any good [BW], we'd have done it 20 years ago; look, they've got Lada cars and we've got Rolls Royces—so they can't possibly do anything any good, we'd have done it years ago'.[87] Furthermore, there also appeared to be an attitude that 'we couldn't make a 20-ton fermenter work, and it's true we couldn't ... the Americans couldn't make plague on more than about a 10 or 20 litre scale, you don't seriously expect us to believe the Russians have got a factory with ten 20-ton fermenters, you must be out of your mind'.[88] Another officer believed the refusal to accept intelligence to be purely a function of the fact that 'the people in the intelligence community didn't know a bloody thing about BW ... I think that came from a complete obscuration of the long-held view that BW was [not] feasible'.[89] Furthermore, 'BW was held at a very high level of security for decades and it was restricted to a very small number of people ... there was no background [knowledge] to BW'.[90]

Finally, and of particular interest given the research focus of this book, this UK attitude appears to relate at least in part to the power and influence that the FCO held at this time in the JIC, but also how the JIC was organised and managed. It has been recorded that 'there was a view that the quality of the DIS civilian staff and much of the military staff was generally inferior to that of the FCO ... therefore there would always be a danger of the FCO carrying the day'.[91] However, it has also been noted that 'the FCO is apt to be too trusting, firstly because in the nature of things they should be, and secondly because ambassadors are apt to fall in love with the country to which they are accredited'.[92] Nonetheless, this provides a useful indication of the perceived quality of FCO personnel. It also perhaps hints at their ability to have their opinions not only heard, but accepted.

The organisational structures in place relating to the tasking, collection and management of UK intelligence in the late 1970s therefore appear to be quite significant here. Intelligence was managed through a very rigid, tall and hierarchical structure. Whilst this will be discussed in more detail in the next section, it is important to note that there were several layers of bureaucracy in place acting as filters for intelligence information collected at the end of this chain—the level of the analyst. Unfortunately for the Scientific and Technical Intelligence Directorate of DIS, it was at the very bottom of this chain: 'there was a tendency to regard that directorate as a scientific dustbin'.[93] Intelligence officers interviewed for the purposes of this book appeared both to accept this view, and universally to identify the barrier to the onwards passage of intelligence product as the JIC.

In terms of the culpability of the JIC in acting as a barrier, there was clear agreement that 'the people that mattered were the people that sat in the JIC committee and the representatives from their departments that would go to the CIG'.[94] Given that all BW analysts worked in the DIS at this time, intelligence had to pass through the assistant director in order to make it to the CIG. One officer explained:

> In ... DI 53 every Wednesday the desk officers would meet with the assistant director—that is Ken Reed in my time—and they would outline to him or to each other any major events which they sort of perceived—very often nothing at all of course, and then he [Ken Reed] would disappear after that to a meeting of the ADIs of DSTI [Assistant Directors of Intelligence of the Directorate of Scientific and Technical Intelligence] and then ultimately the director or the deputy director would go to the ... Chief of Defence Intelligence ... at another sort of top level meeting [CIG,

Central Intelligence Group], and they would recount what had been high-lighted and then presumably they would go to the JIC.[95]

The barrier posed to the passage of intelligence up the organisation towards those capable of affecting policy was therefore immediately challenged because of the presence of a manager who was not prepared to challenge establishment views. The CIG itself posed a major challenge at the next level:

... the CIG would be representatives from the DIS, from GCHQ, SIS, FCO, arms control as it used to be, or non-proliferation as it is now, the countries department, it used to be Russia but it then became Eastern department and then ... the policy arms control section, and then in the old days of course the DTI no interest, Security Service no interest, Customs and Excise no interest. So it was basically MoD, FCO and the Cabinet Office to try and square the circle between the FCO who didn't believe nothing [sic] and the MoD who were saying there's a problem.[96]

The ultimate challenge that intelligence faced at the CIG therefore appeared to be the views of the FCO—the same department responsible for the negotiation of the BTWC, and the same department that, as has already been shown, refused to accept information that there was a Soviet threat because that acceptance ran counter to policy decisions already in place. One intelligence officer was adamant in reiterating arguments already presented: that the FCO had absolute power in the CIG. 'There was always a feeling in the MoD that the FCO ruled the roost and if the FCO wanted a weak paper, we ended up with a weak paper.'[97] Until the FCO view either changed itself, or was forced to change by intelligence so strong that it could not be ignored, there was therefore little chance of intelligence relating to Soviet BW even making it to the JIC, let alone influencing policy there. The issues relating to the interplay between agency and structure here are striking: the organisational structures of both the intelligence agencies and central government appear to have been genuinely limiting the ability of individual analysts to influence or affect policy formation.

Before this section concludes, further analysis of these issues may be enhanced by briefly examining the view of those in the NGO CBW community at this time. Professor Julian Perry Robinson, a leading academic specialising in CBW disarmament issues since the 1960s, cites various reasons for the stance taken by groups such as SIPRI (the

Stockholm International Peace Research Institute). Robinson suggests that the NGO view in the UK was similar to the FCO's: that the focus was entirely on CW, with BW being rarely considered. He explained:

> the information available to us was paltry. The Soviets themselves were secretive in the extreme about their CBW weapons. The British government rarely published anything from the appraisals made within the UK intelligence community, and such information as it did release took on the appearance of bald assertion, un-nuanced, unqualified, without reference to sources, and therefore of little value to nongovernmental analysts except as a snapshot of HMG attitudes.[98]

As a result, NGO opinion in the UK appeared to be largely influenced by information from the US—information which, by and large, was sceptical that a Soviet BW threat existed.[99] The reasons for this US scepticism clearly fall outside the remit of this work, but it is interesting to consider that the UK government attitude was shared by NGOs and actively supported by information originating from the US. Robinson concludes his correspondence by asking: 'Did any of that matter a hoot? Was it good, bad or irrelevant that US officials, not British ones, should have set what became the views of a particular part of civil society?'[100] Perhaps this comment masks deeper questions—not least, was the FCO-dominated government view towards Soviet BW deliberately misleading? Furthermore, might this go some way towards explaining the apparent inability of intelligence agencies at this time to influence foreign policy?

In summary, the UK BW intelligence establishment in the aftermath of ratifying the BTWC was characterised by a belief that the BTWC had ended the BW threat faced by the UK and that, as a result, there was no further need or justification for BW defence expenditure. Evidence strongly suggests that these beliefs were sustained by a refusal to consider intelligence that ran counter to the view that the BW threat had disappeared. The FCO were apparently dominant in setting the tone of this attitude, and it was they who stubbornly refused to allow any challenge to this position. Regardless of the intelligence offered, the FCO always appeared to label product as inconclusive, and always demanded more rigorous intelligence. The organisational structures through which intelligence was managed appear to have played a part in preventing the passage of information up to the JIC, not least because of the views and opinions of line managers. As a result, even by the late 1970s, the JIC considered intelligence relating to the Soviet BW threat to be 'nebulous'.[101] By the end of the 1970s, however, this position was slowly beginning to change.

5

PLAYING THE LONG GAME

CHALLENGE AND PROOF

By the end of the 1970s, CBW experts in the UK intelligence communities were in an extremely difficult position in terms of their ability to have information relating to Soviet BW recognised by their superiors. Analysts with responsibilities for both CW and BW intelligence were adamant that they held powerful evidence of Soviet capabilities, but were faced with strong and rigid attitudes by both immediate superiors as well as senior members of the FCO with responsibilities for all aspects of arms control. From the very end of 1979, over a period of ten years these obstacles were gradually eroded, weakened and ultimately removed due to an increasing ability of analysts of Soviet CBW to present ever stronger intelligence product to their managers—product that it became increasingly dangerous and impossible to ignore. This chapter will provide an analysis of how that transition occurred. This change in attitude towards intelligence on Soviet BW was actually driven by intelligence collected on apparently unrelated incidents: the suspected use of the toxic agent known as 'yellow rain' in South East Asia and the use of CW in the Iran–Iraq War between 1980 and 1988. In addition, both the reorganisation of UK CBW intelligence capabilities along with a change in key personalities—most significantly the arrival of Percy Cradock as chairman of the JIC—were key factors in the overall change of attitude towards Soviet BW.

Challenging the establishment

In November 1979, information began to reach UK intelligence agencies relating to an outbreak of disease at a suspected Soviet BW facility in Sverdlovsk. This incident is often cited by authors (writing retrospectively) as the first hard evidence the West obtained that a Soviet BW programme existed.[1] As demonstrated in the previous chapter, this evidence immediately met resistance from senior government officials who refused to accept its significance. Despite the fact that 'there was low level HUMINT that something very nasty had happened, and there was SIGINT that something very nasty had happened ... the JIC produced an assessment that said we think something *might* have happened but overall we think the Soviet threat is nebulous'.[2] Where the incident at Sverdlovsk was important was in its ability not necessarily to prove that a Soviet BW threat existed, but to draw attention to the incident itself. For the first time this forced consideration of BW as an issue in its own right. Even though 'after Sverdlovsk the papers said it's probable there's been an accident, but you know, it doesn't mean there's an offensive programme, I mean because they might have been making vaccine that they were killing. And it might.'[3] Regardless, this was a major breakthrough for those analysts struggling to get acceptance that there was a Soviet BW threat.

The incident had a similar impact in the US, where official views of Soviet BW closely mirrored those in the UK. Several US intelligence agencies quickly picked up on the fact that 'an accident at a biological warfare institute in Sverdlovsk that resulted in 40 to 60 deaths may have occurred in May 1979'.[4] CIA intelligence reports talked of information that had reached them via a Soviet émigré, yet stated 'despite the proliferation of the rumours of a BW related incident, there is insufficient evidence that the alleged deaths can be attributed to unlawful storage of a BW agent'.[5] The view that there was insufficient evidence to relate the Sverdlovsk disease outbreak to a biological weapons research, production or storage facility is repeated in numerous US intelligence assessments.[6] This came despite a later US DIA report stating that 'the agent released reportedly was a genetically modified strain'.[7] Nonetheless, as in the UK, this incident also drew attention to BW. US concerns were to a degree placated, at least in part, by the assurances of the Soviet ambassador to the UN Conference on Disarmament who stated that 'the Soviet Union had faithfully implemented the BWC'.[8] Whist the Soviet explanations as to the causes of the now confirmed anthrax outbreak at Sverdlovsk were not entirely satisfactory to the Americans, debate and discussions rumbled on for many years, until in 1992 President Boris Yeltsin finally admitted 'our military development was the cause'.[9]

At a similar time that evidence relating to a possible accident with biological weapons at Sverdlovsk were circulating in Western intelligence agencies, so were stories of the possible use of chemical or biological warfare agents by the Soviet Union in Indochina and Afghanistan.[10] Once again, opinion in scientific and academic communities suggested 'if toxic warfare was used in the regions alleged, it is most unlikely that the so called Yellow Rain had anything to do with it'.[11] Intelligence agencies in the US and UK disagreed. In the US, the view was 'there is now no doubt that deaths and casualties have resulted from chemical attacks'.[12] In the UK, the DIS opinion of events in South East Asia was 'no one really has the absolute bottom line about what happened in South East Asia ... there was clearly something being used ... there were people being interviewed who had seen their family die, something was being used'.[13] Even reports of senior Soviet officers such as General Kuntsevich, who was to go on to head the Soviet chemical warfare programme, being seen in Vietnam and Afghanistan at the time of suspicious deaths, were dismissed as coincidental. On one occasion, the visit of Soviet officers known to be associated with chemical and biological warfare programmes to Afghanistan was explained away as interested parties investigating the use of CS gas against Soviet troops. It seems unlikely that such senior officers would show a great interest in the use of a non-lethal tear gas.[14]

By the beginning of the 1980s, political leaders were still unwilling to accept intelligence information, let alone use it to confront the Soviet government, citing a lack of absolute proof in the assessments being made—a view shared by many senior officers within the UK intelligence community as well. But now, attention was clearly drawn to the fact that a BW threat might actually exist, even if that threat came from apparently innocent research into biological agents with potential military application. JIC assessments now began to link 'Sverdlovsk, [which] provides circumstantial evidence ... linking them directly to SE Asia'.[15] It was apparent that a shift in attitude towards BW was beginning to occur. Afghanistan and South East Asia were therefore significant because they began the process of suggesting that a threat might exist. Because the available evidence, albeit circumstantial, could not be explained away, more attention would now slowly begin to be dedicated to trying to establish exactly what BW research was being carried out in the Soviet Union.

From the early 1980s, it is possible to identify three factors that explain the reluctant shift of UK government attitudes towards Soviet BW. Firstly, and perhaps of most significance, was the arrival of Percy Cradock as chairman of the JIC, which brought a new approach to intelligence assessment. This is closely linked to the second factor, of changes taking place in the structure of intelligence, specifically the division of responsibilities between collection and analytical agencies. Third was the use of CW in the Iran–Iraq War, which retrospectively proved the intelligence analysis correct in its reference to the Soviet BW threat. Although these factors took effect across the ten-year period from late 1979, they will be considered in turn.

In 1985, the arrival of Percy Cradock as Chairman of the JIC was to impact on the increasing willingness of the JIC to take seriously the information it was being presented. Cradock was a career civil servant, having joined the FCO in 1954 after graduating from Cambridge. From 1978 to 1984 he had been the UK ambassador to China and had led the negotiations on the Hong Kong Joint Declaration.[16] Cradock was at the same time Foreign Policy adviser to the Prime Minister. He was a strong character whose 'intelligence was intimidating. He was a powerful man in terms of influence, and he completely dominated the intelligence community by sheer force of intellect.'[17]

Cradock took a unique approach to fulfilling his mission. He believed that the key to intelligence success 'lay in the ability to enter the mind of the foreign leader in question. Capabilities could be measured, the number of tanks or aircraft, and their location pinpointed; but intentions were almost always a mystery ... there [is] always the temptation to play safe ... the brave prediction [is] also the most hazardous'.[18] Cradock began the practice whereby individual analysts would be summoned to the JIC to comment on specific aspects of reports being discussed. Even so, there persisted a view that individual departments, 'traditionally the Foreign Office, would ask a question in such a way that was designed to get an answer that would sort of prove that there was no problem'.[19] But whereas CBW analysts might have previously feared that the JIC did not take assessments seriously, assuming their work even got that far, at least there now appeared to be an open ear. As one intelligence officer explained, 'Cradock actually did believe that what we were saying was true. Just because it was a lone voice didn't mean it was untrue.'[20] Cradock also appeared to recognise the political significance of the intelligence on Soviet BW he was receiving, and most significantly that the problem could only be addressed at the highest level.

Cradock's own view was that the problem lay not in the reluctance of the JIC to accept evidence, but with the Prime Minister: 'there was no reluctance on the part of senior officials to accept there was a problem ... [we] were up against the emotions of a powerful lady [Thatcher]'.[21] In particular, whilst intelligence information relating to Soviet biological weapons remained fragmentary, 'the politicians refused to hear the message'.[22] So, whereas intelligence officers at DIS had previously blamed the JIC for being the barrier to the onwards transmission of assessments, now the chair of the JIC was receptive to CBW threat assessments; he perceived the barrier to be a level above him—in the Prime Minister. This problem may relate to the relationship that the then Prime Minister, Margaret Thatcher, had with President Gorbachev. Thatcher had famously stated as early as 1984 that 'I like Mr Gorbachev. We can do business together.'[23] This relationship troubled Cradock insofar as he could influence her willingness to accept that the Soviets posed a clear chemical and biological weapons threat: 'She thought he was a good man, not a cheat ... [she was] emotionally attached, she enjoyed his company and I never shared that view ... [I was always] inclined to believe the worst.'[24] Apparently 'seduced by the reforms that Gorbachev was introducing across the Soviet Union ... no prime minister was prepared to risk a confrontation ... that might change the delicate balance of international relations'.[25] Put simply, Cradock feared that Thatcher's affection for Gorbachev might prevent her from hearing evidence suggesting that he was complicit in Soviet deception relating to the BTWC. Cradock apparently therefore believed that he must push for a confrontation between the two leaders regarding Soviet BW.

In order to deliver the strength of intelligence required to force this confrontation, the existing problems in the structure of intelligence agencies relating to CBW intelligence had first to be addressed. As was considered in earlier chapters, the largest analytic body within UK intelligence was the DIS (Defence Intelligence Staff), a department within the Ministry of Defence. The largest collectors were SIS (Secret Intelligence Service) and GCHQ, under the control of the FCO. There is no department responsible for national assessment, merely the JIC controlling agencies with their own specific focus, interests, budgets and bureaucratic controls, which results in 'some fuzzy boundaries'.[26] That said, it is apparent that the intelligence machinery in the UK seems to be separated from decision-making, and merely gives advice to that process, but with a particular emphasis on forecasting—'on foreign targets it is the government's prophet'.[27]

To illustrate why this structure was problematic, one intelligence officer explained why chemical and biological warfare intelligence brought difficult organisational challenges. Where the SIS are responsible for collecting information, the DIS are responsible for analysing it. But the 'SIS had no one capable of debriefing technical people',[28] so from 1984 onwards the same officer within DIS was also beginning to become involved in the collection of information—a role that should have been fulfilled by SIS. The problem was made worse by the fact that 'because of the way SIS is tasked, it can only go for targets which are identified by the JIC'.[29] But because the JIC assessments did not identify a Soviet chemical or biological weapons threat, taskings were not made to collect specific information on these areas.

The situation was therefore created whereby a DIS officer was also working on behalf of SIS collecting 'intelligence on something for which there was no tasking', something that can be done 'the odd time if it's viewed as valuable, but if it were valuable then it would become a priority'—something which in the early 1980s it was not.[30] Institutionally, UK intelligence did not therefore recognise that a Soviet BW threat existed and therefore did not create taskings to gather intelligence on it. To make matters worse, because this problem partly centred on the fact that one individual was both collecting and analysing the same information due to earlier cuts in BW intelligence after the BTWC was signed, this led to allegations that that individual 'asked the question to get the answer he wants'.[31] This situation clearly raised the possibility of the existence of significant structural problems, not least because it reinforced the risk of problems in the customer and consumer interface of the intelligence cycle, as discussed previously. Now, the barriers between the collectors and the analysers of intelligence were being broken down, yet the JIC was by its own admission not expert enough to provide its own independent analysis of the intelligence it was receiving.

It was the Iran–Iraq War that finally forced the JIC to assign a high priority to the gathering of intelligence on Soviet chemical and biological weapons. This change in attitude came about in a surprising way, however, as one intelligence officer explained:

> I remember when I had to brief X who was DGI [Directorate General of Intelligence] … and Y who was DSTI [Directorate of Scientific and Technical Intelligence] … I was down to brief X when he came on a walkabout around the DIS [Defence Intelligence Staff] and I was told absolutely specifically by Y 'you will not mention Iraq. It's a load of crap, stop wasting our time', because I'd been trying to brief this week after week after week, getting [nowhere], and in this case it was a joke because we did have SIGINT as well of them buying the chemicals.

The visit and briefing went ahead as planned, yet an awkward question was posed, forcing comments to be made on the Iran–Iraq War:

> And when X came round I briefed him about Russian stuff, and at the end of it he said to me, 'What I'm really interested in is is [sic] there any evidence that Iran–Iraq is going to go chemical?' And I said, 'Yes.' He said, 'Who covers it?' I said, 'I do.' 'Well, tell me about it.' And I looked and Y was looking daggers, and I thought 'Well, stuff this' and I told him straight. And X heard me out and he turned to Y and he said, 'Why haven't I heard this before?' And Y said, 'Well, I'm not really sure this is …' 'I want it briefed on Friday, I want a CIG next week, I want a JIC assessment next Thursday.'

The JIC assessment represented a major breakthrough for those analysts working hard to break down the barriers preventing their concerns over Soviet CBW being raised to the highest levels:

> And the JIC assessment came back and said Iraq has got chemical weapons, Iraq will use chemical weapons, and the week after the assessment was made they used mustard in BR 250 WP bombs which I'd said 'and it will be in this'. And the reason we knew that GCHQ wouldn't do anything to collect [was] because they said it's crap. And I finally persuaded a guy to run some of the precursor chemicals that they would have to buy in to make mustard gas … and very quickly they suddenly came up with the orders that were going in to Germany and Holland for all these materials. And it was quite incredible because, you know, chance does happen. Orders that were being shipped—we actually had the photography of the trailers arriving at Samarra where the production facility was, we picked that up pretty quickly from, you know, the German workers who were out there, that there was something fishy, plus the odd Iraqi who was sort of coming out and being loose-tongued.

But in this case the most significant evidence came from the analysis of an extremely subtle piece of evidence:

> We picked up a bit of SIGINT, I don't know, must have been '81 [or] '82, and you know we never know when something's going to come in. There was this really curious piece: they were buying these BR 250 WP [white phosphorous aircraft bombs] from a Spanish firm, and the Spanish firm were told we want them modified for nose filling, and the Spanish firm said but you don't fill WP that way, and the Iraqis said well if you don't want the order we'll go somewhere else. So they said fine, we'll modify them—and I squirreled this away and then we got the buying of thiodigly-col [precursor chemical required to manufacture mustard] and all the rest of it. It could only mean one thing, it was going to be a liquid fill and the liquid at that stage they had was mustard so they were going to use mustard gas.[32]

One week later the JIC assessment was to prove correct as television news stations beamed around the world pictures of dead, injured and blinded Iranian troops.[33] From that point on, chemical and biological issues were given the highest priority by the JIC for the collection of information.[34]

The acceptance of not only the CW threat illustrated by the Iran–Iraq War, but also that UK CBW analysis was actually very, very capable brought with it one last problem which relates back to the previous consideration of organisational issues. As Soviet CBW-related intelligence became a high priority for collection, so the SIS realised that 'you couldn't send a classic intelligence branch officer to interview someone who was in the business of making this stuff, because they don't understand a word they were saying. Unless you could actually talk the same language and establish a rapport, you had no chance of getting information.'[35] The SIS therefore required technical specialists, and so a new unit was set up within SIS specifically for that purpose. The small staff was largely recruited from DIS in order to build on particular expertise which already existed within the UK intelligence community.[36] Now, within SIS, the brother of C [Chief of SIS], X, who headed the department within SIS responsible for technical aspects of collection, began to take an interest in what he was being briefed on Soviet chemical and biological warfare. X 'opened doors that no one else would open'.[37]

Institutional problems did persist, however. SIS is responsible for collection and not analysis, so relocating sole experts from DIS to SIS merely led to further allegations that the same officer who had been 'shouting, hey here's a problem ... all of a sudden [starts] producing intelligence, that proves there's a problem [was merely] cooking the books'.[38] Furthermore, other individuals within government who required further explanation of what intelligence actually meant would telephone SIS and not DIS for comment. Once again, the view of DIS was 'how dare they?'.[39] If one thinks back to comments made previously about the perceived quality of DIS officers against those of the FCO, there is perhaps an air of jealousy and envy about this that goes beyond simple inter-service rivalry. Nonetheless, small successes in the ability of intelligence to affect policy began to have a combined effect in terms of their ability to force the UK intelligence community finally to accept, once and for all, that there was a significant Soviet BCW threat.

First the Iran–Iraq War, then the significant discovery that the UK S6 respirator was ineffective against a new type of Soviet chemical warfare agent challenged the existing dominant mindsets within the UK regarding the CBW threat.[40] There was an increasing recognition of the use, accidental or intentional, of both chemical and biological agents. This drew attention to the potential threat posed by states possessing not just the agents per se, but also the ability to produce them. But even in the mid 1980s, just before the arrival of Cradock, the JIC attitude towards Soviet BW was clear. Intelligence analysts passed reports to the JIC commenting on, for example, 'six facilities [that] pursue R and D on BW and have the capability to produce and store weapons and agents on a considerable scale. All of these facilities are active but it is not known whether agents are still being produced or whether stockpiles exist.'[41] They were to see the same information reflected in JIC assessments, but using markedly toned down language: '[Soviet facilities] conduct wide ranging research in microbiology relevant to medicine, veterinary medicine, agriculture and industry.'[42] They did not comment on 'repeated but undetailed intelligence suggest[ed] as assessing BW relevance'.[43] Cradock therefore inherited a considerable amount of assessment relating to Soviet BW, and he was to be a highly significant figure in his own right in forcing Thatcher to accept that a Soviet threat existed. But he would require a killer piece of evidence if he were to force Thatcher to confront Gorbachev. That killer evidence was to arrive in 1989.

Pasechnik: incontrovertible evidence

In the summer of 1989, as a reward for his overall performance, Vladimir Pasechnik, General Director of the Institute of Ultra Pure Biochemical Preparations in Leningrad, was given permission to travel to France to sign a deal he had negotiated for the supply of advanced laboratory equipment. On arrival in Paris, he contacted the UK embassy, explained his position and announced his desire to defect. The request was accepted. Pasechnik represented a part of the Soviet Biopreperat biological warfare establishment, hidden underneath the cover of organisations involved in ostensibly civilian research. His defection was to provide the evidence required not only to piece together the rather fragmentary intelligence held so far by the UK on Soviet BW, but also finally to provide undisputable proof of the existence of these Soviet programmes.[44]

Up until 1985, when Gorbachev came to power, the foreign policy of the Soviet Union had remained remarkably consistent since the death of Stalin in 1953. At the heart of Soviet foreign policy was a determination to remain militarily strong in the face of the threat from the US-dominated Western world—both in terms of conventional and non-conventional weapons. Although successive Soviet leaders from Khruschev onwards had recognised the massive strain that military spending put on the Soviet economy, there was an absolute reluctance even to consider curtailing military budgets, an issue that was at the heart of the economic problems which the Soviet Union had long faced.[45] Any attempts at reform of the Soviet system always faced the same structural problems: relating to the tension between personalist principles on the one hand, and organisationalist principles on the other.[46] In addition, leaders were often reluctant to drive forwards the type of change programmes that the Soviet economy required: firstly, because of confusion as to where ultimate power lay in terms of the relationship with the president and the Politburo; and secondly, linked to the first point, because of an awareness on the part of most leaders since Stalin of how tenuous their leadership positions could be should they incur the wrath of other Politburo members.[47]

These considerations are important when considering why a secret BW programme was so important for the Soviet Union, because they provide the key to understanding why and how Gorbachev justified deep cuts in nuclear forces to the Politburo. They are also of some use when positing explanations for the eventual rollback of the programme.

Before further considering this point, it is important to note that in areas relating to foreign policy, the Soviet system was unitarily bureaucratic with no bodies that could act independently of the state; it was dominated by 'old school' thinking and hence characterised by a built-in barrier to change.[48] Economic policies were intertwined with all others, meaning that small changes to the economy (such as cuts in defence spending) could have massive implications elsewhere. Furthermore, the economy itself was in such a poor state that any changes could also have huge implications for the general public, which the leadership feared would not be tolerated without immediate visible benefits in terms of improved living conditions.[49]

> The Soviet invasion of Afghanistan in 1979 brought an end to the period of détente. After the death of Brezhnev in 1982, it also marked the start of a period of significant improvement in Soviet relations with the West, although the Cold War did not begin to thaw until 1984–5. The Afghan invasion resulted in an extremely strong reaction from the United States, whereby Carter immediately curtailed grain sales, suspended high technology exports, deferred cultural and economic exchanges, as well as boycotting the 1980 Moscow Olympics. Carter announced that 'the Soviet Union must realise that its decision to use military force in Afghanistan will be costly to every political and economic relationship it values'.[50] By 1982, the cessation of aid and cooperation from the West had forced the Soviet economy into even deeper crisis, accompanied by social unrest and an increasing technology gap between the Soviet and US military forces.[51] It was this that ultimately led to the selection of Gorbachev as president and the start of major reform programmes.

On 11 March 1985, the Central Committee unanimously voted for Gorbachev to become party leader. Whilst they recognised the need to address the stagnating Soviet economy, they were certainly not voting for Gorbachev with the expectation that he would become a radical reformer like Khrushchev had been.[52] There were clues present that Gorbachev believed in a need to reform the Soviet system—the fact that he had been born in 1931 and therefore had no experience of the revolution or Stalin's terrors meant that he was more willing to question the structures of the system; this led him to give public support to reformist measures, particularly in speeches he made in 1984.[53] That said, 'there is not a shred of evidence to suggest that the primary selectorate, the Politburo, endorsed him because of his new thinking, which, in any case, on foreign and defence policy had not yet been revealed'.[54] Even in his acceptance speech, Gorbachev paid tribute to his predecessor and then pledged to continue his policy of 'acceleration of socio-economic development and the perfection of all aspects of social life'.[55] So in general, the early years of Gorbachev's leadership could be characterised as a 'traditional means of approaching the problems of the past ... this assumed that there was nothing wrong with the basics of the Soviet system'.[56] Indeed, some commentators observed that 'from March 1985 to the fall of 1986 [his policies] were noteworthy more for their traditionalism than for their reformism; they were more reminiscent of Andropov's policies than of Khrushchev's'.[57] Take, for example, the failure of the Gorbachev regime to give a prompt, full and honest account of the Chernobyl disaster in April 1986 as an illustration of how little the Soviet system had changed thus far under Gorbachev.[58] An overwhelming amount of evidence therefore suggests that Gorbachev wanted 'to reform the Soviet system, not dismantle it'.[59]

Gorbachev therefore began his work by simply continuing the approach of Andropov, 'attempting to instil greater discipline in the workforce' by addressing corruption and alcohol abuse'.[60] To suggest that Gorbachev was able to dictate policy lacks strong evidence. Institutional factors alone provided constraints to Gorbachev actions: he was accountable to the Politburo, and as General Secretary it was his task to uphold the interests of the party, not undermine them; he could always be removed from post by the Politburo. Structurally he was further constrained by both the Ministry of Defence and the KGB, as well as by the powerful Military Industrial Complex, all of which were highly influential in setting policy, both foreign and domestic.[61] This is not to suggest that Gorbachev was not clever and persuasive in pushing through his reforms. Indeed, 'Gorbachev was often able to take advantage of the old command system's methods, of the residual authority of the party and its general secretary, and of the fact that the conservatives did not immediately catch on to the consequences of the changes they were witnessing and taking part in'.[62] Yet evidence still strongly suggests that Gorbachev set out to revitalise, not destroy, the communist system.[63]

In terms of foreign policy, Gorbachev appears to have recognised the relationship between the poor state of the Soviet economy and defence spending.[64] He also appeared to have recognised the need for a constructive and cooperative relationship with the military in order that his reforms could progress.[65] Some military leaders believed that curtailing military spending was actually a good thing for the army, in order that investment could be made in other, more technologically advanced areas. Evidence suggests that officers such as Marshal N. V. Ogarkov supported Gorbachev's civilian economic reform programmes, recognising the relationship between economic health and a sustainable military.[66] But Gorbachev could only save money on defence spending if he could relax international tensions, so that the Soviet Union could feel secure enough to proceed with cuts in weapons—particularly strategic nuclear forces.[67]

One of the key elements of the foreign policy of Gorbachev's Soviet Union was therefore an emphasis on arms control. His early attempts at positively engaging with the United States, however, began without a fresh strategy.[68] That said, his approaches were driven by a desire to reduce the Western perception of the Soviet Union as threatening.[69] But as Gorbachev began to realise that the pace of his economic reforms was too slow, so too he realised that he needed to change his foreign policy approach to the West. This change would, however, require changes to some key figures dominating the Politburo.

In May 1987, a young German aviator, Mathias Rust, was to provide Gorbachev with the opportunity to purge the heads of those departments resistant to his change programmes. Rust managed to land a Cessna light aircraft on Red Square, having successfully evaded Soviet air defences, which gave Gorbachev an excuse to remove Sokolov, the Minister of Defence, and replace him with Yazov, who was 'far more obedient to Gorbachev'; and replace Akhromeev, the chairman of the KGB, with Kryuchkov.[70] Commenting on Rust, Kryuchkov stated, 'Gorbachev used it ... to strike a blow to the Ministry of Defence, which in his opinion was not wholly subordinate to him, and didn't carry out his will or follow his train of thought'.[71] By purging the conservatives from senior domestic positions, and replacing the Foreign Minister Gromyko with Shevardnadze, Gorbachev succeeded in surrounding himself with people he could trust and who supported his reform attempts.

Gorbachev was therefore able to begin a series of arms control initiatives, aimed at reducing tensions between the Soviet Union and the West. His foreign policy objectives were essentially: to remove Soviet troops from Afghanistan, making it clear to Eastern European leaders that the Soviet Union would not intervene militarily to keep them in office; and to end the Cold War in order to divert resources away from the military and into the civilian sector, as well as to prevent the likelihood of war actually occurring.[72] In addition, Gorbachev refused to allow his desire to end the Cold War to 'become hostage to the sectional interests of the military or the security apparatus'.[73]

One of the greatest obstacles from a Soviet Union perspective to obtaining massive reductions in strategic nuclear forces was the US Strategic Defence Initiative (SDI). The SDI programme had actually been first discussed under President Johnson in the 1960s, but had quickly been found to be technically far too difficult and militarily far too vulnerable. In 1972 when President Nixon signed the Anti-Ballistic Missile treaty (ABM), developments were put on indefinite hold.[74] By 1986, however, under the presidency of Reagan, the ABM treaty was reinterpreted by the US so that 'research involving new physical concepts ... as well as testing, as well as the development indeed, are approved and authorised by the treaty'.[75] SDI deeply worried the Soviet Union. The stated desire of Gorbachev was to eliminate nuclear weapons completely.[76] However, his primary emphasis in arms control negotiations was 'on derailing Reagan's Strategic Defence Initiative'.[77]

Whilst Reagan accepted Gorbachev's proposals to seek the eventual elimination of nuclear weapons, he consistently refused to budge in his policy towards SDI.[78] Almost certainly, part of the Soviet abhorrence towards SDI were the devastating technological and financial implications; regardless, they wanted SDI stopped at any price.[79] But Soviet fears of US military capabilities had been growing over a longer period of time than the SDI time period. These fears were largely the result of disinformation acts by Western governments, most significantly the United States, as well as by the initiation of a binary chemical nerve agent programme. One such example was when in the 1960s the United States embarked upon a programme to mislead Soviet intelligence and military establishments into believing that the US had an advanced and extensive chemical weapons programme. It has been argued that this programme actually resulted in the Soviet 'novichok' programme—an advanced and ultra-toxic nerve agent.[80] It is also possible that these types of activities were at least partly responsible for the Soviet Union deciding to continue with a covert biological weapons programme—in the belief that the United States were doing the same, also in breach of the BTWC.

There is evidence to suggest that the Soviet Union saw their covert biological weapons programme as a potential answer to the US chemical and SDI threat. At a press conference on binary weapons in Europe, General Kuntsevich, a senior figure in the Soviet CBW establishment, commented:

The Soviet Union, in reply to the escalation of chemical weapons, will certainly have to think about having a corresponding alternative. But the Soviet Union is a powerful state which possesses a high scientific, technical and production potential and therefore its equivalent does not have to belong to the chemical sphere. It could take the form of conventional and other types of arms.[81]

Even Gorbachev alluded to alternative capabilities to counter SDI. In a television speech in August 1986, he stated that 'the Soviet Union would respond to defences against Soviet missiles by "making it pointless and useless". He added response would not be "the kind of answer that the US is expecting".'[82] When a former high-ranking KGB officer, Oleg Gordievsky, defected to the West, he passed information to the United States relating to Soviet perceptions of nuclear warfare. Reagan himself read the 50-page report and was reportedly so 'shocked by its contents [that] as a result [he] toned down the "evil empire" rhetoric, one of the principal reasons for the Soviet paranoia'.[83]

The implication of these statements is that the Soviet Union was desperately worried about the sheer cost and resources required to counter SDI in a like for like manner, but that other weapons, perhaps biological, would serve as an acceptable counter should war occur. These biological weapons, if still secret, could also provide an offset to any strategic advantage that SDI might offer the US. This does, however, also raise interesting questions relating to deterrence. Soviet biological weapons could not serve any deterrent value if the United States and her allies did not know they existed. The Soviet Union perhaps therefore only saw a use for biological weapons because they genuinely believed that the United States might one day attack them with nuclear weapons, safe in the knowledge that SDI could counter any Soviet missile response. This does suggest a rather paranoid mentality on the part of the Soviet Union—but any further consideration falls outside the boundaries of this research.

In late 1986, the reforms of Gorbachev began to shift in a more fundamental direction and 'perestroika' took on a more radical hue.[84] Gorbachev expected the same support from his military leaders as from his other ministers: 'Top Soviet generals began to clamber onto the perestroika bandwagon ... those who did not support it wholeheartedly were severely criticised.'[85] By 1987 Gorbachev was in a position where he had surrounded himself by hand-picked ministers who were sympathetic to and supportive of his reforms to the communist system—not the destruction of it. His relationships with the military and KGB were also good, with the Minister of Defence and KGB chairman as well as senior officers within those organisations generally supportive of his efforts. On an international level, Gorbachev had established good working relationships with both President Reagan and Prime Minister Thatcher, having demonstrated a commitment to arms control, negotiating from a flexible and engaging position.

In October 1989, the defection of Dr Vladimir Pasechnik was to result in a significant change in the UK perception of both the Soviet biological weapons establishment as well as the political leadership of Gorbachev. Pasechnik had been the director of the Institute for Ultra Pure Biological Preparations in St Petersburg since 1980, where he had led teams working on the weaponisation of anthrax, plague and smallpox as well as other agents, along with improving the suitability of these agents for dissemination by aircraft and inter-continental ballistic missile. Through lengthy debriefs, Pasechnik confirmed the worst suspicions of those members of UK intelligence who had believed for many years that a Soviet biological weapons threat existed. Essentially, 'the defector was telling the West that the Soviets had created a strategic biological weapons arsenal to which there was no defence, which worked, and which would return the industrialised world to the Middle Ages—to a horse and cart economy, and there certainly wouldn't be enough of them [left] to bury the dead'.[86] The Soviet Union made numerous attempts to discredit Pasechnik, even after the programme had finally been exposed. Speaking in September 1992, General Kuntsevich stated: '[Pasechnik] made up a lot in order to show how important he was ... we are now suggesting to our Western colleagues that Pasechnik come with them to his old institute and show us what he made up'.[87] Pasechnik declined the offer.

In the ten years prior to the defection of Pasechnik, there had only ever really been snippets of intelligence relating to the Soviet biological weapons programme.[88] It is however interesting to note that even after the defection of Pasechnik, strong elements remained within the US intelligence communities who were not only reluctant to believe the accounts they heard, but also keen to discredit them. One SIS officer explained:

... they [the Americans] didn't believe it and they refused to tell people that we had a defector. They claimed it was an agent in place to stop anybody asking questions ... and then eventually as Maggie [Thatcher] hand-bagged Bush, the pressure built on the CIA because CIA didn't want to believe it because of X and the rest of them. [They] sent a team of six experts, unquote, to talk to Vladimir [Pasechnik] and Vladimir said to me afterwards, 'Don't take this wrong, but when you told me that the Americans are sending over a team of six experts I thought, hey, where are they, who are these idiots who have come over to talk to me, haven't they read the reports?' ... There was a guy from Soviet analysis whose one task in coming over to be a member of the US team was to debunk everything that Vladimir said. And he said to me afterwards, 'Well, have I got problems now,' and I said, 'Well, how can you have problems; now you've heard the guy, you know it's true.' 'Oh yes,' he said, 'that's my problem, I've got to go back and tell people, hey it's true'—never saw him again. And the thing the Americans were most interested in was not the programme, but did Gorbachev know. You know, it's absolutely ludicrous—did Gorbachev know—oh no, it's a rogue programme. They wanted to be able to say it's a rogue programme, the MoD, nothing to do with Gorbachev.[89]

The issue of whether or not Gorbachev knew that the Soviet biological weapons programme existed is quite fundamental to understanding why Yeltsin went on to admit that the Soviet Union/Russia had cheated on the BTWC. Opinion on whether, or how much, Gorbachev knew about the programme is divided. The former UK ambassador to Moscow, Sir Rodric Braithwaite, represents one of these schools of thought:

I think one needs to dispel an illusion about authoritarian and totalitarian states, which is that the government knows what's going on, because that's not necessarily the case ... Gorbachev didn't know what was going on ... the generals were bamboozling him, or perhaps some of the scientists in the military industrial complex [were] and I think that explains [it] to my satisfaction. Of course there were people that thought Gorbachev never opened his mouth without telling a lie ... but I don't think that's true. I think that you have to at least take account of the possibility that some things go on in these places which are not matters of government policy at the highest level, it may be the policy of the military, or the industrial scientific complex, or the scientists or something ...[90]

Braithwaite went on to recall a meeting with Chernyayev, foreign affairs assistant to Gorbachev, where he was told, 'Do you think that Gorbachev would want to expose himself to this sort of thing given everything else he's trying to do?'[91] However, a reluctance to expose himself does not mean that he did not know that a programme existed.

With the opposite view are the likes of Sir Percy Cradock, former chairman of the Joint Intelligence Committee; as has already been established, he did strongly believe that a Soviet BW threat existed: 'She [Thatcher] was convinced he was a nice person ... she thought that he [Gorbachev] was being deceived by his generals ... I told her this was about as likely as her being deceived by hers.'[92]

Charles Powell, Thatcher's private secretary, shared her view, noting that when the Prime Minister was first briefed on Pasechnik, she 'was horrified and found it very hard to accept ... she was convinced that Gorbachev had been misled by the military establishment'.[93] The view of the intelligence community, however, now sure that intelligence on Soviet BW was entirely correct, shared that of Cradock:

> Everything said that by the nature of the way the system worked, they wouldn't have necessarily understood what the technical details were, but of course they knew there was a programme. I mean Gorbachev, you know, in terms of awareness of programme, it was quite clear from what Vladimir [Pasechnik] said about the way that meetings were structured, of course they knew. I mean it's impossible in the Soviet Union for them not to know.[94]

Cradock, however, was able to persuade Thatcher that the Soviet threat was real. One SIS officer recounts how 'Cradock had this uncomfortable task of telling Maggie that the man she could do business with was a lying expletive. I mean, to his credit and her credit, he told her and she acted.'[95] Cradock credits the length of his relationship with Thatcher as the key reason he was able to convince her: '[I had] known her [Thatcher] for a long time so she could not just cast my views aside.'[96] Finally, Thatcher agreed to discuss the Soviet biological weapons programme with Bush, and 'actually drag a reluctant American president into a more forceful policy'. It is likely that without her approach, despite the information from Pasechnik, in the US there would have 'been no political will to see it through'.[97]

The UK and US finally approached the Soviet leadership in April 1990 when their ambassadors to Moscow formally issued a joint démarche to the Gorbachev government.[98] It is now known that after this démarche, General Kalinin, the director of the Soviet biological weapons establishment, was asked to prepare a confidential response and propose a way forward; his response was that the Soviet Union should continue denying the existence of any offensive research programme.[99] One must assume that the Soviets had already prepared for this eventuality, given that the most significant evidence behind this confrontation must have come from Pasechnik on his defection. By 8 June, when Thatcher bluntly asked Gorbachev face to face whether the Soviet Union had an offensive biological weapons programme, his denial was absolute.[100] Once again, some in the West linked this denial to a genuine ignorance as to what programmes the Soviet military was actually running. Yet for UK intelligence, evidence continued to mount; and with it grew the determination to force the Soviets not only to prove publicly that they had had a BW programme, but also that they had ended it.

The SIS continued to obtain information, and the resulting assessment 'got stronger and stronger until [it] said they were in breach of the convention unequivocably'.[101] By now, no one appeared to doubt the accuracy of this intelligence. Now, low-level information 'was underpinned by this guy that was in the programme [Pasechnik] and all of these bits fit together and all of a sudden this jigsaw has become a massive jigsaw with all the bits filled in'.[102] Further information, confirming what Pasechnik had earlier told his handlers, also came from two new agents, code-named Temple Fortune and Flamenco, who had worked in the same institute as Pasechnik in St Petersburg and the anti-plague institute at Obolensk.[103] Even Gorbachev's Foreign Minister, Shevardnadze, became implicated in the programme. Pasechnik told his handlers that in 1988 Shevardnadze had chaired a high-level Kremlin meeting where the budget had been approved for the biological weapons programme; a US source confirmed that this approval was personally given in 1990.[104] Once again, though, despite the evidence, the US and UK were apparently reluctant to confront Gorbachev in a more forceful way—probably because of a fear that a refreezing of relations would set back Soviet reforms. After further representations, the Soviet government finally offered the UK and US a chance to visit four sites suspected of being involved in biological weapons research in a process that became known as 'The Trilaterals'.[105]

Hide and seek: inspecting the bear

If one accepts how advanced the Soviet biological weapons programme had been, and how long it had taken Western intelligence agencies to obtain evidence which was strong enough that political leaders could be persuaded to confront Gorbachev, it was extremely interesting that, if a decision had been made to continue the programme, Western visitors should be invited in to inspect some of the most sensitive institutes. The UK ambassador to Moscow, Sir Rodric Braithwaite, suggested a possible motivation for the Gorbachev decision: 'if he proposed it, he must have thought either that he could get away with it, or that his hands were clean, or that this would be a way of putting pressure on his own guys'.[106] But this was not the first time that the Soviet Union had invited inspectors in to secret facilities. In 1987, chemical weapons experts from around the world visited the Soviet chemical weapons facility at Shikhany. Ostensibly this was as a way of demonstrating, as Gorbachev had announced in 1987, that the Soviet Union had given up chemical weapons production prior to striving towards obtaining a worldwide chemical weapons ban; but evidence suggests that the Soviet motivation may have been for other purposes.

UK intelligence had already discovered that a new Soviet chemical agent programme had produced ultra-lethal 'novichok' agents which were not only capable of defeating Western protective and detective equipment, but could also be produced as binary chemicals that could be hidden within any civilian chemical manufacturing plant. The proposed Chemical Weapons Convention (CWC) was to control precursor chemicals required for the manufacture of known agents through a schedule list of chemicals on which all signatory states would agree to tight controls. However, the development of this agent programme may have been a way of side-stepping the CWC, spurred on by the apparent Soviet success in deceiving the West about their BW-related research. As one DIS officer who visited Shikhany commented:

> My personal view is that having established that the new agent programme worked, and they could do it without using scheduled facilities ... you know, facilities that wouldn't be covered by the convention ... that they didn't need live agent any more because, as they'd done with the BWC, ... [they could] continue a programme that would be hidden ... for the chemical [programme] it meant they could move the production to facilities that didn't have to be declared ... there we were hammering away trying to get the convention and the Russians said helpfully, 'Oh don't you think we should name some of these compounds, we don't have chemical weapons, but you know, wouldn't it be helpful to know about some of the chemicals

we're talking about.' And so over a period of years the schedules were developed ... for us they were illustrative, but for the Russians they were absolute, and so it was how you read it, you know these were examples ... 'That's the schedule, so [if] it's not on the schedule, it doesn't ...' Well that's not true, but it's their understanding of it, and unless you can identify specific [unintelligible] and specific factories, there is nothing you can do about it. So my belief is that because they'd had such success with the BW programme, they'd even had Sverdlovsk [anthrax accidental release] and got away with it.[107]

The Soviets could therefore demonstrate at Shikhany weapons, agents and technologies that the West perceived were advanced but were actually redundant due to the development of 'novichoks'. It has been suggested therefore that 'the Russians [only] proposed to fully eliminate ... chemical weapons ... because they have ... mastered a secret production of a still more terrible weapon of mass destruction which might play a decisive role in time of war'.[108] In terms of the Shikhany inspections, however, the view of the officers involved in the inspections was:

The Russians were confident ... they could fool 99% of the people 99% of the time ... I know that when we produced the JIC assessment, X had been one of the four members of the UK team, and he thought it was wonderful until I pointed out that the display of the weapon [which we were discussing], if you looked, the guy had a hole in the glove, and then we were really lucky because somebody had taken some photographs, and you could see the guy had a hole in the glove. And so it clearly wasn't [a] live weapon ... suddenly we were confronted with 'Hey, if you opened your eyes, you could see that there was all sorts of problems', and in fact the JIC assessment ... came out saying ... the Russians had hidden an awful lot but they were still lying, there'd been no complete [display], the weapons were old.[109]

The suspicions from some of the UK inspectors were raised with the Soviet commander of the Shikhany facility, General Kuntsevich. One DIS officer said to him:

Come on, I mean, where are the new weapons? ... Most of these bombs are WW2 bombs; if you use them for external carriage [on an aircraft] the wings will fall off. [He replied] 'What do you know about CW ... you say you've abandoned them all,' and I lulled him along, and eventually he made this comment: 'You don't need sophistication for CW, all you need is a drum of old agent, an explosive charge and you roll it out of a helicopter.'

And I said, 'Oh, sounds just like Afghanistan General,' and he was pulled away because the silly sod had walked straight into it.[110]

Finally, and perhaps most importantly, the Shikhany visits may have given the Soviets the confidence to know that they could deal with intrusive inspections. Together, this evidence suggests that the Soviet Union may have offered the opportunity for Western inspectors to visit suspected biological weapons facilities because they felt confident they could deal with any potential suspicions. Also, given enough notice, sites could probably be cleaned up enough to remove any evidence that might suggest that activities counter to the BTWC were being conducted.

There is another possible consequence of the Shikhany visits: that they signalled to Soviet officers within the biological warfare establishment that it might be possible that they would have to accept visitors from the West one day and must therefore be in a position to convince them that they were not conducting research counter to the BTWC. Another Soviet defector, this time to the US, stated that from 1986 onwards pressure began to mount relating to the possibility of Western visits to biological facilities.[111] Despite the fact that the Soviet biological weapons programme was hidden under the guise of civilian research, the view may well have been: 'the people on the BW programme thought "hell they're going to do the same with us, they're going to open ... we ought to be thinking about this".'[112]

In early January 1991, a team of British and American inspectors began their first visit to suspected biological weapons establishments. The Soviets did a remarkably good job at concealing evidence of their research. One of the inspectors, a serving military DIS officer, believed:

> ... inconclusive proof was the biggest fear, we believed they had a programme, accepted the evidence from Vladimir—it made sense—but we were worried that we needed absolute evidence and it might not be there, or be more ambiguous, but when we went to the inhalation chamber and saw evidence of explosive munitions, this was hard to justify if there was no programme—no reason to have it in [a] defensive programme, this is [a] weapon effect. The other thing was the scale, even though we did not see production facilities. In my own mind I thought they would stop us getting anything that would give the game away, stop at nothing—including violence.[113]

The explosive test chamber, hidden in a facility in Obolensk, was exactly where Pasechnik had said it would be, and despite 'the Soviets nervously resorting to a series of evasions' it brought incontrovertible proof of illegal activities.[114] On their return to London the team reported of 'disturbing evidence which confirmed that the Soviets had a massive, offensive biological warfare programme run by Biopreperat and the military ... specific evidence of disturbing treaty violations emerged [and] Soviet officials had done everything possible to limit the scope of the visits'.[115] General Kalinin surprisingly reported back to Gorbachev that 'the visitors had not found any proof that an offensive BW programme existed in the Soviet Union'.[116]

Gorbachev continued to deny the existence of a biological weapons programme to the West. By the time the Gulf War had ended in 1991, John Major had replaced Margaret Thatcher and continued the drive to gain an admission of cheating from Gorbachev. By August 1991 and the coup attempt by hardliners in the KGB and military, it was apparent to the West that power was beginning to slip from Gorbachev towards Yeltsin, at the same time setting the conditions through which an admission would eventually emerge.

The Yeltsin factor

By the time Yeltsin had been elected president of Russia in June 1991, a situation existed whereby the UK and US were adamant that the former Soviet Union had an illegal offensive biological weapons programme; yet no admission had been made on the part of the Soviet Union, despite overwhelming evidence. Then in January 1992 Yeltsin sent Bush a letter in which he accepted that an illegal programme had existed contrary to the BTWC.[117] It is therefore important to establish why, after six months had elapsed, it suddenly became possible for Yeltsin to make this admission, whereas Gorbachev in the previous years could not.

In terms of whether Gorbachev had known that the programme existed, one must apply the same rationale to Yeltsin. When Braithwaite met Yeltsin on 20 January 1992, he recalled:

> ... and Yeltsin said, open quote, 'I know all about the Soviet BW programme. It's still going ahead even though its organisers claim it's only defensive research, ha ha [*sic*], they are fanatics and they will not stop voluntarily, I know these people personally, I know their names and I know the addresses of the institutes where they're doing the work. I'm going to close down the institutes, retire the director of the programme and set the

others to work at designing something useful, such as a cow with a yearly yield of 10,000 litres. When I've checked for myself that the institutes have in fact stopped work, I'm going to ask for international inspection.' We could do no more than thank him. You couldn't have had a more satisfactory statement.[118]

If Yeltsin knew about the programme within six months of coming to power, it seems plausible to assume that Gorbachev too must have known. In addition, the fact that Yeltsin alluded to genetic engineering also supports what Western intelligence had been told by Pasechnik about the types of genetic research taking place. The comments Yeltsin made would seem to suggest that he knew at least some of the detail of the types of research in which these programmes were involved. Even those supporting the view that Gorbachev as president did not know about the programme could not explain how Gorbachev did not know, yet Yeltsin so quickly found out. When subsequently challenged about how Yeltsin could have found out so quickly where Gorbachev had never known, Braithwaite commented:

> I had not previously thought of your question about Yeltsin, and it is a good one ... I suppose that one answer may be that as an outsider he was psycho-logically and politically predisposed to believe any rumours he heard, or information conveyed to him by whistleblowers, whereas Gorbachev, who was still having to live inside the system was not .... But that is pure specula-tion. How one could ever get real evidence, I don't know.[119]

One SIS officer even went so far as to suggest that 'according to infor-mation ... Yeltsin apparently said that when he was taking over from Gorbachev, Gorbachev said "Well, of course there is this small problem you'll have to take care of, which is our BW programme".'[120] In terms of motivation for the admission, it therefore seems unlikely that the admis-sion was made because Yeltsin, by chance, found out about the pro-gramme where Gorbachev had not. There are, however, other arguments that must be considered when trying to account for the Yeltsin approach towards acting to end the Soviet BW programme.

Investigations into the reasons behind the admission made by Yeltsin suggest that it might in fact be related to the personality of Yeltsin, in particular the difficult relationship that he had had with Gorbachev. Despite the fact that in 1985 Gorbachev brought Yeltsin to Moscow to work in the Central Committee of the Communist Party, Yeltsin quickly turned out to be an immense source of trouble and problems.[121] Yeltsin has been described as an individual with a populist style of leadership:

... he rode the buses and subways, raided stores in search of goods being hoarded under the table, and held public meetings with lengthy question and answer periods ... he called for more unrestrained, public criticism of shortcomings ... [he was] a man of the people who did not accept the traditional ways of doing things ... who did not accept the system of privilege ... and [did] not accept the notion that Moscow's corrupt nobility of Party and state officials was entitled to immunity from exposure and accountability. This was new for Moscow and was a breath of fresh air for those of its citizens who were hoping for a new deal. It was also combustible political material that went beyond what Gorbachev was saying and doing during his stage of political succession.[122]

At the same time, Yeltsin was critical of Gorbachev, who, he believed, 'had no direct, open contact with the people ... The fault lies in his basic cast of character. He likes to live well, in comfort and luxury.'[123] Yeltsin himself had believed from his first years in politics that 'we should, above all, be concerned about people and their welfare, since if you treat people well they will respond with improved performance in whatever their occupation may be. This has remained one of my beliefs.'[124] Other observers are not so kind: the former British ambassador to Moscow, Sir Rodric Braithwaite, described Yeltsin as 'a thug. He was an orthodox party thug. He was always ... a bit of a bad boy and then he jumped on this democratic bandwagon in the 1980s.'[125]

Yeltsin quickly developed a very strong bond with the Russian people.[126] This bond was to become so strong that when in 1987 Yeltsin was removed as Party First Secretary in Moscow and ousted from the Politburo, mass demonstrations probably induced Gorbachev to offer Yeltsin an alternative senior ministerial post.[127] Whilst both Yeltsin and Gorbachev believed in reform, they both had very different views of how to go about it. Gorbachev as leader and as a man desperate to preserve the Soviet system did not have the freedom of manoeuvre that Yeltsin did, and certainly could not appeal to the masses as Yeltsin could.[128] In addition:

the conflict between Gorbachev and Yeltsin is not simply a dispute between two men who do not like each other. There is an objective historical basis for the conflict: a clash of two opposing tendencies—namely, the striving of Russia to find its sovereignty, and the striving of the empire to preserve its former might. The president of the USSR, who does not have his own territorial domain inside the huge country, is, with the loss of power in Russia, in effect losing his power.[129]

As a result, the relationship between the two men gradually grew more and more strained as Yeltsin recognised his potential for power, whilst Gorbachev considered his loss of it.

It is easy to see Gorbachev from a Western perspective as an almost saintly figure, seeking to throw off the chains of communism and end the Cold War. However, there is a great deal of evidence that suggests that Gorbachev was actually not greatly different from those leaders who went before him. It is clear that Gorbachev had 'a tendency towards ruthlessness'.[130] Yeltsin gives several examples of this behaviour in his own memoirs:

> On November 9 [1987] I was taken to hospital with a severe headache and chest pains ... I was pumped full of medicines ... the doctors forbade me to get out of bed and kept giving me drips and injections ... My wife wanted to come and see me, but they would not let her, saying I was too sick to be disturbed. Suddenly, on the morning of November 11, the telephone rang on my special Kremlin line ... It was Gorbachev ... 'you must come and see me for a short while' ... I said I couldn't come because I was in bed and the doctors wouldn't let me get up. 'Don't worry', he said cheerfully. 'The doctors will help you get up'. I shall never be able to understand that. In all my life I have never heard of anyone, whether a worker or a manager, being dragged out of a hospital bed to be dismissed ... However much Gorbachev may have disliked me, to act like that was inhuman and immoral ... I could not understand such cruelty.[131]

Yeltsin goes on to state that after one public 'tirade aimed at me personally ... there can be no doubt that ... Gorbachev simply hated me'.[132] It appears that Gorbachev also made use of the KGB 'to thwart the realisation of Yeltsin's presumed scenario' and 'no scheme or political dirty trick was to be overlooked'.[133] It appears that 'Gorbachev was an assiduous reader of the transcripts of the illegal telephone taps and surveillance reports that the KGB had conducted on his rival [Yeltsin]'.[134] One must perhaps also consider that Yeltsin might have seen the admission of Soviet non-compliance as a means of simply 'getting back' at Gorbachev in revenge for his perceived poor treatment.

Yeltsin appeared to have approached his relationships with international leaders in the same manner as his voting public. His 'chummy pal posture' saw him referring to 'my friend Bill', 'my friend Helmut' and even 'my friend Ryu', referring to the Japanese leader on his first meeting.[135] Braithwaite commented that 'he [Yeltsin] wanted to demonstrate that he was a clean break from the past which made him friends with the West'.[136] Yeltsin's frank revelations about biological weapons to Western leaders, along with his assurances that 'we are firmly resolved not to lie anymore, either to our negotiating partners, or to the Russian or American people [and] there will be no more lies—ever',[137] perhaps seemed to be an excellent way for Yeltsin to cement his relationships as well as mark a clear break from the past days of the Soviet Union, though they 'did not [necessarily] make him friends in Russia'.[138] This desire for friendly relations was probably, at least in part, due to a desire to secure monetary aid and investment in Russia. Viewing Russia as a victim of economic globalisation, Yeltsin managed to secure massive loans to Russia. By 2000, the IMF alone had lent $37 billion.[139] Whilst Gorbachev had realised the importance of Western assistance to ensure the success of his reforms, in particular economic assistance,[140] he had a clear, albeit self-devised, foreign policy aimed at preserving the Soviet system by building trust with the West.[141] For Yeltsin, early in his presidency foreign policy was simply non-existent, until 1993 when 'The Basic Provisions of the Foreign Policy Concept' was published.[142]

Whilst chastising his ministers for a lack of clear foreign policy, Yeltsin himself showed a 'lack of an overarching vision of where he was taking his country ... [he] kept shuffling people at such a rate that implementation became impossible ... [producing] a foreign policy that seemed to lurch from point to point'.[143] Many senior officials no doubt reeled in shock as Yeltsin made promises to the West, such as that 'the Soviet biological weapons programme would be dismantled within a month'.[144]

Yeltsin did attempt to enforce his international promises with domestic legislation. In January 1992 he issued the previously discussed Presidential Decree number 390 (see Chapter 4) entitled 'on ensuring the fulfilment of international obligations in the area of biological weapons'. This decree established that development, production and stockpiling of biological weapons was 'not permitted' in the territory of the Russian Federation.[145] This was soon followed by the April Form F submission to the United Nations.[146] Whilst the lack of an overarching Russian foreign policy may have allowed Yeltsin to act more freely in terms of his acknowledgement of the existence of a biological weapons programme, it is highly likely that he felt as a new president that he could not build workable relationships with Western leaders when their intelligence was so well informed about former Soviet weapons programmes. It was far easier for Yeltsin to accept that the programmes had existed, but were nothing to do with him, in order to show the West that he too was a man they could do business with and, perhaps more importantly, continue to secure the investment that Russia so desperately needed.

One must also consider that Yeltsin was 'vindictive in pursuing Gorbachev' because of his past issues.[147] Through Yeltsin's pro-Western policies, he attempted to outdo Gorbachev's efforts at arms control every way he could. In June 1992 he announced that Russia had already started dismantling SS-18 missiles; he ended subsidies to Cuba and Afghanistan; assumed responsibility for Soviet debts; supported the US Middle Eastern policy; and signalled that he might be willing to renegotiate the ABM treaty.[148] Again though, these promises were underpinned by a desire for Western financial assistance:

> [democracy in Russia has only one chance] there will be no second try ... The reforms must succeed ... If we [that is, you Americans] do not take measures now to support Russia, this will not be the collapse of Russia only, it will be the collapse of the United States, because it will mean new trillions of dollars for the arms race.[149]

Domestically, Yeltsin assumed he could control his military, particularly after the attempted coup, allowing his promises to the West to be fulfilled. In a meeting with the British ambassador, Sir Rodric Braithwaite reports that he had 'started badgering the previous government [about biological warfare] a few years ago, but nothing had happened; perhaps Gorbachev found the politics too intractable. Yeltsin replied with a grin that he has had a lot of trouble with his generals but they find it difficult to stand up to him.'[150] Whilst Yeltsin appeared to break free from past Soviet foreign policy, the Russian military were not so forthcoming in their efforts. The Draft Military Doctrine released in 1992 'was clearly a sample of the old mentality prevailing among the armchair generals. While not naming the USA and NATO as the enemy, it unambiguously pointed to them in referring to some states and coalitions which wished to dominate the world.'[151] Yeltsin did pass orders for the research to stop, but Western intelligence continued to receive information that the programme continued.

Evidence suggests that the West did believe that Yeltsin was trying to stop the biological weapons programme in Russia. In a confidential letter from Douglas Hurd, British Foreign Secretary, and Lawrence Eagleburger, US Secretary of State, dated 24 August 1992, Yeltsin was warned that despite his efforts to ban offensive biological weapons research, programmes are 'being continued covertly and without his knowledge'. The letter went on to state '... this has potentially serious implications ... we have ... acquired information from the measures taken ... to conceal from the UK ... the real nature of activities [at suspect facilities]'. The letter is detailed, naming not only suspect sites, bacteria worked on, but also how the continuing programme is being conducted without the president's knowledge. It concludes by warning that both START negotiations as well as economic packages 'could be affected by this matter'.[152]

To make matters worse, following the Russian Form F submission, Yeltsin appointed General Kuntsevich, former head of Soviet chemical and biological warfare, to oversee destruction of any remaining elements of offensive weapons programmes. The UK took this appointment 'very badly. We all thought that the [Russian] Ministry of Defence had managed to play a blinder and appointed one of their own to protect as much as possible.'[153] As domestic pressures and problems increased, and Yeltsin's health began to deteriorate, the military therefore once again became able to exert its ability to influence decision-making within government.

Despite Yeltsin's admission, fears remained that the former Soviet programme remained in existence in Russia. It is ironic that all attempts to expose Russian research were ended because of the United States' refusal to allow Russian inspectors access to their own facilities which they perceived to be commercially sensitive. Under a new trilateral agreement in late 1992, the US, UK and Russia were to exchange confidence-building inspections, as they had done in 1991. The American refusal gave the Russian military the excuse they needed to bar any further inspectors access to their most sensitive sites. Rumours persist in the intelligence community that:

> ... there was the view that the Brits were a bit of a bloody problem because they were after the truth, whereas there was a, you know, we scratch your back ... I'm sure the Americans perhaps have got things in other areas that they're not too keen on having exposed and it's easier for the two ... to do things without us being involved. And that was part of the problem, we were desperately trying to keep our fingers in the trilateral and there was this sort of awareness that it was rapidly becoming a bilateral ... we had no

programme, we hadn't anything, so you know ... we could actually get up and shout whereas ... who knows in absolute terms what the Americans may or may not have had as emergency contingency plans. I don't know.[154]

The Russians did admit to being in breach of the BTWC, and whilst no complete exposure was given of the programme, this was still massively important. As one SIS officer explained:

... there was this massive injection of money [into BW defence in the UK] ... we spent 100 times more building a facility that could cope with category 3 containment, and to train and recruit people to be able to do the defensive work to make sure that we could develop vaccines, and most importantly trying to develop a method of detection. Essentially we had no defensive measures, we had no vaccine programme. I mean now at least there is a vaccination policy. There are plans for the production of vaccines and all the rest of it. There is a detection capability at the moment.[155]

Perhaps also:

the threat from Russia has gone, because the Russians have realised they don't need to go to war to win anything now. They can destroy us economically because we're dependent on their fuel and oil, so why do they need to fight a war. You know, at the end of the day, they can do far better by not.[156]

Not all intelligence officers share this view. When one senior officer was pushed for a comment on the priority of Russian CBW as an intelligence target in 2008, he commented: 'I quite understand why [you] would like a comment, but I would feel very uncomfortable giving one.'[157]

6

STRANGER THAN FICTION

THE CURIOUS CASE OF SOUTH AFRICA

This chapter will examine the case of South Africa, a country that developed, or is generally acknowledged to have developed, nuclear, biological and chemical weapons throughout the 1970s and 1980s (and arguably the 1990s).[1] She gave up each of these capabilities in turn, gaining the accolade of becoming the only state in the world that has developed nuclear weapons on her own and then chosen to abandon them. Indeed, South Africa also became one of only a small number of states demonstrating the same behaviour in relation to chemical and biological weapons.[2] But for chemical and biological weapons, these actions were not without controversy or an associated degree of confusion; the South African government acknowledged having a regime-sponsored biological weapons programme known as Project Coast, but never declared its existence through submitting confidence-building forms to the BTWC (Biological and Toxin Weapons Convention).[3] It is on that biological weapons programme that the main substance of this chapter is based.

This case study is a curious one. Why would the very ANC (African National Congress) government that exposed Project Coast have failed to acknowledge these same activities in line with international treaty requirements? It also seems strange that the failure of the post-apartheid South African government to shed light on the activities undertaken as part of Project Coast is at odds with its otherwise long-standing commitment to the BTWC, as well as its desire to acknowledge publicly the wrongs of the apartheid regime. At the very least, this certainly does not seem to promote transparency in a region where participation in Form F confidence-building measures was already below average.[4]

Another characteristic of this case study relating to the curious manner in which the programme was exposed is the involvement of UK intelligence agencies, and ultimately the UK government directly. It appears that advice and guidance given from the UK relating to closing down the chemical and biological weapons programmes was at best unclear, raising questions relating to what the reasons behind the involvement of the UK actually was—in particular in the context of the awareness of UK intelligence of the South African programmes. Here, this chapter will reveal that there was UK intelligence focus on a range of complex global security issues, centred around counter-proliferation, yet seemingly driven by national interest in the most traditional sense. The title of a book by Marlene Burger and Chandre Gould, *Secrets and Lies*, documenting the aftermath of these programmes as heard by the Truth and Reconciliation Commission (TRC), seems an appropriate descriptor for a programme which, as this chapter will demonstrate, is at times stranger than fiction.[5]

A gift from a friend: CBW in South Africa

South African involvement in the research, development and manufacture of CBW (chemical and biological weapons) can be dated back to the Second World War, though it appears there is very little direct relationship between the production of 'war gases' and the CBW of Project Coast. Knowledge from these programmes may, however, have been useful in the development of weapons within South Africa later on.

During the Second World War, two factories were built in South Africa for the production of 'war gases': one, the largest, at Klipfontein in North Rand, the other at Firgrove in the Cape. Klipfontein was designed to operate using indigenous materials, whilst Firgrove relied on the import of chemicals from the UK. The entire cost of building Firgrove was met by the UK government, whilst 50 per cent of the cost of Klipfontein was met by the South African government.[6]

A large proportion of weapons filled with chemical agent in South Africa were destined for delivery by aerial bomb, although some artillery shells were also filled—regular inspections and tests were carried out on this ordnance.[7] It appears that safety of personnel within these two production facilities was not rigorously managed. Minutes of management meetings refer to 'the high rate of casualties ... due to [a] lack of complete ventilation'.[8] Other documents give statistics on the level of those casualties: for example, in the six months to 31 December 1942, a total of 417 accidents were reported, of which 341 were to 'toxic workers'.[9]

By the end of the war, 'the bulk of the production from both factories [had been] filled into weapons stored under military control at Port Elizabeth'. Several hundred tons of gas also remained in tanks at each plant. London ordered the disposal of all stocks held in South Africa, under the auspices of the South African authorities, with advice being given that 'it is unlikely that shipping will be available for dumping the charged weapons in Port Elizabeth, and consideration should be given to other methods of disposal such as burning'.[10]

The passage of responsibility for dumping unwanted chemical weapon stocks to the South African government was to prove problematic. In December 1946 communications were sent from the consulate in South Africa to London, reporting that gas containers:

> had found their way into fisherman's trawls ... [and whilst] rumour is a poor source of information ... it is rumoured that these gas containers found their way into the trawls only because of some 'scrimshanking' [sic] on the part of a certain individual ... It is alleged that this individual occupied a sort of Dr Jekyll and Mr Hyde relation to the dumping operation, i.e. he wangled things so that he functioned in the dual capacity of Officer in Charge of the Operation of Dumping, on the one hand, and a sleeping partner in the dumping Contractor's profit on the other. This led to some of the stuff being dumped too near land in order to save ship's time and increase profit.

London were assured that the 'UK was utterly without sin in this matter!'[11]

In terms of the manufacturing factories, at the end of the war it was decided that Firgrove was to be entirely closed, whilst Klipfontein was to be 'retained for a minimum period of 5 years ... available for the emergency production of the special war chemicals for which it was designed'.[12] In that period, it was intended that Klipfontein be entirely converted to the manufacture of industrial chemicals, most significantly DDT, in 'wide demand throughout Southern Africa'.[13] This decision essentially marked the termination of chemical weapon production in

South Africa for war fighting purposes. There is very little evidence that technical knowledge or capability from these wartime programmes was of any significant use in the initiation of Project Coast. Indeed, South Africa only maintained a very small military programme after the war until Project Coast began in 1981, though it is believed that literature from wartime programmes was maintained and used in civilian research projects.[14] One must consider that experience in the manufacture of DDT may have proved useful for the subsequent development of nerve agents—DDT effectively works in the same manner as a battlefield nerve agent would, albeit with a lower toxicity.

The Marxist threat: South African motivations for a CBW programme

Despite the history of chemical weapons production, it appears that there is no evidence that South Africa was involved with biological weapons before Project Coast began.[15] After the war, South Africa was initially interested in developing a nuclear weapons programme, ironically initiated by a UK government approach to the then Prime Minister Smuts to assist in the search for uranium. A survey of South African gold mines found uranium coexisting with gold in virtually every bore hole on the Rand and Free State.[16] The UK and US helped the newly formed South African Atomic Energy Board establish uranium plants from October 1952; by March 1955, sixteen such plants were in operation, capitalising on the massive uranium reserves now believed to be present in South Africa.[17] By 1959, South Africa had begun to establish its own nuclear energy programme, sending scientists overseas for training, financed by the burgeoning price of gold, an element that occurred so plentifully in South Africa.[18] In the mid 1970s uranium enrichment was successfully proceeding at a plant at Pelindaba.[19] By the mid 1980s, South Africa had attained nuclear capability, producing an estimated seven nuclear weapons,[20] aided, at least indirectly, by the UK.

The South African nuclear weapons programme must be seen in the context of both the internal and external security situation that confronted South Africa. In the external context, it was at the Carlton conference in November 1979 that President P. W. Botha first described his plan for a 'constellation' of Southern African states to defeat the Marxist threat,[21] perceived to be present both within South Africa as well as in bordering states such as Rhodesia, Angola, Mozambique and West

Africa (Namibia)—states with strong Soviet and Cuban links.[22] Botha's plan placed South Africa firmly at the centre of this regional power base.[23] The plan, known as the 'Total National Strategy', accepted that 'enemies of the Republic are trying to attack in all fields'.[24] So, in the face of 'total onslaught', a wide range of 'economic, ideological, technological, and even social matters' were required.[25] Nuclear weapons were to be a central part of this strategy, as were the chemical and biological weapons developed under the auspices of the top secret and officially deniable Project Coast in future years.

It is highly significant that the 'Total National Strategy' acknowledged the existence of both internal and external threats to South Africa. Externally, the involvement of South African forces, both overtly and covertly, in bordering areas such as Angola and Rhodesia in support of anti-communist regimes and forces not only reflected the view that Soviet (and Cuban) forces were actively pursuing their plans for a social-ist world order in direct challenge to South African plans for regional hegemony, but they also justified the requirement for a viable nuclear deterrent.[26] Internally, the view of Botha on countering these threats appeared to favour 'the use of widespread coercive force', including 'assassinations, torture and smuggling as well as forgery, propaganda and subversion'.[27] All of these internal initiatives were intentionally deniable, apparently to go along with the desire to present an international view of South Africa as a country where 'apartheid was being softened'.[28] This impression was essential if South Africa was to stand a chance of per-suading regional states that it was in their interests to collaborate with Pretoria in the fight against communism.[29]

Whilst the development of nuclear weapons proceeded well, it quickly became apparent that the survival of apartheid in South Africa was perhaps at greater threat from its internal challenges, against which nuclear weap-ons were of no use. Civil disorder, in particular rioting, along with counter-insurgency operations in Rhodesia, Mozambique and Angola brought significant challenges to the security forces that demanded new and novel responses. It is within this context that the origins of Project Coast lay.

Genesis: the inception of Project Coast

The genesis of Project Coast rests with the adoption of the 'total strat-egy' to ensure the survival of South Africa against the threat of 'interna-tional communism and its cohorts'[30]—the subject of the White Paper on

Defence published in 1979.[31] The very public end to the programme came about in 1995 when the new ANC government began to address a programme that was 'dastardly in its concept and execution ... a reflection of the inherent evil of apartheid'.[32] Information relating to the establishment of Project Coast is at best unclear: 'precisely who knew or did what ... will almost certainly never be known'.[33] It is however apparent that Project Coast violated the commitment of South Africa to the BTWC—a treaty that it signed in 1972. In addition, there are documents that confirm that when South Africa signed the CWC (Chemical Weapons Convention) in 1993, there was a deliberate intention to violate the conditions of that treaty as well.[34] It is perhaps easier to consider Project Coast as having two aims: one relating to providing largely defensive military capability for troops engaged in the Border Wars, the other concerned with supporting internal security agencies. These will both be examined in order to provide an illustration of the aims and capabilities of Project Coast.

It is important to note that there was some justification for a defensive South African programme. The Portuguese military was the first to use both chemical and biological weapons in the 1960s in counter-insurgency warfare in Africa, poisoning wells and drugging then killing prisoners as well as using defoliants.[35] As a result, the South African military philosophy relating to chemical and biological weapons was that they maintained 'the right to reactively use non-lethal chemical warfare ... [which would integrate] chemical warfare into all chemical actions ... [and accept] the use of chemical warfare on a proactive basis to ensure the survival of the state' against the threat posed by revolutionary wars then being fought.[36] This clearly placed demands upon the military, both in terms of research and development of defensive and offensive equipment, as well as in integration into military doctrine.

It was in the late 1970s that South African forces first experimented with the use of biological weapons: anthrax and cholera in Rhodesia, underpinned by the logic that if you 'kill the black man's cattle ... food for the Rhodesian guerrillas dies with them ... kill the cattle and blame the guerrillas and win a psychological victory at the same time ... spread cholera epidemics among the villages and destabilise the guerrillas and their infrastructure'.[37] The fighting philosophy of white forces is powerfully summed up by Colonel Eugene de Kock, veteran of the Rhodesian war, sentenced to serve 212 years in prison for seven murders, who stated 'why keep to the Queensbury rules and fight one boxer, when you can kick them in the balls and kill all three'.[38] During 1979–80, Rhodesia experienced 10,738 human cases of anthrax (a country which would normally expect around 13 cases) following the alleged widespread use of biological agents by South African-sponsored paramilitary groups like the infamous 'Selous Scouts'.[39]

It appears that Project Coast itself was officially initiated in 1981, building at least in part on the already existing South African chemical and biological research and development programmes that had been running since the Second World War, as well as the apparent success in using chemical and biological agents in border conflicts.[40] The South African involvement in border wars clearly provided an ideal opportunity to train personnel, develop tactics and strategies as well as test agents prior to their use against political opponents at home for internal security purposes.[41] Furthermore, the US, UK and other Western governments' fear of Soviet involvement via Cuban troops in Angola made South African success a vital objective. This ironically went some way to facilitate South African efforts to secure both defensive and offensive chemical and biological warfare equipment from the West, despite arms embargoes. As one UK intelligence officer explained:

> ... the fact that South Africa may or may not have been looking for [chemical and biological] kit didn't excite any interest, because with allegations and with concern over potential Russian use in Afghanistan and surrogate use in South East Asia, and with Cubans in Angola, the fact they wanted protective suits and detectors just seemed a sort of insurance policy; after all we had suits and detectors and whatever, and we didn't have a programme.[42]

South Africa could therefore easily justify its desire to procure CBW defence equipment: there was therefore apparently no need for the West to be concerned about the reasons why South Africa required such equipment. A further benefit for South Africa came from the fact that because terrorist groups within South Africa such as the ANC based its military wing, MK, in bordering states, trials could be doubly beneficial and used to target these groups outside South Africa's borders.

Project management: aims and responsibilities within Project Coast

Responsibility for Project Coast, initially under the direction of Magnus Malan, the Minister of Defence, fell to surgeon generals Nieuwoudt and later Knobel. Nieuwoudt appointed a man who was to become central to

Project Coast—the military doctor Major Wouter Basson—to establish a CBW research programme.[43] Basson apparently received the loosest of briefs initially: to provide information on 'the very real threat' of chemical weapons being used by Angolan forces and their surrogates. By gathering information in the international arena, Basson could then advise the South African government on what kind of CBW project to undertake.[44] In terms of the programme itself, Project Coast has been rated as diversely as being the 'second most sophisticated after the Soviet Union' to the analysis that they were based upon 'pedestrian' science.[45] Regardless of its capability, its intent and purpose seem to be clearer. According to a report from UNIDIR (the United Nations Institute for Disarmament Research) published in 2002:

> The chemical and biological warfare programme, code-named Coast, started in 1981 and officially ended in 1995. The purpose of Project Coast can be summarised as follows:
>
> – To develop chemical warfare agents that could be used by security forces to control crowds;
> – To do research into offensive and defensive chemical and biological warfare;
> – To develop chemical and biological weapons for operational use;
> – To develop defensive training programmes for troops;
> – To develop and manufacture protective clothing.[46]

Additionally, speaking before the Truth and Reconciliation Commission, the project officer Wouter Basson explained the aims of the South African programme referring to official documents:

> – Research with regard to the basic aspects of chemical warfare;
> – Research with regard to the basic aspects of biological warfare;
> – Research with regard to offensive systems, both covert and conventional;
> – The creation of an industrial capability with regard to the production of offensive and defensive CBW equipment. In this regard, the project provides access to the basic technology through acting as a middle-man between the local and overseas companies;
> – Support CBW operations (offensive and defensive) through the export of security forces;
> – The conduct of [our] own CBW operations.[47]

Early in his work, Basson quickly realised that no one within South Africa knew much about CBW, and that it fell to him alone to obtain such information. His orders implicitly emphasised the need for 'plausible deniability'.[48] As a result, he began a series of visits around the world, including to the UK, in attempts to obtain such information. Basson was specifically tasked via a meeting held by the South African Defence Minister in 1980, because of his scientific and medical expertise, to 'be sent overseas to determine covertly what the status and capabilities of the Western allies were with reference to chemical and biological warfare and their defensive measures against it'.[49] These visits will be considered in more detail later.

Once the threat from CBW had been established, consideration on the uses of weapons that could be developed then turned towards other areas—significantly methods to control the black population.[50] It is here that Project Coast becomes a rather 'tangled web'.[51] Through the use of civilian front companies such as Delta G and Roodeplaat Research Laboratories (RRL), similar to the way Biopreparat was used by the USSR, Basson developed two aspects of Project Coast. Firstly, having hand-picked scientists and other personnel, he focused on identifying suppliers for defensive equipment, then negotiating contracts, despite the international arms embargo and sanctions against South Africa.[52] Secondly, he began to develop a whole spectrum of lethal, non-lethal and incapacitant agents to be used by the so-called 'third force' to suppress unrest, particularly amongst the black population.[53] A key aim of this aspect of the programme was to develop agents that could be used to kill but leave no evidence post-mortem. A range of poisons and pathogens was researched, developed and tested for this purpose.[54]

Project Coast therefore became the key means by which South Africa attempted covertly to acquire and develop chemical and biological weapons for both offensive and defensive purposes. It was not until 1995 that the true extent of this programme became apparent, along with the extent by which foreign governments were involved, in particular the UK. This chapter will now turn its attention to the UK in the context of Project Coast, in particular to considering the role of UK intelligence in the operation and termination of this programme.

Enter the Brits: UK involvement in Project Coast

UK foreign policy towards South Africa in the context of nuclear, chemical and biological weapons appears to have been, at least on the face of it, relatively consistent from 1980 onwards. In the 1980s, this view was entirely based on:

> ... concern over the nuclear programme, no interest about anything else ... in terms of JIC requirements I think there was only actually a requirement for South African nuclear, I don't think there was a requirement on South Africa B[iological] or C[hemical], but [with] the catch all, 'well if you get any then we'll have it, we don't think there's much so don't bother'.[55]

This view reflected an establishment that, as has already been considered in the previous chapter, was cynical at that point in time about the existence of large and credible offensive chemical or biological weapons in the armouries of any nations. UK intelligence agencies were, however, aware of South African interest in chemical and biological warfare before that date:

> ... there were various allegations from theatres of operations where the South Africans were around, and there were these allegations of use either by or against South Africans, so that raised the awareness slightly; but it was only in the, I suppose, late 80s and early 90s that you start to get any indication that things are going on. I mean, Basson was known about more for the deals, trying to buy protective equipment, you know the CAMs [Chemical Agent Monitors] and whatever, than he was as the leader of a programme; it was only into the 90s before his name emerged as the guy who was running the programme.[56]

In particular, Basson's visits to many countries around the world including the UK, under orders from his Minister of Defence, began to be noticed by SIS (Secret Intelligence Service). In 1981 he visited a conference on CBW in the US where, he reported, '... contact was made with a number of senior military officers ... on first impression most of them were well disposed to the RSA [Republic of South Africa]'.[57] One of his earliest known visits to the UK took place in 1985. In April of that year, Basson visited a stand at a military medical exhibition in London run by a UK-based company called Special Training Services. Here, Basson made enquiries about chemical and biological warfare matters. The meeting was reported by one of the company directors, Jim Shortt, to SIS.[58] UK intelligence 'were ... concerned that there was something going on and that [they] didn't know what it was'.[59] By the mid 1980s, the movement of specialists from DIS to SIS helped them take the CBW threat more seriously within the FCO via the JIC, and this may account for UK intelligence agencies continuing to take note of, if not actively pursue, intelligence on South African CBW.

The UK intelligence agencies continued to obtain information on Basson and his contacts. It became apparent that Basson was operating in the UK under the cover of a front company, WPW Investments. Founded in October of 1986, it later emerged that WPW lent its name to between 50 and 100 companies and close corporations with a wide and diverse range of interests: essentially WPW became a 'multi-national one stop money laundering service'[60] enabling Basson to fund his purchases of arms and equipment and hence circumvent the international arms embargoes placed on South Africa. It must also seem likely that the intelligence agencies of other countries were aware of these issues—not least the US National Security Agency.

Throughout the 1980s, British attention was slowly becoming more focused on South Africa and its CBW programmes. According to one UK intelligence officer:

> the concern about South Africa was that we didn't want them buying our kit, because it was supposed to be on embargo for sale to South Africa ... I mean, if something happened, no one wanted to see on television South Africans running around in British equipment that we were supposed to explicitly not sell to them.[61]

This concern fits well with UK foreign policy relating to counter-proliferation, with intelligence serving as a 'gatherer' of information to inform foreign policy. It is clear that the activities of Basson, carried out on behalf of the South African government, were of concern to the UK. This did however bring with it a problem. At that time all UK arms control monitoring and compliance was entirely intelligence-based, and as a result when it was found or suspected that a state might be in breach of an arms control treaty, deciding upon a course of action was difficult. As one UK Foreign Office official described: 'What can one do? Sources are precious and often intelligence cannot be used, sometimes it is even too classified for ministers to see, sometimes they are simply not willing to act.'[62] As it stood, considering the information held by UK intelligence agencies in the mid 1980s, there was insufficient evidence of non-compliance to generate a high-level political response. This is interesting: in the case of South Africa, the evidence that something might have been going on was not doubted; the problem lay in generating a response. What might be considered sufficient weight of intelligence to compel a political response? There are obvious parallels here with the Soviet case study presented in Chapters 4–5.

Throughout the mid to late 1980s, the UK view of the proliferation threat posed by South Africa continued to develop. UK intelligence carried on obtaining low-level intelligence such as:

> Odd bits of information suggesting that there was something going on. And then it tended to be snippets came out from the offshoots, like Basson's deal ... for CAMs, WPW Investments and whatever. So on the fringes of that, there seemed to be something going on. And then snippets started coming in that the South Africans were doing their own research.[63]

Some of this research referred to a more sinister side of Project Coast. One area of research apparently related to attempts to develop methods for the mass sterilisation of the black population of South Africa, sometimes referred to as 'an ethnic weapon'. Reports on this weapon also appeared in several Western newspapers throughout 1984 and 1985. For example, the *Washington Times* reported:

> The South African Defence Force has refused to confirm or deny charges in a UN Working Paper that it has developed ethnic chemical weapons capable of use against specific races ... the Working Paper said that South Africa had built a research station where these weapons were being tested on prisoners. 'South Africa is researching the development of so-called ethnic biological weapons which could be programmed to affect certain ethnic groups through the use of carefully selected biological viruses directed at the black population', the paper said.[64]

Other reports went into more detail, alleging that South Africa was actively collaborating with Israel in the development of these weapons.[65] Other reports deny this association entirely, suggesting Israel to be concerned about proliferation from South Africa, not cooperation with it.[66]

Whilst one could be forgiven for thinking that newspaper reports relating to the South African development of genetic weapons were espousing the potential for the destruction of the entire black population, UK intelligence views were not as strong: the consensus from BW experts was that 'the rumour about the ethnic weapon was patently rubbish ... all it seemed to be was if we can vaccinate ourselves and we release that organism we kill lots of blacks'.[67] It was therefore suggested that this was not perceived to be genetic warfare, merely the deliberate spreading of disease; this is a massive difference in terms of the counter-proliferation threat, but is nonetheless still biological warfare. The close defence relationship between Israel and South Africa is however well documented, and 'in South African–Israeli relations, what is hidden is much more than what is known'.[68] The South African government even went so far as to state in 1976 that 'Israel and South Africa have one thing above all else in common: they are both situated in a predominantly hostile world inhabited by dark peoples'.[69]

Up to this point, one can accept that the UK foreign policy view towards South African WMD programmes was broadly in line with desired counter-proliferation and arms control objectives. UK intelligence, whilst not directly tasked to seek information on CBW programmes in South Africa, was clearly interested in any information that was available. As this chapter has so far shown, there were enough 'odd bits of information'[70] to interest the intelligence agencies, and perhaps give more priority to South Africa as an intelligence target.

One barrier that perhaps prevented more resources and a higher priority being given to South Africa was that the relatively small number of intelligence officers with expertise in both chemical and biological weapons were, from 1987:

> absolutely drowning in the efforts to debrief [Pasechnik], and with the realisation of new Russian programmes ... the effort available was fairly limited and this just wasn't seen as a high priority ... yes, it was a matter of concern ... but almost all the efforts were expended elsewhere.[71]

This statement is of some interest: the UK government recognised the importance of counter-proliferation efforts, yet the resources were not apparently in place to deal with more than one country or issue at the same time. That said, whilst it can be considered that intelligence relating to South African programmes was apparently passively rather than actively pursued, it was still being collected and passed to intelligence officers with the ability to manage it. It is important to note here that UK intelligence had by now apparently been able to convince the JIC and some of the FCO that the UK faced a significant and serious threat from CBW.

Gaining focus: the developing UK intelligence picture

It seems rather ironic that the priority of South Africa as a target first began to change not because of the direct attempts to gain intelligence, but by the deeds of the South African government themselves. Two incidents are of particular note in the developing UK intelligence picture, and will now be explored: the first was an investigation into the possible use of chemical weapons by South African forces in Mozambique; the second was an internal South African government investigation into Project Coast and associated activities, known as the Steyn Report, and associated with the transition from apartheid to post-apartheid government

The first incident related to investigations by the UK into the possible use of chemical weapons in Mozambique in January 1992. This attack was believed to have occurred on 16 January 1992 near Estompene, close to the South African border. The attack was alleged to have taken place against government troops, and both fatalities and casualties were said to have followed a single airburst explosion that produced thick, dark smoke.[72] It was believed that the South African Defence Forces were responsible for the attack, possibly in an assault against ANC personnel based inside Mozambique.

The initial indication of the attack was reported to the UK ambassador in Mozambique, along with a request for an independent assessment of the casualties and alleged incident. The South African position with regard to this investigation is curious. According to official South African documents, there was concern that 'the sensitive nature of the allegations coupled to the lack of concrete evidence regarding the incident created a situation ripe for political exploitation and unfounded accusations'.[73] As a result, despite their suspected involvement, the South African government 'initiated contact with UK authorities with the objective of conducting a joint, controlled investigation which would ensure international credibility of findings'.[74] This suggests that the South African government had already been informed that Mozambique had requested a UK investigation; if true, this is quite telling of the capabilities of the South African intelligence services, not least in suggesting a considerable ability to extract information from the UK.

On the face of it, this seems like a curious position, especially given the possibility that a UK investigation might find conclusive evidence of South African involvement in the attack. That said, if the South African government were confident of the secrecy of Project Coast and believed (or, indeed, knew) that the UK had little or no intelligence of South African activities in this field, then a joint investigation might seem like a useful way to keep a close eye on the investigation, perhaps influencing its outcome. Equally, the South African government may have believed that it would be capable of directly influencing the result of the investigation. There is some evidence for this: official South African documents state that during direct later negotiations in March 1992 with the UK, 'although they were not forthcoming with many details about their involvement in the Mocambiquan [*sic*] incident, some positive developments regarding SA/UK cooperation did occur, and they seemed to acquire a greater understanding and sympathy with our position and conclusions'.[75]

One must perhaps pause here and consider what this statement might actually mean. There are two possible interpretations. The first and more literal implies that the UK official position was one that wished to keep the details of the investigation secret, but at the same time perhaps acknowledged any South African explanation relating to their involvement that might have been offered. The second interpretation, however, suggests that this statement may actually mean that the South African government had been successful in directly influencing and perhaps obtaining direct assistance from the UK, either unofficially or from individuals passing information in an unauthorised capacity. The implications of this second interpretation will be revisited later in this section.

The South Africans were clearly suspicious of the UK involvement. According to a report by Dr Davey, the UK initially denied that they were involved in any investigation, despite the fact that the South Africans had obtained proof that a UK team had already left for Mozambique. Furthermore, an individual from Porton Down had also told the South Africans that the UK government had recommended that Mozambique report their suspicions to the UN Security Council. This seems an odd course of action for a government to take if it was complicit in South African CBW development as has earlier been suggested—this will be discussed in more detail later. Although a subsequent UN investigation in Mozambique found that 'in the current absence of analytical data, we cannot conclude that a chemical warfare agent was used in the attack', the UK report stated:[76]

> The signs and symptoms of the casualties are entirely consistent with the use of a centrally acting anti-cholinergic CW agent. It is unlikely that traces of agent will be detectable in biological samples taken nearly two weeks after the attack. Given that the analysis of the samples is unlikely to be informative, it can be concluded from the symptoms and signs of the

casualties and the reports of the incident, that it is certainly a possibility that CW was used in the attack ...[77]

Evidence clearly suggests that the UK intelligence agencies took serious note of the outcome of the UK investigation in Mozambique. When the findings of the UK report were obtained by the South African government, they requested a meeting in order to 'discuss these findings which were directly opposed to [their] own'.[78] The meeting was subsequently held at Porton Down under apparently tight security. Once again, there is evidence suggesting that the South African team obtained further information from unnamed individuals whilst on their visit; in particular this evidence relates to knowledge of the identity of previously unnamed persons at the meeting—including UK intelligence personnel—as well as the content of communiqués from the Mozambique government regarding the investigation. This once again suggests that the South Africans were well informed and connected by their own Intelligence agencies inside the UK. It was later to be suspicions over the extent of this involvement, in particular allegations of the leaking of secret documents from Porton Down to South African personnel, along with events related to the completion of the Steyn Report within South Africa that was to change the interests of UK intelligence personnel from a counter-proliferation focus to one that must be described as counter-espionage.

The Steyn Report was the result of the pressing desire of President F. W. de Klerk to respond to allegations made by Judge Richard Goldstone at a press conference on 16 November 1992. President de Klerk had previously appointed Goldstone to head a commission at the end of July 1991 to investigate allegations relating to ongoing violence that threatened to undermine political reform in South Africa. At the press conference, Goldstone announced that investigators from his commission had raided the offices of the Directorate of Covert Collection in Pretoria, subsequently discovering that elements of the South African Defence Forces (SADF) were involved in illegal and unauthorised activities. President de Klerk immediately appointed the Chief of Defence Staff, General Pierre Steyn (a serving army officer), to carry out an investigation into all the SADF's intelligence activities. He also placed Steyn in immediate command of the SADF's intelligence operations, in addition instructing him to ascertain whether there had been any contraventions of the law or of government policy.[79]

On completion of his initial work, Steyn did not hand de Klerk a report as such, but gave a detailed briefing based on contributions from a variety of intelligence sources, including the Directorate of Counter Intelligence. In essence, Steyn argued that elements of the SADF 'had been involved in, and in certain instances were still involved in, illegal and unauthorised activities which could be prejudicial to the security, interests and well-being of the state'. These activities included allegations of murder, fomenting inter-racial violence and the stockpiling of weapons. Steyn added that 'some members of the senior command structure were largely caught up in the momentum of activities of the past ... while others were possibly promoting their own agenda against the interests of the state'—presumably to precipitate the failure of President De Klerk's political change processes.[80] In addition, he specifically raised the activities of Basson, who he believed to have been directly involved in 'chemical warfare attacks ... execution of SADF elimination instructions and that he lives beyond the means linked to his rank'.[81]

The Steyn Commission carried out its investigation at the same time as the Auditor General. This separate investigation was concerned with investigating financial irregularities associated with the funding of Project Coast and other projects managed by Basson. Much of this funding was associated with the commercialisation of the front companies established by Basson, a process that began in 1988. It was perceived that many of these companies could be 'sold to the scientists and management of the company'.[82] Indeed, the SIS subsequently discovered that 'Basson had sold [one of these companies] to his mate and they'd made a lot of money out of the deal'.[83]

Into the shadows: the impact of Project Coast on the UK

It was in the aftermath of the Steyn Report, during which several SADF members and employees, including two generals and four brigadiers, were placed on compulsory retirement,[84] subsequently known as 'the night of the generals', when UK involvement in Project Coast deepened and darkened.[85] It was also then that UK intelligence efforts appeared to switch from dedication entirely to counter-proliferation to what could be described as counter-espionage. This was to bring with it controversy, confusion and a lack of clarity with regard to UK involvement, which still resonates in Westminster today.

This chapter has already discussed how UK intelligence had for some time been receiving 'odd bits of information suggesting that there was something going on'.[86] It appears that from the early 1990s, probably around the same time as Steyn briefed his findings, 'snippets [that] came out from the offshoots' were obtained.[87] Some of this information was significant in terms of illustrating the extent to which Basson had been involved in financial transactions through front companies, some of which were based in the UK; other pieces of information had the potential to place both the UK government and SIS itself into uncomfortable positions.

In terms of intelligence relating to financial matters, of particular note were the dealings of a former army officer and explosives expert, Roger Buffham, with Basson. Buffham had been introduced to Basson via two other business associates, and he was apparently already known to South African intelligence.[88] Reportedly, Buffham became a key aide to Basson; the pair met eight times and made a series of financial transactions together—one netted Buffham's private bank account the sum of £1.5 million.[89] Perhaps of more interest to UK intelligence was the fact that he allegedly secured the supply of stolen blueprints for state of the art CAM devices (chemical agent monitoring equipment) for Basson, originating from the UK company Graseby Ionics,[90] as well as other CBW defence equipment. This painted an interesting picture of Basson in the eyes of UK intelligence: 'money was a huge part [of his motivation] ... he liked wheeler dealing, he liked the jet set lifestyle'.[91] One must consider the importance of money as a motivator for Basson. This indicates the potential for more serious involvement in criminal activities in order to make money. This concern is perhaps important later, when this chapter considers UK fears of Basson's involvement in the sale of CBW knowledge.

Whilst the breaching of sanctions by UK-based companies was serious in itself, other intelligence painted a much more worrying picture. It somehow became apparent to UK intelligence, possibly from information obtained directly from South Africa after the Steyn Report, that sensitive CBW-related material had been passed to Basson and Project Coast. In particular, allegations surfaced that suggested Basson had personally visited Porton Down.[92] One UK intelligence officer described his reaction to this as yet unproven allegation as:

We were genuinely concerned about these comments that Basson had been to Porton. And our nightmare was that a picture would appear on a front page with Basson standing next to, you know, with Dr Death getting his tips from UK ... He could have been there several times under an alias, how would we know? If he'd shaved his beard off, who would have recognised him? If he'd put a wig on and shaved his beard, he could have been anybody.[93]

There was subsequently a major investigation within the UK involving personnel from both SIS and MI5, the Security Service. At a time when the UK was deeply involved and committed to the negotiation of the Chemical Weapons Convention, the damage that would be caused if these allegations were proved true could be devastating. Whether any possible passage of information was sanctioned officially or not, the potential for the UK government to be accused of having assisted Basson and the South African government clearly existed. As a result, both SIS and MI5 were very keen to ensure that the full extent of UK involvement with Basson was established as quickly as possible. There are clearly two sides to an argument here: one, that the UK government had officially sanctioned the passage of information to South Africa and the investigation was a damage limitation exercise; the other that this was a severe shock and it was therefore vital to establish immediately who had been involved and what information they might have passed.

During the investigation, it became apparent that Basson had previously had access to Derek Griffiths, Superintendent of the Physical Protection Division at Porton Down.[94] At the TRC, this evidence was provided:

> ... through Griffiths, Basson had met [others] who knew or were soon made aware that Basson was engaged in sanctions-busting for the South African security forces. Basson claimed that [one of these] had what was known as a 'CBW Mafia'—a group of experts in the field who met monthly to exchange ideas and information ... Basson [was authorised by the Military Intelligence's Chief Director] to attend the monthly meetings. He said it soon became obvious to him that each member of the 'CBW Mafia' had access to the CBW secrets of his own country.[95]

Whilst information here becomes difficult to obtain, it appears that UK intelligence believed that both UK and US 'experts, probably long retired, had been got alongside by South Africans [intelligence services] and there was genuine concern again that, who knows what these people would say'.[96] These views are effectively mirrored by Basson himself, who had commented that 'the British have a peculiar habit of casting aside those who have served them faithfully, and their resentment turns them into willing purveyors of information—old men who are eager to talk about their achievements'.[97] UK intelligence officers commented on past experiences of similar events:

> ... the Russians had shown themselves to be adept at meeting people at conferences and getting them to say things that they shouldn't have done, and we'd seen for ourselves how pathetic some of our people had been ... where they gave away everything and got nothing in return. You know the desire to be seen to be knowledgeable meant they would just tell things that they shouldn't have said, to try to make themselves look important.[98]

In other words, it appears that UK intelligence feared that certain individuals employed, or formerly employed, in UK CBW programmes might have passed official information to Basson. The worst possible outcome for the UK government at a time when it was not only totally committed to counter-proliferation, but also playing a key role in the negotiation of the new Chemical Weapons Convention Treaty was discovering that 'Brits [had] been involved'.[99] Basson had apparently already told General Knobel, the South African Surgeon General, that he had:

> ... penetrated the United Kingdom. And we had wonderful information from them, and some of the scientists who were later on sent to look at our programme were the very scientists who had given us information in the first place ... he went to Porton Down, I'm telling you ... [he] managed to get manuals. Whether he stole them or whether they were given to us, I do not want to elaborate, but they were top secret manuals from ... the British.[100]

Further evidence of UK involvement now appeared: from 1985, it became apparent that 'two British scientists [apparently] on an unauthorised visit from Porton Down helped and advised [on safety upgrades to BL-4 laboratories used in BW development]'.[101] Remarkably, these individuals worked for a company called 'Porton International', a group of former employees of Porton Down.[102]

UK intelligence interest continued to grow when in 1987 it appeared that the South Africans had attempted assassinations of individuals within the UK using biological products from Project Coast.[103] These revelations led to a prolonged investigation by MI5 into the suspicious deaths of up to half a dozen 'enemies of apartheid' who may have been murdered in the UK.[104] All of these deaths from the 1980s and 1990s had similarities: each victim suffered apparent strokes or heart attacks—symptoms closely related to those generated by some of the assassination agents developed by Project Coast. One of those who died suspiciously in 1992 was the SIS officer Peter Martin. Martin had worked on a case where he had direct contact with Basson, relating to BW; he apparently voiced concerns over his personal security shortly before his death.[105] The results of these investigations are still classified.[106]

Basson later had links with an Iranian called Hashemi, through whom he tried to procure equipment of use in the production of biological agents. Hashemi was also working for SIS as an agent, and had been instrumental in the provision of Chinese-manufactured Silkworm missiles to the British in order that counter-measures could be developed for shipping in the Straits of Hormuz against the Iranian missile threat in the mid 1980s. Hashemi came to the attention of UK police when he set up a deal to supply South African-made NBC (nuclear, biological, chemical) suits to Iran. This information came following a tip-off to Metropolitan Police Sergeant Michael Hill, who was subsequently forced to take early retirement after apparently refusing to drop his investigation when SIS connections became clear. Hashemi was subsequently released after a supposed deal designed to prevent SIS operational details being exposed in court.[107] In 1996 evidence was also discovered suggesting that Basson had a network of sympathisers and supporters still active within the UK.[108] These individuals included members from an extreme right-wing South African group called the 'broederbond' or 'Third Force', which had already been linked to attempts to plan a coup against the de Klerk government.[109]

Too close to home: the UK government acts

By the early 1990s the UK clearly appeared to have had ample evidence relating to the activities of Basson and Project Coast. It is therefore interesting to note that, whilst there was clearly concern about the relationship between UK scientists and Project Coast, this did not in itself generate a political response. The overall intelligence picture was strong, yet it appeared that concern was inward-looking rather than outward. This was both in terms of the potential for damage to the reputation of the UK in its counter-proliferation efforts, and in terms of identifying whether or not national security had been damaged—and to what extent—through official secrets having been made available to the South Africans. This is curious, in that it raises questions over what intelligence is primarily for. One might suppose that SIS was directly involved in supporting foreign policy, yet here they might clearly be considered to be acting on behalf of the agendas of other government departments first—specifically the Home Office in a counter-espionage context.

It was to be intelligence relating to the apparent imminence of the takeover of political power within South Africa by the ANC in 1993, as well as suspicions over the involvement of Basson in Libya, that would finally force political action by the UK government. The UK government first formally approached South Africa regarding the proliferation of CBW from Project Coast in the last months of apartheid in 1993. It has been suggested that whilst previously the UK government was closely interested in bringing an end to the South African nuclear weapons programme, it was not until the ANC was poised to take over power that concerns over CBW programmes produced any political activity.

According to one UK intelligence officer, from a UK perspective, 'we [the UK] were concerned that with a handover to the ANC or to a black government there were concerns that that knowledge and technology would spread' although his own view was '[that] the concerns were not so much the ANC per se, but just that if there was stuff [CBW-related material] around, there were those in the ANC that were very pro some not very nice people'.[110] When challenged, this interviewee accepted that this comment related to other states, going on to add 'and if that stuff sort of got sent off to people, either for assassination or for sort of terrorist use or whatever, I mean there were some funny characters around'.[111] The interviewee refused to comment on what those states might be, though it had later become known that Basson had formed a strong relationship with a senior Libyan intelligence agent—Abdur Razzaq—as early as 1984. It may be that Libya was one of those countries of concern, in particular given the Libyan support for the ANC before it came to power; it was always a possibility that the new South African government might wish to reward its friends.[112]

Further investigations by SIS and CIA revealed that Basson had spent a considerable amount of time in Libya. According to one CIA officer:

> It all had a bad smell to it ... Gaddafi had been trying to get a BW programme for years—without success. He had incompetent people in place—that was the only reason he failed to get a BW programme up and

running. Now suddenly we saw him with a man who our source was telling us was South Africa's top BW expert. You can imagine how we felt.[113]

For UK intelligence, the fears were not so great in terms of proliferation of weapons; there was more of a feeling that the South African government must be encouraged to take tighter control over Basson. Whilst the US were fixated on a potential Libyan chemical weapons threat, the UK seemed to be content that Basson had no actual direct involvement with either chemical or biological weapons in Libya. Their view was that the activities of the company 'Libgro', set up by Basson, were not a threat:[114]

> Basson was a smart guy [but] he was never going to get his hands dirty ... if he went to Libya, what could he do? He wasn't an engineer, he couldn't mend the factory, which is what they wanted. They wanted a decent chemical engineer, but Basson could have found them a decent chemical engineer if he had been so motivated. And that was the concern, not that he himself would go and sort the programme out. I mean they had a production facility, it would have worked brilliantly if only they'd had a chemical engineer to make it work. They had all the chemicals, they'd made a bit of mustard. They needed someone to sort out all the crap that the Germans [who built the factory] had left. I mean all the Germans did when they commissioned the plant was distil solvent through it—'There you are, it works fine! Off you go, goodbye.'[115]

One (un-named) Western Intelligence agency apparently even went so far as to suggest to the South African government that the best way to restrain Basson was if 'Basson [were] killed to prevent his knowledge from falling into the wrong hands'.[116] Basson himself certainly alleges that in Tunis, on his way home from a trip to Libya, one of his colleagues was approached by a man he believed to be from Mossad, the Israeli secret intelligence service, and told 'tell your colleague Dr Basson that the next time he is seen in Tripoli he will be dealt with'. Basson recalled, 'Jesus, I was shit scared.' He never returned to Libya.[117]

The UK government, along with the US, next made a series of steps designed to 'bully the de Klerk regime into action'.[118] The UK and US made a number of demands to de Klerk. As General Knobel recorded, these included requirements that:

> Their experts be fully briefed on the details of the SADF [South African Defence Force] programme. Confirmation be given that the programme has been terminated and that no biological weapon systems are in exis-

tence. A public declaration to this effect be made. All cases of alleged abuse of the programme and its products be fully investigated and the results of this investigation be made available to them. That Mr Mandela should be fully informed about this programme.[119]

The quantity and quality of intelligence information held by the UK government was therefore apparently able to allow explicit demands via an official démarche to be made to the South Africans shortly before the election in 1994. These demands appeared to be driven by the desire of the UK to prevent the passage of information relating to CBW either to outside states such as Libya, or to the next ANC government. It has already been established that there were concerns over the motivations behind Basson's visits to Libya. The response to these demands was not necessarily exactly what the UK desired. According to de Klerk, who was later interviewed regarding the first UK approach:

> They were initially quite aggressive. They had a long list of demands and I said that because I could give them certain assurances, that we could not accede to all sorts of demands; that I was [as] concerned as they were that we should prevent the knowledge that had been achieved in South Africa to spread [and] be used elsewhere; that already preventative steps had been taken in that regard and that they could be assured, therefore, that we would deal with integrity within the framework of our sovereignty and we would not allow all sorts of inspections by representatives of other countries; [that] they must accept my word ... but their main concern was the knowledge in the minds of certain individuals who might become ... loose cannons, using that information in other parts of the world.[120]

This acknowledgment by de Klerk of the potential risk posed by Basson effectively selling CBW-related information around the world was ultimately to result in Basson being re-hired by the military in 1995 as a surgeon:

> ... we had to think carefully [about] how to control this man and his knowledge ... it was specifically that, to keep him under control, to put him in a situation where he could be properly managed as far as possible, rather than have him out on a limb, roving the world at his will. We decided to give him employment within the medical section of the defense force where there could be the control.[121]

The logic underpinning this course of action appears to be that it would be easier to control Basson from within the military than if he were a private citizen.[122]

This démarche did result in some cooperation between the UK and South Africa. From a UK intelligence perspective, it appears that a key aim of this cooperation was still to continue to investigate what information had passed from the UK to Basson. This does not necessarily match the priorities given when the original demands were made to the South Africans via the démarche relating to counter-proliferation. As part of this cooperation, two UK intelligence officers 'went over and ... gave the South Africans a full history of our understanding of the programme from way back; our motivations and all that we'd done. And, you know, they accepted this totally.'[123] They also articulated that they 'were genuinely concerned about these comments that Basson had been to Porton'.[124] This may have been a strategy through which the South Africans could be shown that the UK was fully aware of the extent of the programme, but would like to know where information had come from, in particular if it had come from the UK. It may also have paved the way for a new course of action to be taken after the election, when it was presumed that Mandela would be in power.

The agreement also allowed for the visit of UK personnel to South Africa to be further briefed on the programme, as well as to visit facilities. One UK intelligence officer visited some of the facilities involved in Project Coast, and this merely confirmed what the UK intelligence view had been all along:

> Roodeplaat was a nice facility. It was pretty much stripped out: the P3 containment facility was exceedingly small, the reactors were very small, 20 litres or so, very tiny. And I was sniffing round, and on one of the cupboards, someone had obviously a work clothes cupboard, they had got a little sign and it said 'If you want loyalty, buy a dog. I'm here because I get paid.' And that, at the end of the day, summed it all up. But the BW interest? Yes, it was talked up. It was talked up by Basson and others, because it got them money. The reality was it was an assassination programme. There was never any weaponisation. The weaponisation was on bloody screwdrivers and shirts, and it was a way of getting rid of undesirables, rather than it was a sophisticated weapon programme.[125]

This once again raises questions over what the UK primary aims were: were they to stop the programme, or to stop Basson? Knobel later reported to Mandela that 'their scientists and intelligence community did not have any real information on the content of the programme'.[126] This seems to be at odds with the UK intelligence view. One must assume that Knobel was perhaps trying to reduce his own exposure, particularly in terms of the Truth and Reconciliation Commission—as someone who had been involved in the programme. If UK intelligence had not been satisfied, they would probably have pushed the South African government further for greater exposure. Interestingly, Knobel also reported that during these visits 'certain information regarding the Russian and Iraqi programmes was passed on to them, including the identity of the newly prevalent "flesh-eating bacteria" which originated from the Russian programme'.[127]

Making it stop: UK approaches to President Mandela

Mandela did indeed come to power in 1994. He was briefed in August 1994 about Project Coast by Surgeon General Knobel. In a lengthy document, Knobel gave an overview of the programme background, implementation, research and development as well as the winding up of the project. He recommended to Mandela that the records of the programme continue to be kept secret, no public announcement be made, and that a follow-up meeting with the UK and US be held.[128] The UK government met with Mandela and the Government of National Unity who 'welcomed and cooperated with the American and British delegations'.[129] Mandela, despite Knobel's advice, appeared to be happy to accept the demands placed upon him: Basson was re-hired, guarantees were given that all CBW material apart from one copy on optical disc would be destroyed, and commitments were made to submit a Form F as required by the BTWC. Further UK visits took place as a result.

The policy of the Republic of South Africa under Mandela was firmly committed to the fields of non-proliferation, disarmament and arms control relating to conventional arms, weapons of mass destruction and dual-use goods, firearms, ammunition, explosives, pyrotechnics and riot control agents.[130] Indeed, its National Policy emphatically states that 'the adequate protection of rights to life and security of the person against repression and acts of aggression is fundamental to the well-being and to the social and economic development of every country', but at the same time 'it is the duty of every government to protect and safeguard the rights of its people ... [because] every responsible country has the right to acquire arms to equip and defend itself against acts of aggression'.[131] As a result, 'it is South Africa's declared national interest in conjunction with its international obligations and commitments, particularly as these relate to non-proliferation, disarmament and arms control, and the implementation of international humanitarian law, to exercise due restraint in the transfer and trade in weapons and related materials, equipment, technology and services'.[132] This policy therefore represents a commitment to membership of and compliance with a wide range of arms control and proliferation regimes, and significantly, for the purposes of this book, the Biological and Toxin Weapons Convention (BTWC) and the Chemical Weapons Convention (CWC).[133]

The South African government therefore has commitments to those treaty regimes. Like any other signatory state to the BTWC, it is also bound by a requirement to submit a document known as Form F: a fulfilment of requirements under agreements made at the third BTWC review conference in 1991. This document is meant to represent an opportunity to encourage openness and transparency in former state-run offensive and defensive biological weapons programmes. Given that this chapter has already established the extent to which South Africa ran a biological weapons programme, one would expect the South African submission to present information relating to Project Coast. The first (1993) South African Form F submission declared that no offensive biological weapons programme existed prior to 1993.[134] Subsequent submissions from 1994 to 2007 have merely reaffirmed the 1993 submission, i.e. they state 'nothing new to declare'.[135] At least on the face of it, this appears to be misleading: in the 1993 submission, the South African government explicitly states that no efforts had been undertaken to develop biological weapons.[136] This is clearly a somewhat puzzling situation, especially given the apparent commitment of Mandela to transparency.

Whilst submissions of Form F documents, regardless of their perceived accuracy, are entirely consistent, statements from within the South African government are not. At least by implication, some official documents and statements appear to acknowledge that an offensive programme did exist within South Africa. For example, on 15 June 1998, the South African government made a statement relating to the Truth and Reconciliation Commission (TRC) hearings on chemical and biological weapons. This statement referred to 'the apartheid regime's chemical and biological weapons programme'. The TRC itself stated in a 1998 report that 'the military command under the former government [had been] grossly negligent in approving a chemical and biological warfare programme it did not understand'.[137] Why then was no Form F declaration made reflecting the existence of this programme? The answer may lie in the relationship of both the apartheid and post-apartheid governments of South Africa with the UK, although other arguments must also be considered.

One argument suggests that the official view within South Africa might have been that the apartheid regime did run a chemical and biological weapons programme, but that this was somehow not representative of the Republic of South Africa and therefore did not need to be declared on the Form F. In particular, because 'any such offensive uses were done without proper authorization and against official policy',[138] the programme was essentially 'rogue' and therefore not conducted on behalf of the government. This may explain the omission of an acknowledgment of Project Coast from South African Form F submissions.

Arguments drawing on the involvement of outside states, significantly the UK, to possible explanations for the apparent lack of transparency by the South African government appear to be well supported by evidence. But even here positions appear to be inconsistent and certainly confuse attempts to understand UK foreign policy towards South Africa. For example, on 11 April 1994 the UK ambassador to South Africa, Anthony Reeve, met with the State President and Minister of Defence to discuss the 1993 Form F submission made by South Africa. Allegedly, they stated 'that they were fully aware of the contents of the South African Defence Forces CBW programme and that they had certain reservations about the RSA's CBM [Form F] declaration as well as the implications for non-proliferation'.[139] On the face of it, this appears to reflect the official position of the UK government to WMD proliferation: 'to monitor and ensure compliance'.[140] It is, however, also here that UK official views of the South African programme begin to diverge.

It may well be that the objective of this meeting from a UK perspective was to secure access to facilities associated with Project Coast, to ensure that research had ceased. After two further approaches to the South African government from the UK, an agreement was reached whereby UK personnel would both visit CBW facilities and meet with South African officials to 'encourage South Africa to submit a [Form] F which would be credible and not raise more questions than it answered'.[141] The UK delegation was led by Dr Graham Pearson, former head of the Porton Down establishment. Dr Pearson's view is that the reason why South Africa did not submit a Form F reflecting their past offensive programmes may be:

> that they felt that it was not necessary ... and perhaps the UK and US did not press them to do so at a sufficiently high level. It could be that the feeling in the UK and US was that South Africa had shut down their offensive programmes and that the Form F was not seen as important.[142]

It is here that the view from UK intelligence agencies differs though: 'in talking to them [South Africans] after the Pearson ... visit, my attitude ... was quite clear. Because there were never any weapons, they couldn't possibly be seen to have had an offensive programme.'[143]

The key issue that separates those who believe that the South African Form F should have referred to past offensive programmes and those who feel it should not appears to relate to whether or not weapons actually existed. Regardless, one would surely expect the UK government to have a clear and consistent overall view despite this perhaps rather academic distinction. Certainly, General Knobel, the former project manager and surgeon general, believed 'it was spelt out very clearly that in this project we would not embark on creating an offensive capability ... and I can declare quite emphatically to you that at no time were classical chemical, or for that matter, biological weapons developed'.[144] Again, concerns in UK intelligence appear to be that 'if they *had* declared an offensive programme based on assassination, then it was a dangerous track to go down because that potentially put all sorts of people in the mire'.[145] Dr Pearson made comments appearing to support at least one interpretation of this line of argument: 'one reason for not admitting a past programme might have been a fear of national litigation against those involved'.[146] This still assumes that one interprets the South African programme as not having had military application. Again, the SIS view was that 'it was never designed to have military application, it was designed to get rid of the people [they] don't like'.[147] The motivation for this is perhaps sound—'it would have been quite wrong to ... stigmatise the Mandela government who were doing so much to ... get rid of these [programmes]'.[148] If this was the case, it remains strange that given 'there were a number of UK/US approaches to South Africa ... the individuals involved in one approach were generally unaware of the details of the other approaches'.[149]

These differing approaches do suggest different objectives on the part of the UK in terms of foreign policy objectives. One relates to intelligence: gaining assurances and confidence that Project Coast had stopped—the UK intelligence view seems to support this. The visits carried out by Dr Pearson may well have been a fall back. If no confidence was gained that the programme had ceased, the UK was still in a position to apply pressure to South Africa in terms of its Form F submission. The UK may have achieved its own objective from a non-proliferation perspective through the work of SIS, leaving subsequent visits little to achieve. One is however left with a question relating to why UK intelligence were content with such an apparently limited objective, when the normal UK counter-proliferation objective would demand absolute transparency and accountability.

Within the UK, there remained disagreement between SIS and DIS regarding how satisfactory the outcome of this episode had been. In particular, this related to whether or not the South African programme was deemed to have been one that developed weapons. One UK intelligence officer explained:

> there was [sic] disagreeing views. I mean, DIS were all 'oh, they should have declared an offensive programme', where ... the FCO were of the view 'don't be stupid, an offensive programme means weapons. There aren't any weapons.' You know, we've been through this with the Russians who had declared an offensive programme who subsequently said 'Oh sorry, it was a mistake, we didn't really mean to declare it because, you know, we didn't have weapons, we had a notional capability, but we never actually practised.'[150]

The willingness of Mandela to engage with the UK was clearly a valuable asset though. The long-term view of the UK intelligence, regardless of the outcome of disagreements with other agencies and government departments, was that:

> Mandela's the sort of bloke who can sell this to countries who wouldn't listen to us ... this could be really good news because here's a guy who's got such credibility he gets rid of programmes. He actually starts saying the right things about stopping proliferation, controlling problems—you know, it could really have a tremendous boost.[151]

In light of this comment, one could perhaps consider UK intelligence involvement to be an example of intelligence being used for idealistic purposes—actively encouraging another state to close down and open up former weapon programmes. The story relating to Basson and Project Coast did carry on, but by 1997 it was more a case for South Africa's own law enforcement agencies when he was found in possession of classified documents that had supposedly been destroyed. He was later arrested for narcotics offences.[152]

But this case study does not tie up neatly the relationship between intelligence and foreign policy. Indeed, one of the most striking features here seems to be the number of questions that remain after analysis has been completed. Whilst evidence is clear showing there was concern within the UK that sensitive information was passed to the South Africans, there is very little information available in the public domain that proves whether or not there was actually any official involvement here. Certainly, it is striking how seriously UK intelligence attempted to identify the names of those who might have passed that information and what it might have been. But one must also consider the argument that this was for damage limitation purposes, rather than counter-espionage. There is certainly evidence that SIS and MI5 had their suspicions over specific individuals. One of the most vocal proponents of the argument that UK assistance to South Africa was officially sanctioned is the MP Andrew MacKinlay, who on numerous occasions has asked parliamentary questions seeking to confirm what the UK government involvement was in Project Coast.[153] Indeed, some officers within DIS still have concerns that 'we didn't have the full story and some bits didn't fit together'.[154] The UK intelligence view generally remained that 'looking back, we actually came out of it quite well', whilst at the same time acknowledging that 'there is this stigma that somehow or other we had another agenda', that 'obviously we had been involved' or 'we might have been', but 'they were mavericks if they were involved'. Regardless, when the prospect of a potentially difficult political situation arose, UK intelligence quickly worked to protect national interests.

Still further evidence of hidden agendas can be found in some Truth and Reconciliation Commission reports. One document in particular states that 'the development of the programme would not have been possible without some level of international support'.[155] However, this is clearly not the same as saying that the UK was complicit in the development of these weapons. Furthermore, allegations have been made that the UK government put pressure on South Africa to withhold documents from the TRC and hold the hearings in confidence in order to protect issues relating to their involvement.[156] This is perhaps not surprising if one expects UK intelligence to defend UK national interests—in particular, if criminal proceedings might have been pending against UK nationals implicated in the passing of official secrets. What was perhaps more important from an intelligence perspective, certainly for the future, was 'the fact was we had established a very good working relationship with the key people ... and we had wonderful cooperation afterwards in [other] counter-proliferation activities'.[157] This case study therefore provides an interesting example of intelligence interacting with foreign policy in a rapidly changing political environment.

7

GAS AND GADDAFI

LIBYAN CHEMICAL WEAPONS DEVELOPMENT

On 19 December 2003, the Libyan leader Mu'ammer Gaddafi released a statement via his Foreign Minister announcing that Libya would renounce all WMD. In an historic statement, Mohammed Abderrahmane Chalgam reported that his government promised that 'with its own free will [it had] decided to eliminate these [*sic*] materials, equipment and programs so that Libya may be completely free of internationally proscribed weapons'. The statement went on to announce that those steps would be taken in a transparent and verifiable manner, including allowing international inspections. In addition to these intended actions, Libya additionally agreed to be bound by the Nuclear Proliferation Treaty, the safeguards agreement of the International Atomic Energy Agency, the Biological and Toxin Weapons Convention and the Chemical Weapons Convention.[1]

The Libyan statement was hailed by US President George Bush as 'an example to other countries ... Leaders who abandon the pursuit of biological, chemical and nuclear weapons and the means to deliver them will find an open path to better relations with the US and other free nations.'[2] Prime Minister Tony Blair echoed these sentiments, calling the announcement 'an historic one and a courageous one'.[3] However, these statements also masked a secret process of negotiations.[4] Through these negotiations, first between the UK and Libya, then between the US, UK and

Libya, details of a deal to remove sanctions on Libya in exchange for the renunciation of WMD programmes were hammered out. These very negotiations were hailed by the White House to be 'an intelligence victory'.[5] Indeed, Butler also considered Libya to represent 'a major intelligence success', illustrating that 'where intelligence is good it can create its own positive momentum ... increase confidence in the reliability of reporting ... [and] uncover new leads'.[6]

The case study contained in this chapter therefore represents a sequence of events that, on the surface, appears to be a textbook example of the use of intelligence and secret diplomacy to encourage a state to abandon its WMD programmes. However, whilst Butler described Libya as an intelligence success, it will actually be demonstrated here that the outcome was apparently more the result of a wide range of other factors influencing Libyan behaviour. In this sense, the cynic might even argue that the case of Libya, more than any other, represents a 'whitewash' of the true facts. It should be noted by the reader that this case study is relatively recent in terms of events that will be described. As a result, the precise dynamics of the case study are still, to a large extent, extremely sensitive and therefore still classified. Whilst several key UK intelligence and Foreign Office personnel have provided information used in this case study through interviews with the author, it might become apparent in reading the chapter that evidence is at times scant. This is an unfortunate consequence of working with a recent case study that holds international sensitivities. Wherever possible, information obtained through interview for the purposes of this chapter has been either corroborated or triangulated with other sources.

Secret intelligence: negotiations by proxy

Whilst on an initial assessment, the apparent counter-proliferation success shown in this case study appears to be characterised by the use of secret diplomacy through numerous negotiations, in many ways Libya might also be considered to be an example of a state that would have given up all of its WMD programmes voluntarily regardless of intelligence activity. As a result, the UK intelligence agencies might be argued to have constructed a role purely to advance their own reputations through a 'PR coup', at the same time covering up the realities of UK intelligence involvement over a considerable period of time in Libya with a thin veneer of 'intelligence success'. There are, however, other explanations for the Libyan decision to terminate its WMD programmes.

There have been numerous reasons cited for the desire of Gaddafi to rehabilitate Libya. Reasons cited include the perception of Gaddafi that there were significant security benefits to be gained through closer ties to the US: not least because of Libyan concerns about the activities of al-Qaeda in the wake of 9/11.[7] Others have suggested that the 2003 US-led intervention in Iraq, at least in part justified by WMD counter-proliferation concerns, persuaded Gaddafi that he 'had little to gain and possibly a lot to lose' through continuing efforts to acquire those weapons.[8] Some authors have also argued that the economic situation within Libya at the dawn of the twenty-first century under international sanctions was such that the economic resurgence that Libya so desperately needed could only be brought about by positive re-engagement with the international community—and this could only be brought about with the removal of sanctions. This, in turn, entirely relied on Libya renouncing all WMD programmes.[9] Regardless of which of these explanations might best account for the apparent Libyan U-turn with regard to its WMD policies, there are important policy implications here. Significantly, they allow two clear areas to be identified relating to why that decision might have been made: the need to recognise and address Libyan security concerns, and understanding the importance of Gaddafi's personal reputation.[10] To address these two areas required a proactive process of engagement, sweeping away the artificial divides created by sanctions. Intelligence-led diplomacy had a key role to play in addressing these issues: 'where intelligence is good, it can create its own positive momentum'.[11]

One consistent thread in the sequence of events that spans almost a twenty-year period before Libya finally renounced its WMD programmes is the involvement of the UK government and, more importantly for this book, the UK intelligence agencies. From the events that raised initial concerns to the UK government regarding potential Libyan interest in chemical weapons in the early 1980s, through to the secret negotiations initiated at the behest of the Libyan government when contact was initiated with SIS in 2003, UK intelligence appears to have played a consistent and important role in all aspects of the transition from Libya as a pariah state to an accepted member of the international community.[12] It is therefore possible to argue that UK intelligence agencies might be seen to act as ersatz negotiators in this case study.

The involvement of intelligence agencies in facilitating, or indeed conducting negotiations on behalf of government is an important, if neglected, area of study.[13] In a broad conceptualisation, intelligence agencies might be seen to play a significant role in 'operations to influence the world by unseen means—the hidden hand'.[14] This role of secret intelligence services in conducting clandestine diplomacy has been well documented and its value is obvious: it is more readily deniable, and this is particularly significant where the adversary is engaged in armed attacks and/or terrorist activities'.[15] Its strength, because of this, is that it can be used to promote the cause of dialogue and reconciliation.[16] Put simply, where there is a willingness to speak to an adversary, intelligence agencies can provide the ideal channel. Where there is a desire to shroud any engagement from media and public interference, it would seem that this is an attractive option for a government to utilise.[17] It therefore remains clear that 'intelligence ... simply cannot be separated from foreign policy making', even when operating in a clandestine, pseudo-diplomatic role.[18] It is this type of involvement of the UK intelligence agencies within Libya that will be the focus of this chapter.

The development of CW in Libya: motivations and processes

The exact date that marks the venture of Libya, under the leadership of Gaddafi, to embark upon a programme to develop chemical weapons is shrouded in speculation.[19] It is however likely that by the end of the 1970s Libya possessed chemical weapons, or at least pursued its own indigenous production facility. Various theories exist that attempt to explain where Libya received the bulk of the technical assistance it required to develop chemical weapons successfully: Egypt may have transferred some chemical weapons to Libya in 1973, or East Germany may have been instrumental in the developing Libyan programme.[20] There is some confusion here in terms of the available information: some suggest that the Libyans first attained CW through import, others that the Libyans slowly developed their own production facilities. Regardless, it was not until 1986 that Western media sources began to report stories, largely from 'British Intelligence sources', linking Libya to chemical weapons proliferation.[21] Evidence also suggests that it was in the early 1980s that UK Intelligence agencies first became interested in Libya as a proliferation concern.

Libya's reputation as a country of international concern in relation to its support of terrorism had steadily grown since the seizure of power by Gaddafi in 1969. In particular, specific concerns related to Libyan support of various radical Palestinian groups, including the Abu Nidal organisation and Fatah, all known to use terrorism.[22] The CIA had declared Libya to be the world's biggest sponsor of terrorism by 1980, believing her to be supporting groups around the Middle East, Africa, Central America, Philippines, Western Europe as well as in other regions.[23] This support resulted in the imposition of sanctions bringing ever-increasing pain for Libya. By 1986 all economic contacts between Libya and the US had been severed.[24]

Although early concerns towards Libya were characterised by a focus on potential military and political threats towards neighbouring states, these soon changed as it became clear that Libya represented a significant weapons proliferation threat through her support of terrorist groups. In 1981 the US first expressed concerns over possible Libyan intentions to acquire nuclear weapons.[25] In the following years these concerns were expanded to include suspicions that the Libyans were attempting to develop not only nuclear, but also biological and chemical weapons. By the mid 1980s, Western media reports were beginning to report on these suspected Libyan WMD programmes.

In November 1986, the US newspaper *Baltimore Sun* reported that Libya had passed Soviet-made nerve agent warheads for SS 1 Scud missiles to Syria and Iran. Apparently, sources contacted for the report had stated that the 'British intelligence services [had] traced the source of the nerve agent back to the Soviet Union ... [although they] doubted that the Soviets had intended the nerve agents to be distributed in this way'. The report did not confirm that the Soviets had directly supplied CW to Libya.[26] The report was significant because it marked the start of a period of almost twenty years when Libya featured heavily and consistently in the Western media amid concerns over suspected chemical, biological and nuclear weapons programmes. In initial reports, most attention focused on Libyan CW usage or sales: for example, in late 1987, when Libya was engaged in the long-running war with Chad over the Aouzou Strip,[27] the Chadian forces were receiving extensive assistance from both the CIA and the French secret service, the SDECE. Here, reports circulated regarding Chadian accusations of Libyan use of chemical weapons during fighting. Whilst US intelligence sources apparently disagreed about types and levels of CW usage, they did believe that 'Libyan forces dropped chemical weapons from the air'. As a result, the US government supplied chemical defence equipment, including respirators, to the Chadians for defensive purposes.[28] It was not until November 1987 that this apparent Libyan CW capability was directly linked to local production facilities.[29]

By December 1987, US intelligence was reporting that it believed that the Libyans were constructing a chemical weapons production facility. Furthermore, the US believed that the building of this plant was 'consistent with a Libyan pattern of activities involving chemical weapons'.[30] It was to be largely US-led concerns over this plant, later identified to be at Rabta, that would lead to a string of diplomatic and military initiatives designed to persuade Gaddafi to close the plant and renounce chemical weapons. In January 1988 both US and UK intelligence were publicly commenting on the plant at Rabta. The UK Foreign Office said that 'there is no doubt [that the plant was] intended for chemical warfare'.[31] It is clear from research that Western intelligence agencies had actually known about Libyan plans for the construction of a CW facility since 1980—this will be considered in more detail later.

Whilst the Libyan government consistently stated that Rabta was intended for the production of pharmaceuticals, the international community was unconvinced. The public acknowledgement of the discovery of Rabta by Western intelligence agencies coincided with negotiations in Paris that would lead towards the development of the Chemical Weapons Convention. As a result, many nations, particularly those in the West, were probably far more aware of, and sensitive to, issues relating to chemical weapons than they might otherwise have been. Because of the broad international support for the US, their position of robustness in calling for the closure of Rabta was perhaps more likely to result in military action on the part of the US.

US military action against Libya had already been taken in the past. Other than a string of naval and air encounters in the Gulf of Sidra, the most significant US operation against Libya in the 1980s was the bombing of targets within Libya in 1986. The conventional explanation for this bombing raid was that it was in response to the sponsoring of terrorist bombings of US targets in Europe. These attacks probably represented a logical theme within the objectives proclaimed by Gaddafi after he came to power in the 1969 coup. Significantly, these included a strong desire on the part of Gaddafi for the pursuit of Arab nationalism within Libya and the greater Middle East, with him at the head in the role of Nasser's heir. In addition, Gaddafi proclaimed a strong resentment of the West, at least in part due to his perception of Western oil companies and governments interfering in Libyan politics. A strong hatred for Israel, and hence support for the Palestinian cause, was a key part of this theme.[32] One must at least consider the Libyan desire for a range of WMD within this context—these weapons could be seen as both prestigious and of great use in either attacking Israel or retaliating against attacks from other states, including the US.

It has been argued that the Libyan sponsorship of terrorist attacks during the 1980s also coincided with the collapse of the Middle East peace talks, where US President Reagan closely tied the interests of the US to those of Israel. This, it is argued, strengthened and encouraged Arab radicalism—the sponsoring of anti-US attacks by Gaddafi must therefore be seen within this context. The role of WMD in Libyan plans for Arab nationalism here is clear.[33] Indeed, Gaddafi made no secret of the fact that he believed 'Arabs had the right to own poison gas and germ warfare weapons to compensate for Israel's possession of banned arms'.[34]

These issues posed significant concerns for Western governments. As a result of the challenge posed by Gaddafi in his stated desire to achieve WMD, along with the possible aims he might have for the use of these weapons, Reagan faced two possible options in the Middle East. Firstly, he could attempt to defuse Arab radicalism through diplomatic engagement; or secondly, he could use military force against a convenient target in order to deal a 'crushing blow to the forces of Arab radicalism'.[35] After the presidency of Carter, Reagan argued that the US must re-establish its role in the world as the pre-eminent military power. It was power that characterised virtually every aspect of Reagan's foreign policy.[36] This hard-line, militaristic approach to some extent characterised the type of information that was produced by US intelligence in support of the stated US foreign policy. This intelligence was regularly inaccurate, as this chapter will later demonstrate. But the US were not alone in considering the use of force to remove the problem of Gaddafi. Controversially, the former MI5 officer David Shayler has alleged that 'in November 1999, [he] sent the Home Secretary Jack Straw detailed evidence of involvement by MI6 officers in a plot to murder Libyan leader Colonel Gaddafi. Reportedly the assassination failed when attempted in 1996 and innocent Libyan civilians were killed.'[37] It was the US that would be the first to take military action against Libya in response to suspicions that they were complicit in a series of bombings against US targets.

In a manner strikingly similar to some of the arguments put forward to explain the motivations of the US to invade Iraq in 2003, the US bombing of Libya in 1986 can be seen to be a statement to the world, in particular the Arab world, that 'interests were best served by being a friend, rather than a foe, of the United States'.[38] One must also consider that the US bombing was an act of revenge for the bombing of the US Marine barracks in Beirut in 1983. This apparent tit-for-tat activity, including numerous small-scale US–Libyan naval and air engagements, as well as further terrorist attacks such as the bombing of Pan Am Flight 103 over Lockerbie, was also to become a defining feature of US–Libya relations. Placed within this context, it is possible to consider that the existence of the CW facility at Rabta merely provided the US with another convenient excuse to continue the string of military actions already taken against Libya, a country now considered by Reagan to be a 'pariah state'.[39] Equally, one must remember that for Gaddafi these weapons, if they could be acquired in time, might also have been a guarantee of security.

The Rabta facility became a central point of interest for several Western Intelligence agencies, but it was the US commentary that was most frequently reported in the media. US concerns generally linked the CW facility to the supposed intent of Libya to 'give chemical weapons to terrorists',[40] an argument that fitted comfortably with the arguments relating to the US view of Libya detailed above. In addition, many reports detailed the alleged proliferation of CW materials from Libya to states such as Somalia.[41] The Libyans consistently denied that the plant at Rabta was involved in CW production. The Libyan leadership issued statements denying the US allegations to the United Nations,[42] as well as in interviews featuring Gaddafi himself where the US is labelled 'a liar and a cheat'.[43] Whilst the US position towards Libya in 1988 appeared to prefer diplomacy to force, Reagan refused to rule out the use of force against the Rabta plant. Despite reports later shown to be incorrect by US intelligence that the Rabta plant had been destroyed by fire in March 1990, concerns in the West relating to Libyan CW production continued to mount. The US government continued to present their concerns to the media, stating that Rabta would be 'one of the largest chemical arms factories in the world'.[44] By June 1990, US intelligence began to report that the Libyans were constructing a second CW plant buried deep inside a mountain several hundred miles south of Tripoli.[45] Commentators continued to speculate about these underground facilities into 1991, despite the wide availability of reports detailing extensive tunnelling works as part of the 'Great Man-made River Project' which aimed to transform Libyan agriculture by providing mass irrigation systems deep into the arid heart of Libya.[46] By 1991, the US, along with many other states, was focused militarily on Iraq. It is probably in no small part due to this fact that rhetoric from the US stopped short of talk of military action, although this was never entirely ruled out.

From 1991, the first signs began to appear that Gaddafi might be prepared to change his image as perceived in the West. Perhaps due to fears over the type of military action seen by Iraq in 1991, perhaps due to the increasing economic pain felt from the UN-imposed economic sanctions running since 1986, Gaddafi first expelled two militant Palestinian groups from Libya, then donated £250,000 to a UK police charity.[47] This donation came after shots fired from the Libyan embassy in 1984 resulted in the death of WPC Yvonne Fletcher. The collapse of the Soviet Union, an on-off ally of Libya, probably further added to Libyan isolation in the international community. Nonetheless, reports continually appeared in the media linking Libya to continuing attempts to manufacture CW along with missile-based delivery systems.[48] By 1993, US concerns regarding Libyan CW appeared to be being eased somewhat due to the apparent difficulty that Libya was having in acquiring the necessary technology from overseas to continue its development work due to UN sanctions. Even in the realm of biological weapons, the CIA now believed that nothing other than small-scale research could proceed without massive foreign assistance.[49]

It is interesting to note this apparent change in tone from US intelligence. Up to 1993, the US had been entirely reliant on leaked intelligence reports to illustrate the gravity of the Libyan CW threat. It is likely that this approach was taken for two reasons: firstly, to convince both US allies as well as the rest of the international community of the existence of any threat; and secondly because the US may have been preparing both the US public and the international community for military action against Libya.[50] As a result, the efforts made by Gaddafi to make goodwill gestures to the West, as well as not antagonising Western (US) military forces in the Gulf of Sidra, may have been a carefully calculated decision by Gaddafi to prevent any military action being taken. On the one hand, this might simply buy time for the Libyans to complete develop of CW programmes; on the other, it might have signalled that Gaddafi was, even in the early 1990s, being severely affected by economic sanctions. The Libyan economy was, after all, almost entirely reliant on oil exports for its income.

By 1996, the US began to report that the second Libyan CW facility was nearing completion. The Libyan leadership continued to deny that it had anything to do with CW,[51] and it does seem strange that Libya would seek a second facility when it had not yet successfully run its first. Indeed, by April 1996, the very tunnels that US intelligence believed would house secret CW facilities in Libya were finally proven to be part of the Great Man-made River Project.[52] Although the string of false conclusions drawn by US intelligence, including reports of a fire at Rabta, had seriously damaged the credibility of several agencies, the Libyans did apparently work towards attaining CW capabilities. By now it was widely recognised that Libya was both unable to manufacture the required technologies itself and also unable to procure equipment from overseas.[53] Once again, this may account for the lack of appetite on the part of the US to take military action. To all intents and purposes, Libya was contained. This chapter will now turn its attention towards examining the role of intelligence and the UK government in the transformation of Libya as a contained state to a disarmed one.

UK secret intelligence and Libyan CW

It has already been established that Western intelligence agencies had probably been interested in the possibility that Libya was developing a range of WMD programmes since the end of the 1970s. Of all the states involved in gathering intelligence on Libya, the US and the UK feature most prominently in the information that is publicly available relating to their involvement. That said, other Western countries, in particular Germany through its BND (Bundesnachrichtendienst, federal intelligence service), were also involved at various times before Libya renounced its WMD programmes in 2003.

At its genesis, the Libyan CW programme was heavily reliant on importing technology, equipment and personnel from overseas in order to make up for the lack of its own nascent capabilities. It was a matter of course that 'the Security Service always used to talk to people that worked in countries like Libya',[54] and as a result the UK government was able to keep a careful eye on the types of expertise that were being utilised by countries of concern. It is interesting to note that even at the very beginning of the 1980s, Libya was considered by the UK government to be a concern—in particular given the long relationship between the UK and Libya from the end of the Second World War. In the context of CW, UK intelligence agencies were concerned that Libya would acquire CW, quite simply because 'the thought was that [they were] mad enough to do anything with anyone with anything they had'.[55] In particular, specific concerns related to the possible use of CW in the war against Chad, as well as through sponsorship of terrorist groups.[56] The UK Foreign Office believed that Libya's decision in the late 1970s to pursue a CW capability could therefore be quite easily explained: 'nuclear was too difficult ... chemical was the easiest'.[57]

The initial information obtained by UK intelligence that resulted in focusing attention on the Libyan CW programme came about as a direct result of Security Service interviews with personnel who had worked inside Libya. From a UK perspective, one of the most significant individuals associated with Libyan CW was an Iraqi-born businessman by the name of Ihsan Barbouti, who lived in Chelsea, London. 'Dr Barbouti', as he liked to be known, was the director of a company called IBI which in 1984 won the contract to build and equip the Libyan Rabta plant.[58] Barbouti worked as the project manager for the construction of the plant, under a five-year contract that apparently earned him a salary of $200,000 a year plus bonuses, raises and a house in Tripoli.[59] Barbouti had always and consistently insisted that he was contracted to build a pharmaceutical plant for the Libyans. In one interview he stated that 'in four years ... nobody has mentioned or hinted that something secret is there'.[60] Yet from Barbouti, as well as from other site managers who as UK nationals had been interviewed by the Security Service, it quickly became apparent that 'something pretty funny was going on [at Rabta]'.[61]

Of particular interest to UK intelligence was the extent to which European companies were involved in the manufacture and supply of personnel and equipment of use to Libya in the production of CW. The UK government motivation for these attempts to monitor the proliferation of WMD technologies to Libya was part of a foreign policy towards

Libya that had remained entirely consistent from the beginning of the 1980s.[62] Certainly, from a UK intelligence perspective, Libya was 'viewed ... as [the] universal baddie [this is why] we'd helped in allowing the American planes that had bombed Libya to use British bases ... [and] they'd been giving arms to the IRA'.[63] Tracing the contracts and links from these companies to Libya became a key objective, as it allowed UK intelligence to uncover the network of pathways through which chemical, biological as well as nuclear-related technologies were being imported into Libya. As a result, UK intelligence could uncover the extent of the Libyan programme. Attention could then turn towards obtaining information on whether and what it was capable of producing.

Barbouti had told UK intelligence officers that the most deeply involved companies in the construction of Rabta were based in Japan, Denmark and West Germany.[64] Other countries of interest were based in Switzerland as well as East Germany.[65] These revelations were of particular concern to the UK government, as it had acted alongside West Germany in 1986 to 'limit the sale of technology with potential military application to Tripoli'.[66] It was these leads that UK intelligence officers first began to follow.

By the end of the 1980s, through a process of what seems to be pure detective work, UK intelligence had identified the extent to which Western companies were implicated in the supply of CW-related materials to Libya, and also how front companies were used for the transit of materials from countries such as the UK and West Germany where export controls were in place. The contract for the construction of the Rabta plant had been placed by the Libyans, via Barbouti,[67] with the West German company Imhausen. In turn, Imhausen had set up a subsidiary company in Hong Kong called Pen-Tsao-Materia-Medica-Center. This company would receive the necessary exported equipment from Europe under the cover of its supposed management of the pharmaceutical factory 'Pharma 150' in Hong Kong. The plans for the plant were produced by another German company, Salzgitter Industriebau, which claimed that 'Pharma 150' was to be built in Hong Kong.[68] According to one employee of the company, 'it was an open secret that the ominous Pharma 150 was in Libya not Hong Kong'.[69] UK intelligence found it difficult to persuade the German BND that a firm as reputable as Imhausen could be involved in CW proliferation. One UK intelligence officer recounted his experiences in talking to BND:

most of the good intelligence had come from us. I mean, we actually told the Germans [about Rabta] and I remember the Germans saying to me 'Imhausen is a wonderful firm, it has been for many years, it's impossible, they couldn't be involved'. And then we gave them the production instructions [for the plant] and things changed a bit.[70]

The BND were therefore persuaded to join the UK intelligence investigation into Libyan CW procurement efforts. It soon became apparent that the BND had already taken an interest in Libya. As early as April 1980, BND had reported that Gaddafi wanted to establish a domestic CW production installation, and that he was actively trying to obtain the raw materials from European countries.[71] In July 1983, the BND assessed that the Libyans had actually begun the production of mustard gas at a plant near Bu Kemmesh (Abu Kammash), although this assessment was rescinded in 1988.[72] British intelligence did not receive firm human intelligence that Rabta had been built and was capable of producing CW until some time in 1986. The Foreign Office only confirmed that 'we have independent information on the Libyan chemical weapons programme' in a statement on 5 January 1989.[73] This information was passed to the US, along with information relating to West German and Japanese companies implicated in the plant's construction.[74] It is therefore highly likely that UK Intelligence was aware of the completion of Rabta prior to this date.

The UK may have passed intelligence on Rabta to the US because 'they've got all the technical means to be able to look at places'.[75] From the beginning of 1989, Rabta had been placed under 'satellite watch' by the US.[76] The information from this surveillance allowed the UK to link information obtained from human sources to that obtained from technical means. US satellite imagery showed 'the factory being built as the blokes had described it. And then there was the technology centre, the huge great metal workings, the plastics factory, and then the cage behind it. Behind this huge berm was the CW factory.'[77] It is possible to argue that the US reliance on technical means perhaps omitted vital intelligence relating to the plant's capabilities that the UK were obtaining from HUMINT sources. This may have led to the US assessing that a greater threat existed than the UK were being informed from its own sources; the later error of the US intelligence community in reporting a fire at Rabta is a case in point, as will be discussed in more detail later in this chapter. This also perhaps provides lessons applicable to other case studies relating to the vital importance of HUMINT sources.

The German government acted quickly to investigate the extent to which its own companies had been involved in constructing Libyan CW capabilities. The level of this involvement became an acute embarrassment for the government of Chancellor Kohl. After an official investigation by the German Federal Minister for Special Tasks which subsequently published the Schauble Report, it became apparent that information obtained by the BND relating to Rabta had not been passed to the Chancellor because it had been blocked by the State Secretary for Security Affairs. The report went on to state that five months before the US confronted the West German government about Rabta, not only did the German government know that Libya was building the plant, but it also knew that Imhausen was deeply involved, yet it failed to act. Unfortunately, the vague language relating to 'probable' involvement by German companies made it impossible for the state to begin legal proceedings.[78] As far as UK intelligence were concerned:

> they [Imhausen] knew full well what they were doing. But you know the bottom line was they claimed that they didn't know what the compounds were because the Libyans did this 'react compound A with compound B to produce compound C' ... the Germans had done a very smart job to cover their backs ... but all they did at the end of the day was to distil solvent through the system and say 'there you are, it all works, goodbye!'[79]

US and them

Despite the fact that UK intelligence were sharing intelligence on Libya with the US, there were significant disagreements over what the plant was actually capable of producing. US statements regarding the capabilities of the plant varied widely. In one report, US sources said that Rabta could produce 5 tons of mustard a day;[80] other reports stated that figures could be between 22 and 84 tons of mustard and nerve daily.[81] The UK intelligence view of these US figures, given publicly to the press, was that 'they were absolutely ludicrous'.[82] This disagreement led to heated exchanges between UK intelligence and CIA officers. One UK intelligence officer recounted:

> I had this furious row with them. If they had 40 tons a day, they'd have to refill the tank farm four times a day. The tank farm was designed to sustain

operations for six months, so how can it be ... it was just stupid, and again it was this situation where the analysts that were producing this nonsense didn't seem to have any understanding that this ... would drive potential military action against it ... there was almost a prize for coming up with the biggest number. And I had row after row with them. 'How can you possibly say, when we've given you the production instructions ... you know, we know how much liquid is in the tanks, because we knew from somebody we were running how much was in the tanks.' [We knew] how much [the tanks had] gone down, so we knew they'd produced virtually nothing ... and they were only making mustard gas because they'd bust the pumps and they'd had to bastardise the equipment to get one reactor working to make mustard gas.[83]

Not only did UK intelligence disagree with the methodology used by the US to give production capability figures, a method that when applied to much larger Soviet CW plants actually gave lower figures than Rabta;[84] there were also strong disagreements regarding the interpretation of satellite imagery.

In March 1990, US analysts reported that the Rabta facility had been shown by satellite imagery to be on fire. The US rapidly briefed the president as well as a hastily assembled press conference to that effect.[85] UK intelligence had a very different interpretation of what the images showed:

[When] our PI [photographic interpreter] looked at it, he said, 'Hang on ... don't brief it, don't brief it, just ignore it because we don't believe it's burned at all.' And anyway, there was a rain shower and it washed the paint, so you could see it had just been painted. But I mean, that's the ... problem, you see our PIs would tell you very different from what the Americans would tell you, because the Americans were doing this quick, 'Oh great big news, we'll go and brief it, aren't we wonderful.' You know, there's nothing worse than briefing the fact that it had burnt down, oh no it didn't, it was actually painted black marks on the roof ... but this was what the Libyans basically did ... paint the roof with black marks all over it.[86]

By April 1990, the US were forced to admit that they had indeed been the victim of a hoax—Rabta had not burned down at all.[87] The painting of the roof of Rabta in order to resemble fire damage may have been a very intelligent move by Gaddafi. If it had been his intent to delay what he perhaps saw as imminent military action, he was certainly successful. In addition, whilst UK intelligence was providing very accurate information, none of this was released to the media. All public information was coming from the US, and their falling for the Libyan trick almost certainly damaged the credibility of US intelligence, in particular if it was to be used to make the case for military action. Despite this, it still appeared to be the view of 'plenty of people in Whitehall who would much rather believe the Americans'.[88]

From this point onwards, the US appeared to lose their appetite for taking military action against Libya. This may be at least in part due to the efforts of President Bush (Snr) to build a coalition of forces to deal with the Iraqi invasion of Kuwait. Nonetheless, the Libyans continued in their efforts to develop a CW production facility, closely monitored by UK intelligence. By the early 1990s, when information was received that the Libyans were now constructing the underground Tarhunah complex, UK views continued to diverge from those of the US. Yet again, UK human intelligence sources not only provided UK intelligence details of the planned plant, they also revealed the companies involved in the building. Once more, a German company, Westfalia-Becorit, was at the centre of concerns.[89] One of the key scientists involved in the development work, Dr Sauer, denied any possibility of the work being for WMD development purposes. His counter to allegations of any wrongdoing was: 'If you sleep with a woman, it is possible that you manufacture the next Hitler. Whatever you do in this world, it can be used for good and bad.'[90] Whilst the UK was concerned that Libya had defied UN sanctions to obtain the components for this new facility,[91] UK intelligence was content that the tunnels were for irrigation purposes—as indeed they were later proved to be. UK intelligence 'knew about the plans that they were going to build an underground factory, but ... that never materialised'.[92] As a result, the UK government was content to wait for sanctions to take effect, rather than push the US for military action.

It is perhaps tempting here to try to draw parallels between Libyan efforts to procure WMD-related technologies and the efforts of other states, such as Iraq, to do the same. However, what is apparent from the analysis presented so far is that Libya had no apparent local nascent WMD manufacturing capability. As a result, the Libyan government had been trying to procure its capability in its entirety from international markets. This may have meant that whilst a degree of crosspollination of expertise may have taken place between Libya and other states attempting to acquire similar capabilities, Libya was actually keen on maintaining as much secrecy as possible around its true intents; this may have actually reduced cooperation between Libya and other states. Other than in its nuclear programme, information regarding Libyan cooperation with other states for CBW procurement remains thin.[93]

While the US painted pictures of terrorist attacks sponsored by Libya using CW, the UK Foreign Office remained in a position where they could not 'condone any action that doesn't have a proper basis in international law'.[94] Furthermore, the UK continued to refuse to provide information obtained by UK intelligence. The FCO stated that 'the usual problem of evidence from secret sources [means that] those who you are working against can very often identify where you have got the information from if you leak it in any detail, and then you lose the source of the information. It's the classic problem of intelligence.'[95] Not only were UK intelligence keen to protect their sources, but the FCO was clearly more than happy with the level and accuracy of intelligence being provided, regardless of the fact that it did not match that being regularly leaked from Washington. This apparent relationship between intelligence and foreign policy in the UK is interesting: UK intelligence are clearly confident and comfortable with the fact that whilst intelligence might assist and inform decision-makers, it will not be used for public affairs advantage. As a result, the UK intelligence reliance on human sources for intelligence could continue safe in the knowledge that sources would not be compromised for political purposes.

It is perhaps of use to pause briefly in the analysis of UK intelligence involvement in Libyan CW in order to consider Libyan attempts to develop biological weapons. Information relating to Libyan efforts to develop BW is scant. That said, the US and UK each had their own view of the risk posed; and once again those two views differed. US officials were adamant that Libya did have a 'nascent biological programme', although they also believed that this was 'mired in the early stages of research and development'.[96] The UK seemed to possess more specific information relating to the BW threat, again coming from human intelligence sources. UK intelligence had been aware that:

[A] Libyan scientist wrote to some bloke who he met at a conference in England asking for strains of all the ... top BW agents ... [so] the Foreign Office brought this alert warning system in ... because basically until they were controlled any idiot could write in for a strain and they would be given it, no questions asked—you know, 'I'm doing research in [x], please give me a strain.' And they would have. I mean, this [Libyan] asked for smallpox ...[97]

Whereas the US stated connections between Wouter Basson and the covert South African BW programme, UK intelligence could once again explain away problems that US intelligence could not:

> I mean, there was concern because he [Basson] had actually gone to Libya. But he ... was involved in all sorts of business deals, and one of the things he was involved with was rebuilding this Tripoli Egypt railway line ... he was involved with all sorts of big financial people. But at some stage during his trip he and Philip Myberg had been asked if they ... had any interest in trying to make this 'medicine factory' work. And basically, Basson said [no] ... there was no interest [because] there was no money in it. You know [the research was] always going to be crap because the Libyans are totally useless at doing anything.[98]

Although the US made connections between the visits of Basson and later arms deals agreed between Libya and South Africa,[99] their analysis could never provide any level of evidence in support; the US view seemed to be consistently characterised by assumption and speculation. Another connection made by the US was that Saddam Hussein had sent weapons microbiologists to Tripoli in the late 1990s—something that Libya and Iraq denied.[100] The interviews conducted for this chapter suggest that these concerns were never shared by UK intelligence personnel. Indeed, in contrast to the US, the amount of low-level human intelligence available to the UK and its ability to provide accurate assessments seems to be quite staggering. The UK assessment of Libyan BW therefore remained consistent and supported by evidence:

> They had a toe in the water. But it was lab thinking about it—not that there was ever any serious plans to [scale it up], in fact, as far as the intelligence we had [was concerned] ... the scientists themselves made sure it was never going to go anywhere, because they knew full well that if they did, they were going to get the shit bombed out of them. And they probably let it run down because ... they're pretty scared of the Israelis—and their ability to rub people out.[101]

The evidence considered so far in this section essentially provides an analysis of Libyan CBW development from the perspective of British intelligence during the time period that any efforts to run that programme could be considered to have been taking place.

Cracks appear: the end of the Libyan CW programme

It now appears to be widely recognised that UK intelligence played a significant role in the process of negotiations that led to the statement by Gaddafi that he wished to end his WMD programmes. It is however difficult to identify and consider the exact reasons behind this decision without also looking at the socio-economic situation in Libya over the same period. Whilst this chapter has so far provided an analysis of the role of UK intelligence in monitoring the Libyan CBW programmes, attention will now turn to considering the events from the late 1990s onwards that led to the Libyan renunciation of CBW.

Prior to 2000, Gaddafi faced a wide range of problems, both domestic and external, of varying seriousness. Throughout the mid to late 1990s, Gaddafi had been forced to suppress dissent from both military and tribal groups. He had also been required to confront the growing support for Islamist groups, increasingly frustrated by his alleged undermining of the religious authority of local leaders and repression of Islam. In April 2000, Gaddafi had ordered the execution of several individuals considered to be Islamist militants. The tribes and individuals that were seen to have harboured these individuals were also collectively punished.[102] Moreover, Libya had seen its influence across the Arab world decline rapidly, in particular due to its deteriorating relationship with Egypt. The personal impact of all this on Gaddafi, in particular when considered alongside apparent progress in the Middle East peace process—especially the warming relationship between Israel and Egypt— was deep and profound.[103]

The unilateral economic sanctions imposed by the UN in 1992 had hit Libya particularly hard. Oil was absolutely vital to the Libyan economy: when Gaddafi came to power in 1969, oil represented almost 99 per cent of revenue and almost 100 per cent of exports, though the oil industry itself employed only 1 per cent of the population.[104] By 1998, it was estimated that sanctions had directly cost Libya $24 billion but, perhaps more importantly, the living conditions of the Libyan population had deteriorated sharply,[105] at least in part due to rampant inflation that reached 50 per cent during the 1990s.[106] These internal problems and dissent, combined with the ever-increasing risk of military action by the US—in particular after UN-sponsored action against Iraq from 1991 and the increasing willingness of the international community to intervene in crises of breach of state sovereignty—posed Gaddafi with stark choices if he was to maintain his grip on power. There had been chaotic discussions within the Libyan government about how power could be maintained by the Gaddafi regime. There were two main views as to how to proceed: pragmatists argued for structural and economic reforms, whilst hardliners argued that defiance of the West was at the heart of the regime's legitimacy. Although strangely quiet during these discussions, by 1998 Gaddafi resolved the debate in favour of the pragmatists.[107] In a radical turn-around, Gaddafi first purged the very Revolutionary Committees that had been so central to his power, then announced that 'we can no longer stand in the way of progress ... the fashion now is the free market and investments'.[108] Slowly but surely, from the start of 1999 onwards, Gaddafi began to provide the international community with the evidence that Libya was fit to return as a full member. In April 1999, Gaddafi accepted UN demands for the extradition of the Lockerbie bombing suspects, acknowledging that 'the world has changed radically and drastically. The methods and ideas should change, and being a revolutionary and a progressive man, I have to follow this movement.'[109]

In a speech in 2000, Gaddafi publicly stated that his long-standing anti-imperialist struggle was over.[110] During this same period of time, secret talks were set in place with the Clinton administration in parallel with the trilateral Lockerbie negotiations. It is believed that whilst the WMD issue was not addressed here as a key problem to resolve if sanctions were to be lifted, these contacts clearly put in place a useful framework—an important step for Libya in improving relations with the US.[111]

The impact of the 11 September 2001 terrorist attacks on the Libyan leadership is not entirely clear. Gaddafi's son, Saif-al-Islam, believed that his father changed course because he had to: 'Overnight we found ourselves in a different world ... So Libya had to redesign its policies to cope with these new realities.'[112] Others have argued that the Libyan decision was driven by the realisation that WMD programmes were becoming an acute risk in the post 9/11 world, especially given the apparent willingness of the US to use preventative military force.[113] The UK intelligence view certainly seemed to echo some of these arguments. As one UK intelligence officer put it: 'It was a response to the fact that they'd ... already been bombed once and so Gaddafi knew that if he didn't change his ways he'd be [attacked again] ... let's face it, he sleeps on a different bed every night, it's not much of a life really.'[114]

What seems clear from the evidence considered so far is that prior to 9/11, Gaddafi had already realised that he would have to change his position with regard to the West if he was to survive in power. There is also very strong evidence to demonstrate that Gaddafi had initiated contact with Western intelligence agencies in order to progress his negotiations. This point is absolutely key when considering a counter to the arguments recounted earlier in this chapter that suggested that the 2003 Iraq War was the key factor in persuading Gaddafi to give up his WMD programmes or face military action.

Whilst the Lockerbie negotiations provide evidence of determined Libyan engagement with the US, there is also evidence of engagement with the UK prior to 9/11. Whilst before 9/11 'there had been various attempts to try to talk to them [Libyans]',[115] evidence suggests that towards the end of the 1990s the UK Security Service had held direct discussions with Libya. These negotiations had largely focused around Libyan support for the IRA, and the provision of weapons to that same group. The gist of these discussions seems to have been that the Libyans were told, 'Why don't you get sensible? Why don't you ... try and join the mainstream and all sorts could flow.'[116] In particular, in the autumn of 2002, UK emissaries had discussed Libya's WMD with Gaddafi at the same time that his son, Saif-al-Islam, had been trying to develop back channels for further talks. The UK personnel involved in these talks reportedly assured the Libyans that Blair would raise the matter with Bush in his September 2002 Camp David talks.[117] At a similar time to the US-led invasion of Iraq, the timing of these talks led to the inevitable arguments that the Libyans feared a similar US action if they did not renounce WMD. Apparently one senior Libyan intelligence officer told the UK that Gaddafi wanted 'to clear the air' about WMD programmes, as well as obtain assurances that Libya would not be attacked.[118] Whilst the timing of these events is close to the timing of the US invasion of Iraq, it has already been demonstrated that the Libyans had already indicated that they wished to give up WMD prior to this event. Indeed, some have argued strongly that the Iraq War did not force the hand of Gaddafi at all.[119]

In the context of Libya's CW programmes, it was on 20 March 2003 that an intermediary made a telephone call to a senior intelligence officer in the headquarters of SIS at Vauxhall Cross. In this call, the message given was that 'Saif-al-Islam Gaddafi would like to arrange a meeting'.[120] The same intelligence officer as had been involved in the Lockerbie discussions, Musa Kusa, was once again central to the discussions that followed. Gaddafi's son apparently believed that these negotiations on WMD were 'a card in our hands', and immediately after the Iraqi invasion was clearly 'the best time to play that card'.[121] This certainly appears to be a clever diplomatic move on the part of Libya. The West could hardly invade Iraq on the pretext that it would not give up WMD and then refuse to deal with Libya in a more cooperative manner with regard to its own weapons programmes.

This type of contact and request for discussions was not entirely unusual for SIS. One interesting example of SIS-facilitated negotiations is seen through the actions of a senior officer called Michael Oatley. Whilst employed by SIS, Oatley allegedly 'played an important role over eighteen years in Northern Ireland, developing secret channels through which MI6 could cooperate with the IRA'. Oatley had once been described as 'an Irish Lawrence of Arabia' for his part in establishing these networks.[122] Oatley is therefore apparently widely considered to have been responsible for 'having helped pave the way to the Good Friday agreement, decommissioning, peace and power-sharing'.[123]

The negotiations themselves appear to have progressed quickly. Whilst many of the details of meetings—both in the UK at the Travellers Club in Pall Mall, as well as in Switzerland—remain secret, the role that intelligence played can be identified. It seems that the Libyans were less than frank about the extent to which they had developed WMD. Indeed, it took 'considerable prodding'[124] for the Libyans to be convinced that they must be entirely open. It is here that the utility of the intelligence held by the UK can be seen. According to one Foreign Office official, the role of secret intelligence was vital. It was revealed very slowly during negotiations that the UK government knew exactly when the Libyans were telling the truth.[125] The UK intelligence view here was that 'if we hadn't had the same level of intelligence, I think we would probably have been inherently more suspicious about the fact that the programme really wasn't very good'.[126] In particular, for the Foreign Office, an absence of that detail of information would have meant that when locations were selected for visits in order to verify Libyan disarmament, the UK would not necessarily have known what it wanted to see.[127] In short, this provides a striking illustration of the role of UK intelligence in supporting foreign policy. A detailed account of the negotiations will not be covered here, though information is now widely available, in particular in the context of nuclear weapons programmes.[128]

Politically, it seems that the UK government saw the Libyan moves with a mixture of scepticism and caution.[129] Libyan attempts to establish exactly what was known about their problems suggested to some that their intent was not entirely clear. Indeed, this may have been an attempt to carry out some form of damage control exercise, and also one through which the extent that secrecy still protected their programmes could still be established. It may well be for this reason that the UK gave its negotiators no mandate to negotiate.[130] The Libyan government did however prove that its intentions were honourable. By the end of 2003, the Libyan decision to disarm was made public. The UK, US and Libyan governments established a trilateral steering group to facilitate the commitments made by Libya. This would include international verification that plants such as Rabta, suspected of being involved in WMD production, had ceased working.[131] Libya subsequently signed the CWC later in 2004.

But it is perhaps also worth considering briefly what the Libyans got in return for their efforts. Most significant, given the state of the Libyan economy, was the lifting of all sanctions and the removal of Libya from the list of states known to sponsor and support terrorism. This enabled Libya to sign a series of lucrative exploration contracts with Western oil companies. In addition, Gaddafi received high-profile visits from leaders such as Prime Minister Tony Blair, Chancellor Schroeder and President Chirac, signalling new confidence in Libya as a country for investment. Furthermore, the unfreezing of assets held in the US allowed Gaddafi to find desperately needed cash for investment within the country.[132] Finally, Gaddafi obtained promises of commitments to set out the assistance that Libya would receive if attacked. All in all, these gains provided cash, investment, political engagement and security—things that Gaddafi desperately needed if he was to retain power in a country crippled by sanctions and international isolation.

But was Libya a true intelligence success? On reflection, one must probably conclude that this judgement is too shallow and does not reflect the realities of the long process of engagement between the UK and Libya, as well as the wide range of other factors impacting on Libya's eventual decision. In particular, the 2003 Iraq War led by the US, economic problems within Libya, as well as Libyan attempts to stem al-Qaeda and other radical Islamist activities within Libya could all be seen as factors that influenced the Libyan decision. Clearly, UK foreign policy towards Libya in the context of all WMD programmes was remarkably consistent. It also reflected a desire to cooperate in the attainment of foreign policy success, not to confront. This was, at least initially, very different to the track pursued by the US in its relations with Libya.

The UK clearly had very accurate and very specific intelligence relating to the Libyan efforts to pursue CBW programmes. This intelligence had been collected over a considerable period of time, providing a deep and relatively detailed knowledge base from which to draw. It is because of this library of intelligence, along with the growing credibility of UK CBW intelligence amongst policy-makers demonstrated in previous chapters, that such a positive contribution was apparently made by the intelligence agencies in facilitating the disarming of Libya. Evidence suggests that much of this intelligence came from well-placed human sources within various elements of the Libyan programmes. In contrast, the US not only appeared to rely on technical intelligence, they also regularly briefed uncorroborated information, often resulting in embarrassing U-turns and admissions of serious errors.[133] UK intelligence seems to have been accurate, consistent and secret: this protected both sources and the extent to which the UK was capable of gathering intelligence on Libya. The importance of HUMINT sources in this case study is abundantly clear: without level input from sources within Libya, it would have been very difficult to track Libyan CBW development accurately using just technical means.

Persuading the Libyans to acknowledge the extent that their CBW programmes had progressed was a key part of the negotiations between the UK and Libya. From an admission, the conditions could be set through which international organisations such as the OPCW (Organisation for the Prohibition of Chemical Weapons) could verify that disarmament and compliance had taken place. To this end, intelligence can be considered as a tool through which momentum can be generated in discussions through the empowerment of negotiators. Intelligence essentially told them when the Libyans were telling the truth. Without the detailed intelligence held, the UK would have been far more suspicious of Libya. Intelligence did not achieve results in its own right, but it accelerated a successful end being reached in negotiations. Perhaps part of the reason for this was the fact that the UK intelligence agencies may be seen to have had an inherited credibility from the past case studies examined earlier in this book. One must ultimately remember, though, that the end result appears to have been achieved simply because Gaddafi wanted it to be. Whilst Libya could be largely contained through sanctions, there is insufficient evidence to argue that either US military action in the 1980s or the Iraq War in 2003 forced the Libyans into the course of action on which they embarked. Evidence clearly shows that the Libyans had already engaged with the UK, and already stated their intent to disarm well before the end of the 1990s. So, where it has been argued that Libya provides a model for how to persuade a state to disarm,[134] this may not actually be entirely accurate.

8

BEFORE INTELLIGENCE FAILED

WAS IRAQ A WATERSHED?

This book began by considering the role of UK intelligence in the formulation of foreign policy during the lead-up to the 2003 Iraq War. Having described the mechanics of this relationship, subsequent chapters presented three other examples of CBW-related foreign policy problems. Attention was focused on attempting to understand how the intelligence and foreign policy relationship proceeded in each of these case studies. This final chapter now aims to draw together the more significant observations from these case studies in order that overarching conclusions can be drawn relating to intelligence and foreign policy interaction within the UK. Fundamentally, this chapter aims to consider whether the intelligence and foreign policy interface identified in the three case studies presented within this book is different to that seen during the lead-up to the 2003 Iraq War. It will ask whether or not intelligence was used differently by the Blair government before the war from how it had been used by policy-makers in the past. Put simply, was Iraq an intelligence watershed?

The intelligence and foreign policy nexus

The decisions over foreign policy leading to and following the 2003 Iraq War are still perhaps the most significant and controversial made by the

Blair government throughout its twelve years in power. The publication of four inquiries into the use of intelligence by the UK government in the run-up to the 2003 Iraq War, as well as the more recent Chilcot Inquiry, have provided a unique opportunity to gain an insight into the normally hidden world of UK secret intelligence.[1] In general terms, the plethora of both evidence and commentary relating to these inquiries provides a detailed, though perhaps rather general insight into how intelligence was used in the formulation of foreign policy in that period. As a result, this gives a reference point against which the other cases of intelligence on WMD programmes and their interface with foreign policy can be compared. The results of this comparison allow us to establish whether the 2003 Iraq War marked a watershed (or transition) from how intelligence was used in those earlier examples.

Several observations relating to the use of intelligence in the lead-up to the 2003 Iraq War are immediately of interest in this concluding chapter. Firstly, as Lord Butler notes, 'the government's conclusion in the spring of 2002 that stronger (although not necessarily military action) needed to be taken to enforce Iraqi disarmament was not based on any new development in the current intelligence picture on Iraq'.[2] Secondly, there was no recent intelligence that would itself have given rise to a conclusion that Iraq was of more immediate concern than the activities of some other countries.[3] And thirdly, the UK government, as well as being influenced by the concerns of the US government, saw a need for immediate action in Iraq because of the wider historical and international context.[4]

Essentially, these comments suggest that in the case of Iraq the toughening UK foreign policy was not related to new intelligence; no new intelligence in itself would have caused that toughening stance; and furthermore, the changing foreign policy was being directly influenced by other, broader factors. Chilcot was clear here: 'after the invasion... [there was] mounting evidence that there had been failings in the UK's pre-conflict collection, validation, analysis and presentation of intelligence on Iraq's WMD'.[5] Put simply, it might be argued that the Blair government used 'intelligence evidence stretched to the outer limits'.[6] It might also be argued that these Iraq-specific observations cut straight to the heart of the differences in the theories of intelligence suggested by Kent and Casey and described earlier in this book (Chapters 2–3). Essentially, in the Iraq example, there seems to have been no relationship between changing foreign policy positions and intelligence. It is in this observation that the analysis presented within this book is focused: how much are intelligence and foreign policy ever connected, and just what is the mechanism and under what conditions does intelligence influence foreign policy?

It is important to note that other important observations relating specifically to the use of intelligence in the lead-up to the 2003 Iraq War stand out from the range of available official reports: a small number of human intelligence sources were key to the JIC in the formulation of assessments;[7] technical issues made assessments of Iraq's WMD capabilities difficult;[8] and finally, the government broke new ground in the way it produced and presented public documents by explicitly drawing on material produced by the JIC.[9] Fundamentally, the key issue for investigation appears to be whether or not the way intelligence was used to support a foreign policy decision to go to war in 2003 differs from the way intelligence was used to support foreign policy in similar situations in the past. It is towards this question that attention will now turn.

Before and after Iraq: the purpose of intelligence

This book discussed at some length several differing definitions of intelligence. Whilst this discussion will not be restated here, the in-depth case studies focused on several issues that it is useful to review before beginning a broader discussion of their results. In particular, it is interesting to consider what the three case studies say in general terms about what intelligence is, and what it is actually for.

Considering its purpose, initially: each of the case studies does seem to reflect the official UK government view of intelligence, that its purpose is to inform policy-making in support of national security policies.[10] In general terms one can consider that, at least from the government's perspective, UK national interests must be closely related to UK national security: pursuing national interests can therefore be considered to mean pursuing policies that directly benefit national security. This may seem a rather vague way of understanding intelligence, yet when intelligence is considered within the context of government, it is not really surprising that one would find a direct relationship between national interests, national security and intelligence.

It is also worth considering the alliance dimension of UK intelligence here. Whilst not the focus of the research presented in this book, there is an important relationship between UK and US intelligence agencies in each of the three case studies. Indeed, at times UK intelligence seems to have been quite influential to US intelligence assessments, contributing valuable HUMINT in particular to complement the generally strong US technical intelligence. The dynamics of this relationship have not been fully explored here, but it is clear that the relationship does exist and is one that has endured over a long period of time.

By considering UK foreign policy relating to CBW as being in the national interest, one must conclude that the UK government believed that the pursuit of these policies was directly linked to UK national security. Indeed, the pursuit of these types of policies remains a remarkably consistent feature of UK CBW policy from the early 1970s, as demonstrated through the case studies presented in this book. Over that period of time, the UK government appears to have pursued either disarmament, or arms control, or counter-proliferation as its end goal. In each of the three case studies in this book, intelligence seems to have been used in the pursuit of a clear national interest that was wholly consistent with these key tenets of foreign policy.

In each of the three case studies, national interest and national security are therefore clear and obvious explanatory factors for the reasons why intelligence was required by the UK government. With the Soviet Union, throughout the Cold War, intelligence worked to provide warning of CBW threats and to help ensure preparedness. With Libya, intelligence allowed monitoring of the effects of sanctions and provided warning of attempts to continue the development of WMD in the midst of them. This ultimately seems to have directly assisted negotiations with the Libyan government and ensured that the termination of those programmes was absolute. With South Africa, the importance of national interests is perhaps even clearer: the potential for damage to the international reputation of the UK in the midst of what was in effect a counter-espionage investigation was profound. Furthermore, in this case, the UK apparently used intelligence to encourage the post-apartheid government to address residual concerns relating to Project Coast.

When one returns to assessing the way in which intelligence interacted with foreign policy in the lead-up to the Iraq War, however, there appear to be significant differences in the purpose of intelligence compared with the case studies considered above. Specifically, in the case of Iraq, intelligence seems to have been demanded by policy-makers to support desired positions and policies. Yet in the three case studies in this book, intelligence agencies appeared to work independently: they sought intelligence to describe and analyse possible threats and risks, leaving it to the policy-makers to decide, over time, based on the strength of their findings, whether these threats and risks should inform foreign policy. In effect, evidence relating to the use of intelligence in the lead-up to the Iraq War suggests that intelligence was used as a secondary support of decision-making in the way that Casey suggested. Whilst in this case one might consider intelligence supporting foreign policy to mean a rather more extreme type of support—selective use in order to justify foreign policy decisions—in reality it marks a fundamental shift from the apparent purpose of intelligence seen in the three case studies.

The findings of the three case studies within this book also suggest some interesting and notable differences between how intelligence was defined within the first chapter and how it might be described within the context of the case studies. Firstly, intelligence definitions often seem to imply that intelligence exists as a physical product that by definition has value in its own right. One common characteristic of each of the three case studies is the long period of time that passed before intelligence was seen to have demonstrable value by policy-makers. One might therefore argue that intelligence could be considered to be of value only if it actually has an effect, whether that be on foreign policy or elsewhere. Intelligence may well be knowledge and foreknowledge of the world, but equally it is not immediately of value because of this.[11] Intelligence product may also develop and grow over a period of many years before it gains sufficient weight to effect some decision or change. In short, intelligence is not a panacea simply because it is intelligence: it may actually only hold value when it provides reassurance to policy-makers in terms of the policies being formulated or pursued. The value of intelligence must therefore be considered as a result of its observable impact on, for example, foreign policy decision-making, not purely because of what it is.

These comments suggest a very complicated relationship between intelligence product and the consumer—in the case of this book, the foreign policy decision-maker. It seems a gross over-simplification to say that intelligence is simply for the purpose of informing policy-making.[12] Whilst Kent argued that intelligence must be independent from decision-making, defining the purpose of intelligence in this way masks a wide range of issues, not least in the implicit assumption that there is an automatic, immediate and direct relationship between intelligence and changes or influences in policy-making. As a result, it is therefore suggested that there is an interesting dynamic between something that might be considered to be intelligence and its effect, or indeed lack of effect, on policy and decision-making. This is clearly an area for further investigation and research.

Finally, to return to the case of the UK government, there seems to be a more complex relationship at play between the officially offered definition of intelligence and the way in which it actually functions, based on the evidence collected in this book.[13] Certainly, this definition loosely supports the evidence collected from the three case studies: intelligence provided an insight into potential threats and risks; it was probably fragmentary and incomplete; and it was treated cautiously when the evidence was not particularly weighty. However, intelligence was always gathered to attempt to support foreign policy. At times it might be argued that intelligence was perhaps gathered just for the sake of being gathered, but nonetheless it was always specific to UK counter-proliferation policy objectives. This would seem to suggest that, as Casey argues, intelligence must support decision-making and always be aware of the needs of policy-makers in order to work effectively.

Whilst the theories of both Kent and Casey have gone some way to supporting the observations drawn from the case studies, there is some difficulty in using them fully to explain the use of intelligence in the 2003 Iraq War. In the lead-up to the war, intelligence was actively sought in order to support foreign policy decisions that had apparently already been made. Furthermore, intelligence was selected or disregarded based on its ability to provide that support. All of this was despite the grave misgivings of former members of the international weapons inspection community. David Kelly was famously reported as saying:

> that no stockpiles of weapons of mass destruction will be found in Iraq, and coalition leaders were wrong in their assessment of Saddam Hussein's arsenal. His comments came a day after Prime Minister Tony Blair appeared to suggest that the Iraq Survey Group may cite evidence of such weapons when it gives its next report.[14]

The issue apparent in the Iraq example therefore appears to be not whether or not intelligence directly supported foreign policy decision-making, but whether or not it was used selectively in order to give that support. Each of the three case studies demonstrates intelligence activities that were separated from policy-makers, which acted independently, and which were authoritative in their own right, fitting the theory of intelligence suggested by Kent. Yet each of the three case studies also ultimately facilitated foreign policy decision-making and action as described by Casey. So, whilst each case study might ultimately demonstrate aspects of both Kent and Casey's theories, the 2003 Iraq War appears to take a far more extreme position in terms of how intelligence was actually used to support decision-making. In simple terms, one might argue that this was due to the fact that foreign policy decisions had already been made; intelligence was needed in order to justify these positions, not support them.

Evidence for this observation can be found in the Butler Report. Here it is stated that the manner in which Blair built his case for war had placed 'more weight ... on intelligence than it could bear'.[15] The suggestion therefore is clear: intelligence was being used to support decisions that had already been made. Harsher critics of the 2003 Iraq War support these opinions, but also argue that to make the case he did, in the way he did, Blair must have been either 'mad' (with an unreasonable belief in the existence of WMD in Iraq), 'bad' (lying to the UK public about their existence) or 'had' (being lied to or tricked by the UK intelligence community).[16] Either way, these events perhaps provide some fascinating insights into Blair's character, as well as his possible perception of the utility of intelligence. Indeed, it has been stated that 'Tony Blair honestly and sincerely thought Saddam was a very bad and dangerous man who had stockpiled chemical weapons, who may have biological weapons and was trying to acquire nuclear weapons'.[17] As a result, he apparently said to the UK intelligence community, 'you may not have much evidence, but for goodness sake go out and find it'. Lord Butler certainly believed that the intelligence agencies might have subsequently been a little 'over-eager to believe the intelligence they came up with because of the pressure'.[18]

Speaking to the Chilcot Inquiry, Tony Blair's former security coordinator, Sir David Omand, said that some intelligence figures were 'queasy' about publishing intelligence details in the way that they did, adding that some were simply 'local colour'.[19] Former Foreign Secretary Robin Cook took a rather stronger view: 'selected for inclusion [in the case for war] were only the scraps of intelligence that fitted the government's case. The net result was a gross distortion.'[20] Some simply call what subsequently happened 'intelligence failure'.[21] One might also argue that to use intelligence in this way was counter to many perceptions of how the foreign policy and intelligence nexus should exist. Whilst Casey suggests that intelligence agencies should always be responsive to the needs of policy-makers, Iraq perhaps suggests that this position is only a whisker away from intelligence being misused or abused in order stubbornly to justify a desired position. If a policy-maker needs to use intelligence selectively to justify decisions that have already been made, there currently appears to be no constitutional barrier to prevent them doing so.[22] One thing is certain though, as Chilcot states: the aftermath of the Iraq War has 'produced a damaging legacy, including undermining trust and confidence in Government statements, particularly those which rely on intelligence which cannot be independently verified'.[23]

Before and after Iraq: the collection of intelligence

This book has suggested that whilst the UK had been involved in gathering intelligence relating to CBW since at least the mid 1920s, including through the ALSOS (Army Logistics Support to Other Services) project in the lead-up to the end of the Second World War, it was not until the early 1970s that a specific, albeit evolving, CBW intelligence establishment can be identified within UK national intelligence.[24] In many ways, therefore, the Soviet case study in this book can be seen to represent the genesis of contemporary UK CBW intelligence capabilities. It also represents the first case study since those relating to Project ALSOS towards the end of the Second World War for which sufficient information is available to produce a detailed analysis of the UK intelligence establishment.[25]

One characteristic of the Soviet case study relating to intelligence collection is the relatively low level of sources used to obtain information. In the early stages of intelligence work on the Soviet Union's BW programme, these sources were from émigrés discussing, for example, several rings of fences around suspect facilities. Later, in the Libyan case study, these sources were workers providing tank farm readings at suspect facilities. In South Africa, much early intelligence came from information passed to intelligence officers from individuals suspicious of foreign contacts made with them for business purposes. Certainly, with the Soviet Union, it is highly significant to note that much of what came to be considered irrefutable evidence of Soviet non-compliance with the BTWC came from HUMINT sources. The importance of HUMINT is equally clear in the Libyan and South African case studies. This observation is interesting: the UK has consistently spent a large proportion of the budget allocated to the intelligence agencies on electronic intelligence, in particular SIGINT, yet the bulk of useful intelligence in each of the three case studies in this book appears to have come from HUMINT sources.[26]

Another striking feature of the case studies in this book is how HUMINT was used in what one former chairman of the JIC described as 'the jigsaw puzzle approach to intelligence'. Here, one interviewee conceptualises an intelligence target as:

> a big jigsaw, and you find all the little pieces and they make up a big picture ... of course that's a false analogy, the pieces may be the wrong pieces and they may not fit together anyway, but you've got to start somewhere ... this process of collecting little bits of information is ... a necessary process.[27]

It is here that the value of intelligence from other sources can be seen: not just because they add value in their own right, but because they are able to corroborate the information obtained from HUMINT sources. As an example, the BW-related accident at Sverdlovsk provides a useful illustration of how electronic intelligence was ultimately able to substantiate intelligence obtained from HUMINT sources.

But intelligence from HUMINT sources does not always require corroboration from other sources. In the Soviet case study, the defection of Vladimir Pasechnik in 1987 was regarded as a means through which 'killer facts' of Soviet cheating could be demonstrated, also finally permitting the bringing together of all the pieces of intelligence collected over preceding years into one single completed 'jigsaw puzzle'. Whilst it can be considered that this means by which previous intelligence could be verified was more the result of a 'windfall' than an intelligence coup per se, it still demonstrates how corroboration can work by using skilful debriefing techniques, even when the only available method to check information is from similar sources. In the Libyan case study, even when US partners appeared to be almost entirely reliant on SIGINT for intelligence-gathering, the UK intelligence agencies remained characterised by the dominance of their skilful acquisition and analysis abilities in HUMINT. With Libya, in particular, the different approaches to intelligence-gathering are striking: between UK intelligence efforts with their reliance on HUMINT, and the US with their reliance on SIGINT and ELINT. That said, the benefit of hindsight certainly suggests that the UK were far better able to build accurate assessments in the long term, as opposed to the US who provided what were essentially just snapshots of specific occurrences at specific points in time. The UK use of and reliance on HUMINT remain true in the South African case study. One must therefore conclude that a key reason for the apparent success of UK intelligence agencies in each of the three case studies in this book is the dominance of HUMINT in the collection stage of constructing an overall intelligence picture.

When one considers the criticisms made in the wake of the Iraq War relating to reliance on only a few HUMINT sources, the case studies in this book are particularly notable by their almost absolute reliance on HUMINT. In the context of Iraq, many authors raised concerns about the possible consequences of relying on a small range of available sources—in particular when conclusions are drawn from what only one or two people have said.[28] In cases where intelligence is required under very tight time constraints, for example as with Iraq, where it could be argued that the UK and US wished to gain intelligence in order to justify taking pre-emptive military action, this issue may become a profound problem. At an extreme, this may result in decisions being made based solely on the word of one or perhaps two human sources in the absence of any means of corroborating that information. The case studies in this book show that policy-makers were not prepared to make decisions without a wide and diverse range of sources to draw from; whereas, once again, the opposite seems to have been true in the lead-up to the Iraq War.

Whilst it is easy to be critical of the way in which limited HUMINT was used to support the UK case for war in 2003, this issue raises particular problems relating to the role of intelligence in WMD counter-proliferation. In particular, when intelligence effort is directed against non-state actors such as terrorist groups, the only available evidence may often be from single sources that cannot be corroborated from elsewhere; yet that evidence may be required to justify, *in extremis*, pre-emptive military action. This will clearly place significant pressure on intelligence agencies as well as on policy-makers who must perhaps act quickly, sure in the knowledge that they will need to draw on intelligence that they can trust.

Despite the obvious problems of drawing conclusions from only a few sources, one must also consider that defectors may have a tendency to tell their de-briefer exactly what they think they want to hear. The open-minded intelligence officer is then faced with corroborating that information from further sources—something that may be quite difficult. Yet it is here that the value of the 'jigsaw puzzle' approach taken in the three case studies can be seen. The problem remaining is that, as has already been seen, this approach may take a great deal of time—time that may not be available in the contemporary challenges that intelligence agencies may face. This suggests a clear change in the way that intelligence is being forced to adapt to operate effectively in the current strategic environment (post 11 September 2001), which will be further considered later in this chapter.

It is important to consider the comments made so far relating to a reliance on HUMINT in the context of the countries from which intelligence was sought. The Soviet Union, Libya and Apartheid South Africa were all, to varying degrees, closed states. UK intelligence officers therefore faced particular problems when operating within them. It is clear that closed states, and indeed police states, might be very difficult targets for intelligence-gathering. Indeed, it could be argued that where one 'knows' that a state will deny and deceive, intelligence almost becomes something of a chimera. Furthermore, it should be considered that where an intelligence officer might expect denial and deception from a specific state, this in itself poses a danger to the subsequent attempts at accurate intelligence analysis: denial and deception might be seen as a given, rather than as a hypothesis to be tested.[29] Once again, though, one could consider the long timescales over which intelligence was gathered as something of a counter to this problem: the more time is available, the more pieces of the jigsaw puzzle can be collected, and the more the overall picture is accurately established because of the continual challenging of intelligence analysis. It is perhaps only cases like Iraq—where too few HUMINT sources were used over a very short timescale, not supported by other sources, to support a desired political decision—that illustrate the dangers of reliance on the collection of intelligence in this manner.

Nonetheless, the Soviet Union, Libya and to a lesser degree South Africa did in some ways present clear opportunities to the intelligence agencies. Certainly, they were all clear and obvious targets with a direct link to UK national security and national interests. The Soviet Union was the single largest perceived military threat to the UK from the end of the Cold War until the collapse of the Soviet Union: it is only common sense to expect the intelligence agencies to have made great efforts to collect any information relating to specific threats and risks. In the same way, Libya proved itself to be a willing sponsor of terrorism, some of which was directed against the UK, throughout the 1980s. This, along with its suspected links to the IRA, also made Libya an obvious target. When one considers the possible threat posed by terrorist groups obtaining Libyan-produced chemical or biological weapons, intelligence efforts are once again justified.

These countries, as targets, also raise questions relating to how intelligence is, and should be, prioritised to allocate adequate resources to targets. Clearly, during the Cold War it could be argued that the Soviet Union should always have been the main focus of intelligence effort. Yet the case studies presented in this book illustrate how important proliferation threats were being considered in other states where intelligence effort was also required. At times, for example in the South African case study, it was only on the initiative of individual intelligence officers that those threats were detected at all. Targeting is an important issue in the intelligence cycle. It cannot always be reactive to customer needs, particularly in the post Cold War world where threats may appear from non-state groups very quickly, presenting clear and direct threats to the UK and her interests. Once again, this places significant challenges on intelligence agencies.

Whilst South Africa may be seen as a rather different case because there was no clear and direct threat to the UK, there is ample evidence to suggest that UK national interests were indirectly threatened by the proliferation of knowledge or materials from South African CBW programmes, once again justifying intelligence efforts. One further factor of note here is that not only did these three case studies represent obvious targets for the intelligence agencies, but they also reflected long-term and consistent trends in UK foreign policy towards CBW. These facts go some way to explaining why intelligence was collected in the way it was over long periods: the actual threats were likely to present themselves over equally long periods, and foreign policy towards the states in question would probably not be radically altered as a result of intelligence unless significant breaches of international treaties or other major initiatives took place. All of this presents a rather comfortable view of how intelligence worked in support of UK foreign policy.

Perhaps a defining characteristic of the 'jigsaw puzzle' approach, particularly when relying on HUMINT, is the sheer length of time it takes to collect intelligence and build an actionable case from it. In particular, the time taken to identify and cultivate agents in order to obtain useful intelligence may be considerable. This may not be a problem when those proliferation problems about which intelligence is required are constant and long-running, but when only short periods exist for the collection of compelling material to support foreign policy actions, this presents challenges. To that end, it could be argued that the case studies in this book suggest that intelligence is better able to generate appropriate foreign policy changes when robust cases are built over a long period of time. Given the apparently successful outcomes of the three case studies for UK national interests, regardless of the frustrations that might be faced by individual intelligence officers in trying to get their cases heard, it appears that the 'long game' allows far more effective, accurate and non-politicised cases for action to be built, rather than the short-term cases produced as a result of political needs in the case of Iraq.

In summary, when considering how intelligence was collected in each of these three case studies, one striking theme apparent from each is the importance of HUMINT in the cases assembled by UK agencies. This characteristic is perhaps all the more surprising when one considers the difference in budgetary allocation between HUMINT collection efforts and technical or SIGINT efforts. In 1994, GCHQ was receiving an allocation of £1.1 billion, while the other two agencies were receiving about £225 million. Moreover, we know that much SIGINT spending is 'hidden' in other budgets. It would not be unreasonable to assume that SIGINT of one kind or another accounts for close to 85 per cent of UK intelligence spending.[30] On a pound for pound basis, HUMINT perhaps represents far better value for money than other means, therefore, though it seemingly cannot be relied on to deliver usable intelligence quickly. Although the Butler Report in particular was critical of an apparent over-reliance on HUMINT during the lead-up to the Iraq War, it is interesting that when considered within long-running cases, HUMINT apparently builds the backbone of assessments. Once again, the striking difference between the apparent intelligence successes of the three case studies in this book and the 2003 Iraq War example seems to be the influence of time on the accuracy of assessments, along with the driver for the requirements of that intelligence—supporting decision-making or allowing an already made decision to be justified. The 'long game', as demonstrated by the three case studies in this book, appears to pay dividends.

Factors affecting the analysis of intelligence

Analysis marks an important means by which information can be differentiated from intelligence.[31] The case studies in this book illustrate many topical issues relating to the analysis of intelligence, reflecting both organisational and individual factors. This section will therefore draw together general conclusions relating to the analysis of intelligence, ultimately placing them within the context of the 2003 Iraq War in order to suggest how the analysis of intelligence might have differed between the early 1970s up to the early 2000s and then from 2003 onwards. There are several important areas for consideration here: organisational issues, establishment-related issues, and also how intelligence agencies might be seen to learn—all this analysis will be placed within the context of the wider debate relating to the Iraq War.

From across the three case studies in this book, it is striking that there have been relatively few individuals who were seemingly directly involved in CBW intelligence-gathering and analysis across the UK intelligence agencies. In some cases, the same individuals have been responsible for all aspects of intelligence-gathering and analysis over the entire period of time spanned by the case studies. This means that at times there was no separation between those individuals collecting intelligence from those responsible for its assessment; in the case of the Soviet Union, the same officer was responsible for both functions. This seems to be a peculiar situation in several senses. First, there was (and perhaps still is) clearly a very small pool of individuals within the UK with the knowledge and experience of CBW necessary for the levels of analysis required for political decision-makers to act upon these findings. This raises questions over just how vulnerable and sensitive intelligence agencies might be in terms of having enough analysts with skills to deal effectively with highly technical subject areas. In addition, if relatively few individuals are responsible for CBW intelligence, they might perhaps be more susceptible to political pressure due to their need to justify their presence in niche roles within intelligence organisations.

In the context of Iraq, as well as other possible cases in the future where there is a desire to use military power pre-emptively, this may be a significant problem when it comes to providing rapid and accurate analysis. Next, when there is no separation between the collection and analysis function, it is possible that the final intelligence product could be open to accusations of being less than objective; again, they might also be considered as being more susceptible to politicisation. These issues are apparent in the Soviet Union case study, where one analyst is accused of producing analysis that suits the raw intelligence that has been collected. This is obviously a real problem: in an ideal world, there would be a clear separation between collection and analysis, but in highly technical areas such as CBW this may simply not be possible. It is here that the credibility of analysts as well as their consistency in producing accurate product become particularly important: in a 'long game', the lengthy duration of cases would go some way towards addressing this issue.

The long timescale associated with the Soviet case study, before definitive political action was taken by the UK, could actually be a function of the time required for those individuals within UK intelligence agencies to develop the credibility required in the eyes of policy-makers to support the analysis they are presenting, and in particular for it to be considered to be accurate and reliable enough to act upon; after all, the consequences of policy-makers acting upon incorrect analysis could be severe. Essentially, one might argue that a small number of intelligence officers had to spend many years building their own personal credibility through demonstrably accurate analysis before policy-makers were willing to trust them to provide analysis on threats with significant strategic implications. Once again, in contemporary security challenges concerning WMD, trust and credibility should be an important factor in the acceptance of intelligence by policy-makers. In the case of Iraq in 2003, the political desire for specific product to be provided by intelligence agencies perhaps assumed that the information would be sound because it always had been in the past. There is therefore a clear need for intelligence agencies to force policy-makers to accept the confidence of intelligence agencies in the overall quality of product, not allow product to be used to carry 'more weight ... than it could bear'.[32]

The Soviet case study also suggests that the organisational changes that occurred within UK intelligence, resulting in the move of personnel from DIS to SIS, were a key feature in developing the credibility of UK CBW intelligence. Restructuring the UK intelligence agencies, in particular in the early stages of the Soviet case study, might be seen to have been crucial in putting the right people in the right places where they could have maximum impact in intelligence-gathering and analysis. One might even argue that DIS and SIS both failed for considerable periods of time to recruit the correct levels of technical experts into those organisations. That said, it has been suggested that restructuring also brought with it problems: Philip Davies has argued that organisational changes within SIS from the mid 1970s pushed 'responsibility further down the organisational pyramid. The question has to be asked as to how far down can one push a function in an organisational hierarchy before it is deprived of any influential voice at the decision making levels.'[33] Lord Butler also noted in the aftermath of the invasion of Iraq in 2003 that 'the ability of [junior officers] to challenge the validity of cases and their reporting was ... reduced'.[34] Certainly, for junior intelligence officers one might consider that it is quite right that a CIG (Current Intelligence Group) or the JIC (Joint Intelligence Committee) might disregard their analysis—in particular when a consensus of more senior officers disagrees, yet one must consider the possibilities of the 'what if' when that junior officer is correct.

The Soviet case study therefore provides an interesting account of the difficulties faced by intelligence officers in passing analysis that is contrary to established views and policies up to political masters. The key consideration here is whether this type of organisational structure might actually serve to prevent politically sensitive analysis reaching policy-makers who might be forced to make awkward decisions because of it. Certainly, as has already been discussed, there is a fair argument that states that junior intelligence officers must be properly managed and prevented from passing on unsubstantiated or unproven assertion; indeed, the record of the JIC itself is not one of perfection and effectiveness.[35] That said, one would expect intelligence agencies to be structured in such a way that the appropriate information was passed to policy-makers; indeed, one of the purposes of the JIC is to act as such a conduit. The apparent strength of the FCO in particular in influencing what the JIC endorses and passes on to policy-makers is significant here: it was certainly instrumental for a considerable period of time in blocking the passage of Soviet CBW threat-related assessments.

The Soviet case study illustrated a period of many years when a single intelligence officer was consistently 'hushed up' or just ignored because his analysis did not fit the organisational view of the Soviet BW threat. Years later, when that same intelligence officer was a much more senior officer in another intelligence organisation, one might argue that the opposite problem existed: no one disagreed with the analysis of that officer and the time taken to force political action on the South African case study was therefore greatly reduced. One might even argue that this growth of personal credibility was accompanied by an increased willingness of policy-makers to accept intelligence analysis after subjecting it to far less rigour than might have been expected in the early years of the Soviet case study. Personality and interpersonal relationships are therefore crucial across the three case studies in this book.

It is even possible to argue that this increasing willingness to accept intelligence is also related to a decreasing level of rigour in the analysis itself; this might certainly be seen to be true when considering the role of intelligence in building a case for war prior to the invasion of Iraq in 2003. By contrast in the case of the Soviet Union, the first evidence relating to Soviet breaches of the BTWC was collected in the mid 1970s; but it was not until the end of the 1980s that senior political figures were prepared to accept the overarching intelligence picture relating to Soviet non-compliance and take specific action. Whilst it could be argued that political pressure rather than the politicisation of intelligence product has been a factor apparent throughout each of the case studies in this book, in the case of Iraq there seem to have been particular factors that allowed politicisation to take place. Not only was there a remarkably short time available for the intelligence agencies to present intelligence that could be used to allow political leaders to justify their desired actions; there is also evidence that policy-makers were willing to accept any evidence that provided support for their already determined foreign policy. The comments of Lord Butler, stated earlier in this chapter, where he comments that the intelligence agencies may have felt pressured to present specific rather than objective intelligence product, certainly seem to give weight to this argument.[36] The apparent 'informality and circumscribed character of the Government's procedures which [was seen] in the context of policy-making towards Iraq' only perhaps further reduces 'the scope for informed collective political judgement ... in a field ... where hard facts are inherently difficult to come by and the quality of judgement is accordingly all the more important'.[37] To a degree, then, political positions of policy-makers have always affected whether or not intelligence has been used. What is seemingly different about the Iraq case is that here policy-makers demanded specific information to fit their desired course of action, whereas in the other cases they were just selective in how they accepted and used intelligence.

Before finishing discussion on this issue, one must also bear in mind that an organisation that relies on small numbers of specialist officers may face severe problems when those individuals retire. It may perhaps be no coincidence that the officers featuring across the three case studies in this book retired around 2001—before the debacle concerning the use of intelligence in the lead-up to the 2003 Iraq War. It does seem appropriate to consider here the issue of 'over-learning', as discussed by Robert Jervis.[38] Jervis argues that significant events in intelligence—for example, the success against the Soviet BW programme—might leave deep imprints on audiences. As a result, people will be sure not to repeat the same mistakes again (here, in ignoring the threat for so long) by 'over-correcting', and as a result become more likely to commit the opposite error. Jervis uses the example of poor assessment of Iraqi WMD in 1991 to explain what he perceives to be an apparent over-estimation in 2003. This is clearly an interesting concept, and also one that can be applied when attempting to explain the increasing ability of intelligence officers to generate foreign policy action in the case study of Libya as well as South Africa. Furthermore, it may explain why intelligence of such apparently lower rigour was accepted at the highest level in 2003: if success and personal credibility in the Soviet case study led to continued success in Libya and then South Africa, it is possible that the reputation that was built by individual intelligence officers was perceived by policy-makers as being the same thing as success and credibility of the department within the agency. As a result, when those individuals responsible for those successes retired, policy-makers still perceived those departments as retaining that credibility. They might therefore have placed more trust in intelligence collected and produced by new and less experienced officers, resulting in the issues observed by commentators on the 2003 Iraq War. Organisational structures and learning issues are therefore seemingly significant across the case studies considered in this book. Furthermore, there is certainly enough evidence in this book to argue for a need for specialised pools of technical personnel within UK intelligence, along with training, learning and development programmes to sustain, maintain and develop those individuals. These factors become particularly important when considering the link between the intelligence producer and its consumer.

The producer and consumer linkage

Many authors have argued that intelligence is one of the key elements of foreign policy decision-making.[39] Whilst it may not be correct to suggest a specific role of intelligence in foreign policy formulation and enactment, existing literature does articulate the view that intelligence is a key element of foreign policy decision-making. This observation would certainly seem to be borne out by the case studies in this book. In particular, it has been argued that the quality of the intelligence, its ability to reach political leaders, leaders' judgements and the independent actions of the intelligence community are all key factors affecting this relationship.[40]

If intelligence is to serve a useful purpose within a democratic society, it must provide accurate assessments, regardless of political agendas. It is, however, important to note early on in this section that because intelligence assessments must ultimately interface with political systems, the risk of politicisation of intelligence must always be considered as a risk. Clearly, if a policy-maker desires specific intelligence to support a particular course of action—for example, to build a case for pre-emptive war, as in Iraq in 2003—politicisation of intelligence may be a considerable risk. If an intelligence system is managed effectively, there should be no question of intelligence analysts being forced to choose between 'the painful value trade-off between pleasing policy makers and following professional standards'.[41] Indeed, the case studies within this book suggest that the analysts involved did, until the immediate period before the 2003 Iraq War, maintain the highest professional standards, regardless of the potential for adverse impact on their careers, to guard against attempts to politicise product. That said, one might argue that the very defining characteristics of each of the three case studies meant that use of intelligence for abusive political gain was never likely to occur. More contemporary examples of how intelligence is used to support political action may present very different circumstances, where assessments are required over very short time periods, so politicisation, or just political interference, may be a real risk. This seems to be the legacy of the Iraq War: how can intelligence be obtained quickly enough to support decision-making under extreme time constraints? Regardless, it is clear that politicisation of assessment will always be a risk. Politicisation might then be considered to be 'like fog. Though you cannot hold it in your hands, or nail it to the wall, it does exist, it is real, and it does affect people.'[42]

Where the interface between intelligence and foreign policy does not mesh effectively, for whatever reason, there is a risk of incorrect assessments being made and used by policy-makers in the formulation of policy. At its very worst, this may lead to what might be called an 'intelligence failure'. Intelligence failure has been defined as 'a mismatch between the estimates and what later information reveals to have been true'.[43] The use of the term does seem to be rather one-sided, often bringing with it blame for specific intelligence process failures. It might, however, be argued that the case studies presented in this book, certainly by virtue of the fact that they ran for such long periods before political action was taken, suggest that there must be an opposite term to 'intelligence failure'. Where intelligence is 'wrong', it captures the attention of policy-makers and the public alike; yet what happens where intelligence is 'right' and the policy itself is 'wrong'? In this book, three case studies, to greater or lesser degrees, show that policy-makers have been placed in situations where they have been forced to change policies because of the intelligence presented to them—it is they who have been 'wrong'. It would certainly appear that the case studies in this book are successes, in that they forced foreign policy changes in order to ensure outcomes of benefit to the security of the United Kingdom.

It therefore seems that the level of political willingness to accept and act on intelligence is another key factor in impacting on the intelligence and foreign policy nexus. There are several issues in particular that it is important to draw out here. Firstly, in the case of the Soviet Union, the long timescale before the UK government confronted the Soviet government appears to be related to the lack of political acceptance and interest in a Soviet BW threat. Regardless of the intelligence gathered over a considerable period of time, policy-makers refused to confront the Soviet Union over BW development until absolutely incontrovertible intelligence was given to political masters, making it impossible for them not to act upon it. With South Africa, whilst political interest was once again initially low, when it became clear that the UK may have been involved in the development of South African CBW, that interest rapidly grew—because UK national interests were directly threatened. Only in the case of Libya, where political interest was already high, was there a much shorter timescale between the accumulation of CBW-related intelligence and political action.

Based on the case studies in this book, the CBW threat identified by intelligence agencies on each occasion appeared to be acted upon only when it became a subject of political interest. It therefore could be argued that policy-makers only act on CBW intelligence when it is in the national interest to do so. One must also consider the relationship between intelligence and foreign policy as a function of its currency as a political issue within the context of a time period in question. The case of the Soviet Union reflected a considerable proportion of the timescale of the Cold War. Here, foreign and defence policy towards the Soviet Union remained consistent across governments and time. Soviet BW represented only another part of the already well-acknowledged and accepted Soviet threat, and for policy-makers as well as the general public in the UK that threat could be seen as simply representing a way of life. Whilst intelligence could perhaps inform foreign policy in this case, if it did not, then no real change in perception of that Soviet threat would occur. Only in the subsequent case studies does it become clear that if policy-makers ignored intelligence, it might impact domestically. This would suggest that the producer and consumer relationship perhaps needs a far more robust system of management. Whilst it is the prerogative of individual policy-makers to ignore intelligence, surely a system of management should be strong enough to ensure that relevant intelligence is at least considered?

In a sense, in the case studies of South Africa and Libya, the UK experienced a fusion of foreign and home policy: intelligence became important in the pursuit of foreign policy objectives, but ignoring it, in particular if it was subsequently found to be correct, would have risked impacting on home policies. Whilst the Soviet case study demonstrates an important development in the credibility of analysts and the intelligence they can produce, it also marks the start of a time when intelligence moves from a position where it might only inform foreign policy to one where it could be considered to determine it. What becomes interesting as a result of this is a consideration of why, certainly in the case of the Soviet Union, the FCO seemed so resistant to consider intelligence relating to a threat from what was at the time arguably the greatest single existential threat to the UK. One might argue that during the Cold War the FCO consistently worked to justify its own inaction, as opposed to after the Cold War when it worked to justify action. Issues discussed in the previous section relating to personal and organisational issues seem to go some way towards positing explanations for this apparent inaction. Certainly, at a general level, this book provides some evidence that rivalries between not only different intelligence services, but also other government departments (in particular the role of the Foreign Office and the apparent subservience of other government departments and agencies to its wishes on the JIC) might be seen to have had an impact on the intelligence and foreign policy nexus across each of the case studies considered. Additionally, evidence in this book suggests that the credibility and abilities of individual officers across the intelligence apparatus are also important factors.

So, although it may seem obvious to suggest that UK intelligence is only used in support of UK national interests, in the context of CBW the UK has a much broader range of responsibilities, and the case studies in this book suggest a rather more complicated relationship at work. National intelligence should be expected to inform policy-makers of issues of which they might not otherwise be aware, as within these case studies it certainly seems to do. Intelligence should also be expected to provide warning of likely or even only conceivable threats to both national security and national interests. Again, evidence from the case studies supports this. One might even argue that the intelligence agencies within the UK have a moral obligation to provide such warnings—even if these might be counter to the views and wishes of policy-makers. Once more, evidence in particular from the Soviet and South African case studies suggests that this could be so. For the UK, counter-proliferation efforts seem to be not just for the good of the UK, but also for the good of the international community as a whole.[44] It is interesting to consider that key interviewees in this book considered their responsibility to be towards making the world a better place, free of CBW, rather than purely in the national interest. One might therefore consider intelligence to contribute to state power in two ways: first, through enhancing the range of options open to policy-makers to advance national security interests; but secondly, through facilitating the passage of norms and values relating to arms control and counter-proliferation. This is not necessarily an attitude associated with staff of a national intelligence agency. It also seems appropriate to consider the role of UK intelligence on CBW across the case studies in this book as evolutionary—both in terms of changes and developments across time, as well as in terms of increasing ability to produce analysis that directly influences foreign policy.

Intelligence and WMD in the contemporary world: new problems?

The three case studies in this book occurred at a time when the context of each was largely related to the environment of the Cold War world. As pointed out in the introductory chapter, the 2003 Iraq War provides a more contemporary environment against which the intelligence and foreign policy nexus can be examined. But how and why does the relationship between intelligence and foreign policy differ between that Cold War period and the 2003 Iraq War?

Whilst the three case studies in this book played out over considerable time periods, one characteristic of the 2003 Iraq War is that contemporary counter-proliferation problems seem to have much shorter times available for responses to be generated by governments such as the UK. Indeed, probably one of the most significant challenges for the intelligence agencies in the contemporary world is acting at speed to gather, analyse and provide intelligence assessments relating to WMD threats in order to support pre-emptive military action. Arguably, the very existence of the Butler Report is testament to the significance of this challenge.

The case studies in this book therefore suggest that it may not actually be possible for intelligence on CBW proliferation to operate accurately in the time constraints imposed on contemporary problems such as Iraq in 2003. The Butler Report certainly provides detailed commentary on the apparent shortfalls in intelligence analysis in the lead-up to the Iraq War. These are linked to political demands for rapid production of assessments to suit policy decisions. Butler also suggests the possible complicity of the intelligence agencies in providing product of questionable reliability to support existing policy decisions relating to a desire for military action. In order to suggest that these problems may be directly related to time pressures, one must return to the mechanisms through which intelligence operated in each of the three case studies.

Firstly, one striking characteristic of the UK intelligence agencies involved in CBW analysis in the case studies is the sheer length of time required to gather sufficient evidence to draw credible conclusions; whereas pre-emptive military action demands quick intelligence analysis—perhaps as quick as several weeks—in order to provide conclusive proof of a threat that is to be dealt with by military force. This book suggests that UK intelligence has never been capable of providing that type of intelligence on CBW programmes in a timescale shorter than several years.

Next, it could be argued that this long duration for intelligence-gathering efforts, arguably within states where one could reasonably expect that type of threat to dissipate anyway, suggests that UK intelligence agencies were not even particularly good at this type of operation. Take, for example, the role of 'windfall' high-level defectors who provided conclusive proof of the existence of threats; neither an intelligence agency nor a government can rely on that type of source to deliver conclusive proof of a threat significant enough to justify pre-emptive war. Credibility of individual analysts in UK intelligence is another factor here, and one that has already been discussed previously, yet the retirement of key personnel in 2001 suggests that credibility was supposedly transferred from individual analysts to their departments. Intelligence might therefore have been considered sound because of where it had come from, rather than from whom.

Any desire for pre-emptive war certainly places significant challenges onto the intelligence agencies. One must consider the concerns voiced by Lawrence Freedman: that this type of situation might be driven by theory and ideas, perhaps originating in the intelligence agencies themselves, about what might or could happen.[45] Intelligence agencies that cannot fulfil the time-sensitive demands placed on them must be more sensitive to this type of dilemma. As Freedman argues, 'intelligence agencies do themselves no favours when they appear to fall into line and they do governments no favours when they fail to draw their attention to real doubts and uncertainties in evidence'.[46]

Pre-emptive war clearly requires a government to take the initiative in its international relations; and the consequences of taking an initiative based on wrong intelligence are grave. One must, however, consider that in light of the findings of the research presented in this book, UK intelligence currently seems incapable of meeting the time-sensitive demands of a government needing to construct cases rapidly for pre-emptive war. Whilst foreign policy might demand that UK intelligence make the transition from an organisation focused around providing independent advice to policy-makers, separated from the political process, to one actively and proactively supporting policy-makers, it must also ensure that this transition sees a parallel development in the abilities of those organisations to guarantee the accuracy and reliability of the intelligence they provide. War is a high price to pay for flawed analysis; these flaws may be the regrettable result of intelligence failure.

NOTES

1. INTRODUCTION: OBSESSING ON INTELLIGENCE

1. See, for example, www.forbes.com: Asher Hawkins, *Bond's Markets: The Man With The Golden Franchise* (28 May 2008).
2. See http://www.legislation.gov.uk/ukpga/1994/13/contents for the text of the 1994 Intelligence Services Act; and http://isc.independent.gov.uk/committee-reports/annual-reports for Intelligence and Security Committee reports.
3. Nigel West, 'Fiction, Faction and Intelligence', *Intelligence and National Security*, Vol. 19, No. 2 (June 2004), pp. 275–89, this pp. 275 and 276.
4. See, for example, Steven Kettell, *Dirty Politics: New Labour, British Democracy and the Invasion of Iraq* (London: Zed Books, 2006).
5. For an overview of the current legislative frameworks relating to UK intelligence agencies, see *National Intelligence Machinery* (London: The Stationery Office, 2006), p. 3.
6. In 2000, the UK government released a short brochure entitled *Central Intelligence Machinery* (London: The Stationery Office, 2000), offering some basic details.
7. *Active Diplomacy in a Changing World: The UK's International Priorities* (London: The Stationery Office, 2006), p. 28.
8. *Review of Intelligence on Weapons of Mass Destruction* (London: The Stationery Office, 2004), p. 1.
9. *Report of the Inquiry into the Circumstances Surrounding the Death of Dr David Kelly C.M.G* (London: The Stationary Office, 2004), p. 2.
10. See David Isenberg and Ian Davis, *Unravelling the Known Unknowns: Why no Weapons of Mass Destruction have been Found in Iraq* (British American Security Information Council, BASIC Special Report 2004.1, January 2004).
11. Simon Rogers (ed.), *The Hutton Inquiry and its Impact* (London: Politico's Guardian Books, 2004), p. 9.

12. For detailed information on the various dossiers utilised by the government, see *Review of Intelligence on Weapons of Mass Destruction*, 2004.

13. Ian Davis and Andreas Persbo, 'After the Butler Report: Time to Take on the Group Think in Washington and London', *BASIC Papers: Occasional Papers on International Security Policy*, No. 46 (July 2004), accessed at www.basicint.org/pubs/Papers/BP46.htm on 6 February 2009.

14. The committee concluded that this area involved striking a 'difficult balance' and required 'further thought'; Cm 6510, ISC, *Annual Report 2004–5*, April 2005, p. 31, para. 88.

15. The official website of the Chilcot Inquiry details the precise terms of reference for the inquiry and can be found at www.iraqinquiry.org.uk

16. Updates on the progress of the Chilcot Inquiry can be found at http://www.iraqinquiry.org.uk/news.aspx

17. See, for example, https://www.theguardian.com/uk-news/2016/jul/06/iraq-inquiry-key-points-from-the-chilcot-report

18. See, for example, Brian Jones, *Failing Intelligence* (London: Biteback Publishing, 2010).

19. *Review of Intelligence on Weapons of Mass Destruction*, pp. 17–26.

20. Ibid., p. 15.

21. See, for example, Tom Mangold and Jeff Goldberg, *Plague Wars* (Basingstoke: Macmillan, 1999), especially pp. 91–7 and 242–3.

2. INSIGHTS INTO INTELLIGENCE

1. See Gregory Treverton, Seth G. Jones, Steven Boraz and Philip Lipscy, *Towards a Theory of Intelligence Workshop Report* (Santa Monica, CA: RAND Institute, 2006), especially p. 10.

2. Stuart Farson, 'Schools of Thought: National Perceptions of Intelligence', *Conflict Quarterly*, Vol. 9, No. 2 (1989), pp. 52–104, this p. 56.

3. *National Intelligence Machinery* (London: The Stationery Office, 2006), p. 37.

4. These three building blocks are: collection and analysis, covert action and counter-intelligence, as described in Loch K. Johnson, 'Bricks and Mortar for a Theory of Intelligence', *Comparative Strategy*, Vol. 22, No. 1 (2003), pp. 1–28.

5. J. Ransom Clark, *Intelligence and National Security* (London: Praeger Security International, 2007), p. 1.

6. *National Intelligence Machinery*, pp. 20 and 37.

7. Loch K. Johnson, 'Preface to a Theory of Strategic Intelligence', *International Journal of Intelligence and Counter Intelligence*, Vol. 16, No. 4 (2003), pp. 638–63, this p. 641.

8. David Kahn, 'An Historical Theory of Intelligence', *Intelligence and National Security*, Vol. 16, No. 3 (2001), pp. 79–92, this p. 90.

9. Sherman Kent, *Strategic Intelligence for American World Policy* (Hamden, CT: Archon Books, 1965), p. xxiii.

10. Michael Herman, *Intelligence Power in War and Peace* (Cambridge: Cambridge University Press, 1996), p. 2.

11. Roger Hilsman, 'Intelligence and Policy-Making in Foreign Affairs', *World Politics*, Vol. 5, No. 1 (October 1952), pp. 1–45, this p. 2.

12. Abram N. Shulsky, *Silent Warfare: Understanding the World of Intelligence* (Washington, DC: Brassey's, 1993), p. 1.

13. Andrew Rathmell, 'Towards Post Modern Intelligence', *Intelligence and National Security*, Vol. 17, No. 3 (2002), pp. 87–104, this p. 102.

14. Alan Dupont, 'Intelligence for the Twenty-First Century', *Intelligence and National Security*, Vol. 18, No. 4 (December 2003), pp. 15–39, this p. 16.

15. Michael Herman, *Intelligence Services in the Information Age* (London: Frank Cass, 2001), p. 10.

16. Ibid., p. 284.

17. Ibid.

18. The intelligence cycle is most often described as a cyclical series of five steps: first, the intelligence user (or policy-maker) sets a requirement for specific intelligence, prompting planning and direction; second, intelligence agencies collect and collate data; third, that data is evaluated for reliability and credibility before being processed to make it usable by analysts; fourth is analysis and production as intelligence products; fifth, that analysed product is then reported and disseminated, as a result leading to a new requirement for intelligence being set. The cycle then repeats itself.

19. Robert M. Clark, *Intelligence Analysis: A Target-Centric Approach* (Washington, DC: CQ Press, 2004), p. 14.

20. Arthur S. Hulnick, 'What's Wrong with the Intelligence Cycle?' in Loch K. Johnson (ed.), *Strategic Intelligence, Vol. 2: The Intelligence Cycle* (London: Praeger, 2007), p. 1.

21. Ibid., p. 2.

22. Gregory Treverton, *Reshaping National Intelligence in an Age of Information* (Cambridge: Cambridge University Press, 2001), p. 179.

23. Ibid., p. 192.

24. Ibid., p. 183.

25. These ideas were put forward by Sir David Omand during a workshop on 'The Future of Intelligence and Special Operations' held on 7 May 2008 at the University of Warwick. They are now available in D. Omand, *The National Security Strategy: Implications for the UK Intelligence Community*, (London: Institute for Public Policy Research, 2009).

26. Carmen Medina, 'What to do when Traditional Models Fail', in Christopher Andrew, Richard J. Aldrich and Wesley K. Wark (eds), *Secret Intelligence: A Reader* (London: Routledge, 2009), pp. 108–15.

27. Herman, *Intelligence Power in War and Peace*, p. 285.

28. Hulnick, 'What's Wrong with the Intelligence Cycle?', p. 3.

29. Ibid., p. 3.

30. Philip Davies, 'A Critical Look at Britain's Spy Machinery: Collection and Analysis on Iraq', *Studies in Intelligence*, Vol. 49, No. 4 (2005), https://www.cia.gov/library/center-for-the-study-of-intelligence/csi-publications/csi-studies/studies/vol49no4/Spy_Machinery_4.htm, accessed on 7 June 2009.

31. Ibid.

32. Treverton, *Reshaping National Intelligence in an Age of Information*, p. 199.

33. Herman, *Intelligence Power in War and Peace*, p. 285.

34. Sherman Kent, 'Producers and Consumers of Intelligence', in Douglas H. Dearth and R. Thomas Goodden (eds), *Strategic Intelligence: Theory and Application* (Washington, DC: US Army War College, 1995), p. 129.

35. Clark, *Intelligence Analysis: A Target-Centric Approach*, p. 16.

36. Ibid., p. 17.

37. Ibid., p. 17.

38. Herman, *Intelligence Power in War and Peace*, p. 295.

39. Bruce D. Berkowitz and Allan E. Goodman, *Best Truth: Intelligence in the Information Age* (London: Yale University Press, 2000), p. 72.

40. Ibid., p. 74.

41. Omand, *The National Security Strategy*.

42. Berkowitz and Goodman, *Best Truth: Intelligence in the Information Age*, p. 22.

43. Ibid., p. 22.

44. Harold P. Ford, *Estimative Intelligence: The Purposes and Problems of National Intelligence Estimating* (Lanham, MD: University Press of America, 1993), p. 98.

45. Shulsky, *Silent Warfare: Understanding the World of Intelligence*, p. 180.

46. James J. Wirtz, 'The Intelligence–Policy Nexus', in Johnson (ed.), *Strategic Intelligence, Vol. 1: Understanding the Hidden Side of Government*, p. 141.

47. Ibid., p. 141.

48. Ford, *Estimative Intelligence: The Purposes and Problems of National Intelligence Estimating*, p. 98.

49. Ibid., p. 137.

50. Wirtz, 'The Intelligence–Policy Nexus', p. 141.

51. Ford, *Estimative Intelligence: The Purposes and Problems of National Intelligence Estimating*, p. 98.

52. David A. Charters, Stuart Farson and Glenn P. Hastedt (eds), *Intelligence Analysis and Assessment* (London: Frank Cass, 1996), p. 41.

53. Wirtz, 'The Intelligence–Policy Nexus', p. 142.

54. Treverton, *Reshaping National Intelligence in an Age of Information*, p. 208.

55. Wirtz, 'The Intelligence–Policy Nexus', p. 143.

56. Ibid., p. 143.

57. Ford, *Estimative Intelligence: The Purposes and Problems of National Intelligence Estimating*, p. 98.

58. Treverton, *Reshaping National Intelligence in an Age of Information*, p. 208.

3. PUTTING IRAQ INTO CONTEXT: UK INTELLIGENCE AND
    CHEMICAL AND BIOLOGICAL WEAPONS

1. *National Intelligence Machinery*, (London: The Stationery Office, 2006), p. 2.
2. See ibid. for an official though brief overview of UK intelligence.
3. See, for example, Philip Davies, *MI6 and the Machinery of Spying* (London: Frank Cass, 2004).
4. Michael Herman, *Intelligence Power in War and Peace* (Cambridge: Cambridge University Press, 1996), p. 113.
5. *Terms of Reference for the Joint Intelligence Committee*, JIC (57) 101, 1 October 1957, in CAB 158 30, UK National Archive, Kew, cited in Philip Davies, 'A Critical Look at Britain's Spy Machinery: Collection and Analysis on Iraq', *Studies in Intelligence*, Vol. 49, No. 4 (2005), https://www.cia.gov/library/center-for-the-study-of-intelligence/csi-publications/csi-studies/studies/vol49no4/Spy_Machinery_4.htm, accessed on 7 June 2009.
6. Davies, 'A Critical Look at Britain's Spy Machinery: Collection and Analysis on Iraq'.
7. Gregory Treverton, *Reshaping National Intelligence in an Age of Information* (Cambridge: Cambridge University Press, 2001), p. 213.
8. Ibid., p. 213.
9. Robert Dover, 'For Queen and Company: The Role of Intelligence in the UK's Arms Trade', *Political Studies*, Vol. 55 (2007), pp. 683–708, this p. 684.
10. *National Intelligence Machinery*, p. 17.
11. Timothy Gibbs, 'Studying Intelligence: A British Perspective', in Loch K. Johnson (ed.), *Strategic Intelligence, Vol. 1: Understanding the Hidden Side of Government* (London: Praeger, 2007), p. 41.
12. David A. Charters, Stuart Farson and Glenn P. Hastedt (eds), *Intelligence Analysis and Assessment* (London: Frank Cass, 1996), p. 26.
13. Percy Cradock, *In Pursuit of British Interests: Reflections on Foreign Policy under Margaret Thatcher and John Major* (London: John Murray, 1997), p. 44.
14. Herman, *Intelligence Power in War and Peace*, p. 140.
15. John Dickie, *The New Mandarins: How British Foreign Policy Works* (London: I. B. Tauris, 2007), p. 103.
16. Ibid., p. 103.
17. Michael S. Goodman, 'The Dog That Didn't Bark: The Joint Intelligence Committee and Warning of Aggression', *Cold War History*, Vol. 7, No. 4 (2007), pp. 529–51, this p. 533.
18. Michael Herman, 'Diplomacy and Intelligence', *Diplomacy and Statecraft*, Vol. 9, No. 2 (1998), pp. 1–22, this p. 14.

19. John Dickie, *The New Mandarins: How British Foreign Policy Works* (London: I. B. Tauris, 2007), p. 82.

20. Philip Davies, 'Organisational Politics and the Development of Britain's Intelligence Producer/Consumer Interface', in Charters, Farson and Hastedt (eds), *Intelligence Analysis and Assessment*, p. 116.

21. Reginald Hibbert, 'Intelligence and Policy', *Intelligence and National Security*, Vol. 5, No. 1 (2008), pp. 110–28, this p. 113.

22. Ibid., p. 120.

23. Ibid., p. 125.

24. Cradock, *In Pursuit of British Interests*, p. 44.

25. Ibid.

26. Ibid.

27. See, for example, *Review of Intelligence on Weapons of Mass Destruction* (London: The Stationery Office, 2004).

28. Mark Curtis, *Web of Deceit: Britain's Real Role in the World* (London: Vintage Books, 2003), p. 210.

29. Ibid., p. 298.

30. Ibid., p. 1.

31. For a detailed overview, see Erhard Geissler and John Ellis van Courtland Moon, *Biological and Toxin Weapons: Research, Development and Use from the Middle Ages to 1945* (Oxford: Oxford University Press, 1999), p. 168.

32. Stockholm International Peace Research Institute, *The Problem of Chemical and Biological Warfare, Vol. 2: Chemical Weapons Today* (New York: Humanities Press, 1971), p. 189.

33. Darryl Howlett, 'UK Arms Control and Disarmament Policy on Chemical and Biological Weapons', in Mark Hoffman (ed.), *UK Arms Control in the 1990s* (Manchester: Manchester University Press, 1990), p. 151.

34. Ibid., p. 152.

35. Stockholm International Peace Research Institute, *The Problem of Chemical and Biological Warfare, Vol. 2: Chemical Weapons Today*, p. 189.

36. Geissler and Moon, *Biological and Toxin Weapons*, p. 168.

37. Howlett, 'UK Arms Control and Disarmament Policy on Chemical and Biological Weapons', p. 157.

38. See David Goldman, 'The Generals and the Germs: The Army Leadership's Response to Nixon's Review of Chemical and Biological Warfare Policies in 1969', *Journal of Military History*, Vol. 73 (April 2009), pp. 531–69.

39. Howlett, 'UK Arms Control and Disarmament Policy on Chemical and Biological Weapons', p. 158.

40. Information remains sparse in the public arena relating to these binary 'novichok' agents. Probably the definitive document containing information relating to these agents is Lev Federov, *Chemical Weapons in Russia: History, Ecology, Politics*

(Moscow Centre of Ecological Policy of Russia, 27 July 1994). For general background information, see Vil Mirzayanov and Lev Fedorov, 'A Poisoned Policy', *Moscow News Weekly*, No. 39 (1992); and Pal Aas, 'Future Considerations for the Medical Management of Nerve-Agent Intoxication', *Pre-hospital and Disaster Medicine*, Vol. 18, No. 3 (2003), pp. 208–16, especially p. 210.

41. Howlett, 'UK Arms Control and Disarmament Policy on Chemical and Biological Weapons', p. 162.

42. Ibid., p. 163.

43. *Active Diplomacy for a Changing World: The UK's International Priorities* (London: The Stationery Office, 2006).

44. Ibid., p. 18.

45. Ibid., p. 52.

46. Tony Blair, Speech to Trades Union Congress Conference (Blackpool, 10 September 2002), from www.number10.gov.uk

47. For the Australia Group and its efforts to harmonise international export controls in order to counter chemical and biological weapons proliferation, see www.australiagroup.net. Further information on the organisations listed here is available from the relevant websites: www.nuclearsuppliersgroup.org, www.mtcr.info/english/index.html and www.sgpproject.org (for G8 Global Partnership).

48. For further details on this, see http://www.fco.gov.uk

49. See http://www.fco.gov.uk. BERR was formally known as the Department for Trade and Industry (DTI).

50. *The Report of the Iraq Inquiry: Executive Summary* (London: The Stationery Office, 2016), para 806.

51. UNSC Resolution 687 was the 1990 Gulf War ceasefire resolution calling on Iraq to destroy all WMD programmes. Resolution 1441 was the 2002 finding of the Iraqi 'material breach' of Resolution 687; essentially this retrospectively authorised force to be used.

52. *Review of Intelligence on Weapons of Mass Destruction*, p. 42. UNSCOM is United Nations Special Commission and IAEA is International Atomic Energy Agency.

53. Ibid., p. 13.

54. *The Report of the Iraq Inquiry: Executive Summary*, paras 501 and 506.

55. *Review of Intelligence on Weapons of Mass Destruction*, p. 150.

56. Ibid., p. 34.

57. Ibid., p. 35.

58. *The Report of the Iraq Inquiry: Executive Summary*, para 507.

59. *Review of Intelligence on Weapons of Mass Destruction*, p. 150.

60. Ibid., p. 108.

61. *The Report of the Iraq Inquiry: Executive Summary*, para 514.

62. Ibid., para 518.

63. *Review of Intelligence on Weapons of Mass Destruction*, p. 107.

64. Ibid., p. 107.

65. Ibid., p. 152.

66. *The Report of the Iraq Inquiry: Executive Summary*, para 538.

67. *Review of Intelligence on Weapons of Mass Destruction*, p. 110.

68. *The Report of the Iraq Inquiry: Executive Summary*, para 807.

69. For a full report on this comment, see http://news.bbc.co.uk/1/hi/uk_politics/2721513.stm, accessed on 6 January 2010.

70. Steven Kettell, *Dirty Politics* (London: Zed Books, 2006), p. 3.

71. Bryan Burrough et al., 'The path to war', *Vanity Fair*, May 2004, p. 110.

72. Taken from http://www.number10.gov.uk/Page1712 on 6 January 2010.

73. Ibid., p. 113.

74. David Isenberg, *See, Speak and Hear No Incompetence: An Analysis of the Findings of The Commission on the Intelligence Capabilities of the United States Regarding Weapons of Mass Destruction* (British American Security Information Council BASIC Special Report, Special Report 2005.1, October 2005), this p. 19.

75. *Review of Intelligence on Weapons of Mass Destruction*, p. 153.

76. Percy Cradock, *Know Your Enemy—How the Joint Intelligence Committee Saw the World* (London: John Murray, 2002), cited in *The Report of the Iraq Inquiry: Executive Summary*, para 845.

4. FROM REFUSAL TO DISBELIEF: THE SOVIET UNION

1. For a detailed account of these events, see Tom Mangold and Jeff Goldberg, *Plague Wars: The Terrifying Reality of Biological Warfare* (New York: St Martin's Press, 1999), pp. 158–69.

2. Ibid.

3. Extract from 'Review Conferences: Second Review Conference: 8–26 September 1986', www.opbw.org/rev_cons/2rc/2rc_sum.htm, accessed on 16 April 2007.

4. Ibid.

5. A request for a copy of the Russian Federation Form F made to the UK FCO generated the following response: 'I am unable to send you a copy of the Russian Confidence Building Measures (CBM). CBMs are shared between governments and are not public documents.' Email correspondence, Wilkinson/FCO, 15 September 2006.

6. *Russian 1992 Confidence Building Measures Form F*, Box E1352, Harvard Sussex Project Archive, University of Sussex.

7. For a detailed overview of the Russian Form F submission in a publicly available source, see Nicolas Isla, 'Transparency in past offensive biological weapons programs: An analysis of Confidence Building Measure Form F 1992–2003', Occasional Paper No. 1, Hamburg Centre for Biological Arms Control, June 2006.

8. *Russian 1992 Confidence Building Measures Form F*, Box E1352, Harvard Sussex Project Archive, University of Sussex.

9. Ibid.

10. Ibid.

11. See Mangold and Goldberg, *Plague Wars: The Terrifying Reality of Biological Warfare*, pp. 106–7.

12. 'Yeltsin arms reduction statement', BBC News Monitoring, R920129049, CTV1E, 0900 hrs, 29 January 1992.

13. 'Decree of the President of the Russian Federation: On Ensuring Fulfilment of International Obligations in the Area of Biological Weapons dated 11 April 1992', US National Security Council Collection Files, document provided courtesy of Dr Ron Manley (formerly of the Organisation for the Prohibition of Chemical Weapons, The Hague).

14. Statement by Deputy Foreign Minister Berdennikov, Official Kremlin International News 1992, cited in Jan T. Knoph and Kristina S. Westerdahl, 'Re-Evaluating Russia's Biological Weapons Policy, as Reflected in the Criminal Code and Official Admissions: Insubordination Leading to a President's Subordination', *Critical Reviews in Microbiology*, Vol. 32, No. 1 (2006), pp. 1–13, this p. 4.

15. For a detailed overview, see Erhard Geissler and John Ellis van Courtland Moon (eds), *Biological and Toxin Weapons: Research, Development and Use from the Middle Ages to 1945* (Oxford: Oxford University Press, 1999).

16. From http://www.iemrams.spb.ru:8100/english/fort.htm on 29 May 2005.

17. Ken Alibek and Stephen Handelman, *Biohazard* (London: Hutchinson, 1999), p. 32.

18. Roger Roffey, Wilhelm Unge, Jenny Clevström, and Kristina Westerdahl, *Support to Threat Reduction of the Russian Biological Weapons Legacy—Conversion, Biodefence and the Role of Biopreparat* (Swedish Defence Research Agency, Stockholm, 2003), p. 97.

19. National Archive, Kew, Box WO 188/784, *Soviet Russia, Bacteriological Warfare*, page CX 9767, dated 17 January 1927.

20. Anthony Rimmington, 'Invisible Weapons of Mass Destruction: The Soviet Union's BW Programme and its Implications for Contemporary Arms Control', *Journal of Slavic Military Studies*, Vol. 13, No. 3 (September 2000), pp. 1–46, this p. 4.

21. Ibid., p. 4.

22. Igor Domaradskij and Wendy Orent, *Biowarrior: Inside the Soviet/Russian Biological War Machine* (New York: Prometheus Books, 2003), p. 127.

23. Barton Whaley, *Covert German Rearmament, 1919–1939: Deception and Misperception* (Lanham, MD: University Publications of America, 1984) p. 125.

24. Ibid., p. 101.

25. Walter Hirsch, *Soviet BW and CW Preparation and Capabilities (Hirsch Report)*, National Archives, Washington, USA, Reference (NAW) RG 319 G2, P-Project File, Box 3, p. 101. This report is widely considered in both academic and government circles to be the definitive document regarding both Soviet and German CBW

programmes: despite some shortcomings, its importance as a source document should not be underestimated.

26. Ibid., pp. 111–12.

27. National Archive, Kew, Box WO 208/4277, 'Report on the Interrogation of Professor H. Kliewe May 7th—11th 1945', by Major H. M. B. Adam, Major J. M. Barnes, Captain W. J. Cromartie, Captain Carlo Henze and Lieutenant J. W. Hofer, Reference A-B-C-H-H/149, page 7, dated 13 May 1945.

28. See both Alibek and Handelman, *Biohazard*; and Geissler and Moon (eds), *Biological and Toxin Weapons*, p. 165.

29. William E. Lexow and Julian Hoptman, *Studies in Intelligence* (CIA), Vol. 9 (Spring 1965), pp. 15–20, this p. 15.

30. From *The Soviet BW Program* (CIA, Scientific Intelligence Research Aid, Office of Scientific Intelligence, 24 April 1961), p. iii. (Obtained as a Freedom of Information Act document from www.cia.foia.gov on 10 September 2005.)

31. Mark Popovsky, *Manipulated Science* (New York: Doubleday, 1979), p. 72.

32. E. S. Levina, 'Eksperimental'naya Biologiya v Sisteme Bezopasnosti Rossii Vtoroi Polovinoi XX Veka: Biologicheskoe Oruzhie ili Zdravookhranenie?' (Experimental biology in the system of Russian security of the second half of the twentieth century: Biological weapons or healthcare?), in R. S. Golovina et al. (eds), *Nauka I Bezopasnost' Rossii: Istorichesko-Nauchnie, Metodologicheskie, Istorichesko-Tekhnicheskie Aspekty* (Science and security of Russia: Historico-scientific, methodological, historico-techical aspects) (Moscow: Nauka, 2000), p. 373, cited in Mark Wheelis, Lajos Rozsa and Malcolm Dando (eds), *Deadly Cultures* (Cambridge, MA: Harvard University Press, 2006), p. 134.

33. Domaradskij and Orent, *Biowarrior: Inside the Soviet/Russian Biological War Machine*, p. 143.

34. Wheelis, Rozsa and Dando (eds), *Deadly Cultures*, p. 135.

35. Ibid., p. 137.

36. National Archive, Kew, Box DEFE 44/205, Report from Ministry of Defence: Defence Intelligence Staff, Directorate of Scientific and Technical Intelligence, titled 'Reports, Notes and Memoranda', dated September 1960.

37. Confidential document 1.

38. National Archive, Kew, Box FCO 66/313, Report from Foreign and Commonwealth Office: Disarmament Department and Arms Control and Disarmament Department, titled 'Chemical and Biological Warfare', dated 16 July 1971.

39. Ibid., dated 4 February 1971.

40. Ibid.

41. Ibid., dated 16 March 1971.

42. Ibid., dated 9 December 1970.

43. Report to the National Security Council, *US Policy on Chemical and Biological Warfare Agents*, submitted by the Interdepartmental Political Military Group in

response to NSSM 59, dated 10 November 1969, Top Secret, Freedom of Information Act request obtained from http://www.gwu.edu on 19 April 2007.

44. Ibid.

45. Adam Roberts and Richard Guelff, *Documents on the Laws of War* (Oxford: Oxford University Press, 2004), p. 155.

46. National Archive, Kew, Box FCO 66/227, Foreign and Commonwealth Office: Disarmament Department and Arms Control and Disarmament Department, Registered Files (DS Series), undated.

47. From *Soviet Chemical and Biological Warfare Capabilities (NIE 11–11–69)* (CIA, National Intelligence Estimate, 13 February 1969), p. 9. (Obtained as a Freedom of Information Act document from www.cia.foia.gov on 10 September 2005.)

48. Ibid.

49. Jeanne Guillemin, *Biological Weapons* (New York: Columbia University Press, 2004), p. 126.

50. Mangold and Goldberg, *Plague Wars: The Terrifying Reality of Biological Warfare*, p. 53.

51. Ibid., p. 58.

52. National Archive, Kew, Box FCO 66/313, Foreign and Commonwealth Office: Disarmament Department and Arms Control and Disarmament Department, *Chemical and Biological Warfare*, dated 30 March 1971.

53. For a detailed examination of communism and arms control theory, see P. H. Vigor, *The Soviet View of Disarmament* (London: Macmillan Press, 1986).

54. Aleksand' G. Savel'yev and Nikolay N. Detinov, *The Big Five: Arms Control Decision Making in the Soviet Union* (Westport, CT: Praeger Publishers, 1995), p. 1.

55. Paul Bennet, *The Soviet Union and Arms Control* (Westport, CT: Praeger Publishers, 1989), p. 5.

56. Savel'yev and Detinov, *The Big Five: Arms Control Decision Making in the Soviet Union*, p. 7.

57. Jozef Goldblat, *Arms Control* (London: Sage Publications, 2003), p. 142.

58. Mangold and Goldberg, *Plague Wars: The Terrifying Reality of Biological Warfare*, p. 59.

59. Guillemin, *Biological Weapons*, p. 126.

60. President Richard Nixon, cited in Mangold and Goldberg, *Plague Wars*, p. 53.

61. National Security Adviser (Henry Kissinger), *Talking Points—Briefings for Congressional Leadership and Press*, dated 25 November 1969 (Top Secret), US NARA, Nixon Presidential Materials, NSC Files, Subject Files, Box 310, Chemical and Biological Warfare (Toxins etc.), Vol. 1.

62. See, for example, Wheelis, Rozsa and Dando (eds), *Deadly Cultures*; Leonard Cole, *The Eleventh Plague* (New York: Henry Holt and Co., 1997); and Judith Miller, Stephen Engelberg and William Broad, *Germs: The Ultimate Weapon* (New York: Simon & Schuster, 2001).

63. Arkady N. Shevchenko, *Breaking with Moscow* (New York: Alfred A. Knopf, 1985), p. 179.

64. Popovsky, *Manipulated Science*, p. 229.

65. For a definitive account, see Joseph D. Douglass, Jr, *Why the Soviets Violate Arms Control Treaties* (Washington, DC: Pergamon Brassey's, 1988), in particular ch. 6, Cheating and Deception.

66. Ibid., p. 63.

67. Confidential Interview A.

68. National Archive, Kew, Box DEFE 44/205, Ministry of Defence: Defence Intelligence Staff, Directorate of Scientific and Technical Intelligence: Reports, Notes and Memoranda, dated September 1960.

69. Confidential Document 1.

70. Churchill Archives Centre, The Papers of Vice Admiral Sir Louis Le Bailly, LEBY, Box 7 (6), Memorandum, The Development of a Defence Intelligence Staff Stage II: 1970–1975, p. 3.

71. Confidential Interview A.

72. Confidential Document 1.

73. Churchill Archives Centre, The Papers of Vice Admiral Sir Louis Le Bailly, LEBY, Box 7 (6), Memorandum, The Development of a Defence Intelligence Staff Stage II: 1970–1975, p. 13.

74. Confidential Document 1.

75. Confidential Interview A.

76. Confidential Interview B.

77. Confidential Interview A.

78. Confidential Interview B.

79. Confidential Interview B.

80. Confidential Interview A.

81. Confidential Interview A.

82. Ibid.

83. Ibid.

84. Confidential Interview A.

85. Ibid.

86. Ibid.

87. Confidential Interview A.

88. Ibid.

89. Confidential Interview B.

90. Ibid.

91. Churchill Archives Centre, The Papers of Vice Admiral Sir Louis Le Bailly, LEBY, Box 7 (3), Private note dated 20 January (year not annotated), pp. 1–2.

92. Ibid., p. 2.

93. Churchill Archives Centre, The Papers of Vice Admiral Sir Louis Le Bailly, LEBY, Box 7 (6), Memorandum, The Development of a Defence Intelligence Staff Stage II: 1970–1975, p. 9.

94. Confidential Interview A.
95. Confidential Interview B.
96. Confidential Interview A.
97. Confidential Interview B.
98. Written correspondence Wilkinson/Robinson dated 11 February 2008.
99. See *Soviet Chemical and Biological Warfare Capabilities (NIE 11–11–69)*, (CIA, National Intelligence Estimate, 13 February 1969), pp. 9–10. (Obtained as a Freedom of Information Act document from www.cia.foia.gov on 10 September 2005.)
100. Written correspondence Wilkinson/Robinson dated 11 February 2008.
101. Confidential Interview A.

5. PLAYING THE LONG GAME: CHALLENGE AND PROOF

1. See, for example, Jeanne Guilleman, *Anthrax: The Investigation of a Deadly Outbreak* (London: University of California Press, 2001), especially pp. 183–4.
2. Confidential Interview A.
3. Ibid.
4. See DIA Weekly Intelligence Summary, Excerpt: Soviet Biological Accident Rumoured, dated 9 November 1979, Secret, Defence Intelligence Agency; Freedom of Information Act request obtained from http://www.gwu.edu on 19 April 2007. For detailed accounts of the Sverdlovsk outbreak, see Guillemin, *Anthrax*; and Joshua Lederberg (ed.), *Biological Weapons: Limiting the Threat* (Cambridge, MA: MIT Press, 2001), especially pp. 193–210.
5. CIA Intelligence Report, *Biological Warfare—USSR: Additional Rumours of an Accident at the Biological Warfare Institute in Sverdlovsk*, dated 15 October 1979, Top Secret, Central Intelligence Agency; Freedom of Information Act request obtained from http://www.gwu.edu on 19 April 2007.
6. For other declassified intelligence reports, see Robert Wampler and Thomas Blanton, *US National Security Archive Electronic Briefing Book No. 61, Vol. V: Anthrax at Sverdlovsk, 1979*, 15 November 2001, at http://www.gwu.edu, accessed on 16 August 2006.
7. DIA Defence Science and Technology Study: *Biological Warfare Capabilities—Warsaw Pact*, dated March 1990, Secret, Defence Intelligence Agency; Freedom of Information Act request obtained from http://www.gwu.edu on 19 April 2007.
8. Victor Israelyan, 'Fighting Anthrax: A Cold Warrior's Confession', *Washington Quarterly*, Vol. 25, No. 2 (2002), pp. 17–29, this p. 17.
9. Victor Israelyan, *On the Battlefields of the Cold War* (Pennsylvania, PA: Penn State University Press, 2003), p. 315.
10. For official intelligence reports, see CIA Special National Intelligence Estimate, *Use of Toxins and Other Lethal Chemicals in Southeast Asia and Afghanistan*, Vol. 1: Key Judgements, dated 2 February 1982, classification deleted, Central Intelligence

Agency; Freedom of Information Act request obtained from http://www.gwu. edu on 19 April 2007. For other narrative and investigative accounts, see Grant Evans, *The Yellow Rainmakers* (London: Verso Editions, 1983); and Sterling Seagrave, *Yellow Rain* (New York: M. Evans and Co., 1981).

11. Julian Perry Robinson, *Chemical and Biological Warfare Developments: 1985* (Oxford: Oxford University Press, 1986), p. 13.

12. CIA Special National Intelligence Estimate, *Use of Toxins and Other Lethal Chemicals in Southeast Asia and Afghanistan*, Vol. 1: Key Judgements, dated 2 February 1982, classification deleted, Central Intelligence Agency; Freedom of Information Act request obtained from http://www.gwu.edu on 19 April 2007.

13. Confidential Interview A.

14. Ibid.

15. Confidential Interview B.

16. For a detailed autobiographical survey of his experiences whilst chairman of JIC and foreign policy adviser to the Prime Minister, see Percy Cradock, *In Pursuit of British Interests: Reflections on Foreign Policy Under Margaret Thatcher and John Major* (London: John Murray, 1997)

17. Mark Urban, *UK Eyes Alpha* (London: Faber and Faber, 1997), p. 4.

18. Cradock, *In Pursuit of British Interests*, p. 42.

19. Confidential Interview A.

20. Ibid.

21. Interview Wilkinson/Sir Percy Cradock, 17 January 2007.

22. James Adams, *The New Spies* (London: Random House, 1994), p. 275.

23. Thatcher Archive, TV Interview for BBC at 10 Downing Street, London, John Cole and Margaret Thatcher, 17 December 1984.

24. Interview Wilkinson/Sir Percy Cradock, 17 January 2007.

25. Adams, *The New Spies*, p. 275.

26. Michael Herman, *Intelligence Power in Peace and War* (Cambridge: Cambridge University Press, 1996), p. 33.

27. Ibid., p. 34.

28. Confidential Interview A.

29. Ibid.

30. Ibid.

31. Ibid.

32. Confidential Interview A.

33. For a history of the Iran–Iraq War, see Dilip Hiro, *The Longest War* (London: Paladin, 1990).

34. Confidential Interview A.

35. Ibid.

36. Stephen Dorril, *MI6: Fifty Years of Special Operations* (London: Fourth Estate, 2000), p. 764.

37. Confidential Interview A.

38. Ibid.

39. Ibid.

40. Ibid.

41. Confidential Interview B.

42. Confidential Document.

43. Ibid.

44. There are numerous accounts of the defection of Pasechnik; see, for example, Tom Mangold and Jeff Goldberg, *Plague Wars: The Terrifying Reality of Biological Warfare* (New York: St Martin's Press, 1999), especially pp. 91–105; Adams, *The New Spies*, pp. 270–83; and Urban, *UK Eyes Alpha*, pp. 129–42.

45. Robert Donaldson and Joseph Nogee, *The Foreign Policy of Russia* (New York: M. E. Sharpe, 2002), p. 94.

46. Graeme Gill and Roger Markwick, *Russia's Stillborn Democracy? From Gorbachev to Yeltsin* (Oxford: Oxford University Press, 2000), p. 21.

47. F. S. Northedge, *The Foreign Policy of the Powers* (Faber and Faber, London, 1968), p. 93.

48. Gill and Markwick, *Russia's Stillborn Democracy?* pp. 21–3.

49. Ibid.

50. Transcript of President's State of the Union Address to Joint Session of Congress, *New York Times*, 24 January 1980, cited in Donaldson and Nogee, *The Foreign Policy of Russia*, p. 100.

51. Donaldson and Nogee, *The Foreign Policy of Russia*, p. 101.

52. Richard Herrmann and Richard Ned Lebow (eds), *Ending the Cold War* (New York: Palgrave Macmillan, 2004), p. 37.

53. Gill and Markwick, *Russia's Stillborn Democracy?* p. 26.

54. Herrmann and Lebow, *Ending the Cold War*, p. 37.

55. Stephen White, Alex Pravda and Zvi Gitelman (eds), *Developments in Soviet Politics* (London: Palgrave Macmillan, 1990), p. 18.

56. Gill and Markwick, *Russia's Stillborn Democracy?* p. 27.

57. George Breslauer, *Gorbachev and Yeltsin as Leaders* (Cambridge: Cambridge University Press, 2002), p. 53.

58. Donaldson and Nogee, *The Foreign Policy of Russia*, p. 105.

59. Herrmann and Lebow, *Ending the Cold War*, p. 49.

60. Donaldson and Nogee, *The Foreign Policy of Russia*, p. 104.

61. Herrmann and Lebow, *Ending the Cold War*, p. 39.

62. Pavel Palazchenko, *My Years with Gorbachev and Shevardnadze: The Memoir of a Soviet Interpreter* (Pennsylvania, PA: Penn State University Press, 1997), p. 81.

63. White, Pravda and Gitelman (eds), *Developments in Soviet Politics*, p. 286.

64. Christopher Bluth, *New Thinking in Soviet Military Policy* (London: Pinter Publishers, 1990), p. 23.

65. Ibid., p. 23.

66. Carl Jacobsen (ed.), *The Soviet Defence Enigma: Estimating the Burden and Costs* (Oxford: Oxford University Press, 1987), p. 170.

67. Gill and Markwick, *Russia's Stillborn Democracy?* p. 37.

68. Donaldson and Nogee, *The Foreign Policy of Russia*, p. 104.

69. Francois Heisbourg (ed.), *The Strategic Implications of Change in the Soviet Union* (London: Macmillan, 1990), p. 35.

70. Herrmann and Lebow, *Ending the Cold War*, p. 44.

71. Ibid., p. 44.

72. Ibid., p. 49.

73. Ibid., p. 44.

74. Michael Krepon, *Arms Control in the Reagan Administration* (Lanham, MD: University Press of America, 1989), p. 171.

75. Ibid., p 199.

76. Ibid., p. 210.

77. Donaldson and Nogee, *The Foreign Policy of Russia*, p. 105.

78. Jack Matlock, *Autopsy on an Empire* (New York: Random House, 1995), p. 96.

79. Margaret Thatcher, *The Downing Street Years* (New York: HarperCollins, 1993), p. 450.

80. For a full account of this example, including information on the 'Top Hat' and 'Fedora' agents, see David Wise, *Cassidy's Run* (New York: Random House, 2000), pp. 188–95.

81. Text of reportage from press conference (SU/8061/A1/6) shown on Soviet television at 14.45 hrs GMT on 19 September 1985, from University of Sussex, Harvard Sussex Project information bank archive, file: USSR.

82. Peter Samuel, *New York City Tribune*, 28 August 1986, p. 1.

83. Adams, *The New Spies*, p. 35.

84. Gill and Markwick, *Russia's Stillborn Democracy?* p. 37.

85. Dale Herspring, 'On perestroika: Gorbachev, Yazov and the military', *Problems of Communism*, Vol. 36 (July–August 1987), pp. 99–107, this p. 103; cited in Bluth, *New Thinking in Soviet Military Policy*, p. 32.

86. Mangold and Goldberg, *Plague Wars: The Terrifying Reality of Biological Warfare*, p. 93.

87. News Chronology, *Chemical Weapons Convention Bulletin* (Journal of the Harvard Sussex Program on CBW Armament and Arms Limitation), No. 18 (December 1992), p. 15.

88. Confidential Interview A.

89. Ibid.

90. Interview Wilkinson/Sir Rodric Braithwaite, 6 February 2007.

91. Ibid.

92. Interview Wilkinson/Sir Percy Cradock, 17 January 2007.

93. Urban, *UK Eyes Alpha*, p. 133.

94. Confidential Interview A.

95. Ibid.

96. Interview Wilkinson/Sir Percy Cradock, 17 January 2007.

97. Mangold and Goldberg, *Plague Wars: The Terrifying Reality of Biological Warfare*, p. 104.

98. Ibid., p. 106.

99. Ibid., p. 108.

100. Ibid., p. 111.

101. Confidential Interview A.

102. Ibid.

103. Ibid.

104. Mangold and Goldberg, *Plague Wars: The Terrifying Reality of Biological Warfare*, p. 111.

105. Ibid., p. 114.

106. Interview Wilkinson/Sir Rodric Braithwaite, 6 February 2007.

107. Confidential Interview A.

108. News Chronology, *Chemical Weapons Convention Bulletin* (Journal of the Harvard Sussex Program on CBW Armament and Arms Limitation), No. 7 (February 1990), p. 12.

109. Confidential Interview A.

110. Ibid.

111. Ken Alibek and Stephen Handelman, *Biohazard* (London: Hutchinson, 1999), p. 145.

112. Confidential Interview A.

113. Confidential Interview C.

114. Mangold and Goldberg, *Plague Wars: The Terrifying Reality of Biological Warfare*, p. 111.

115. Ibid., p. 139.

116. Ibid., p. 140.

117. Ibid., p. 158.

118. Interview Wilkinson/Sir Rodric Braithwaite, 6 February 2007.

119. Email Wilkinson/Braithwaite dated 8 February 07 as follow-up question to Interview Wilkinson/Sir Rodric Braithwaite, 6 February 2007.

120. Confidential Interview A.

121. Breslauer, *Gorbachev and Yeltsin as Leaders*, p. 31.

122. Ibid., p. 110.

123. Boris Yeltsin, *Against the Grain* (New York: Summit Books, 1990), p. 165.

124. Ibid., p. 64.

125. Interview Wilkinson/Sir Rodric Braithwaite, 6 February 2007.

126. John Dunlop, *The Rise of Russia and the Fall of the Soviet Empire* (Princeton, NJ: Princeton University Press, 1993), p. 38.

127. Ibid., p. 39.

128. Breslauer, *Gorbachev and Yeltsin as Leaders*, p. 40.

129. *Komsomol'skoe znamya*, 7 June 1991, cited in Dunlop, *The Rise of Russia and the Fall of the Soviet Empire*, p. 24.

130. Dunlop, *The Rise of Russia and the Fall of the Soviet Empire*, p. 11.

131. Yeltsin, *Against the Grain*, p. 199.

132. Ibid., p. 128.

133. Dunlop, *The Rise of Russia and the Fall of the Soviet Empire*, p. 23.

134. 'Yeltsin byl pod kolpakom u Kryuchkova', *Rabochaya tribuna*, 7 January 1992, cited in Dunlop, *The Rise of Russia and the Fall of the Soviet Empire*, p. 23.

135. Breslauer, *Gorbachev and Yeltsin as Leaders*, pp. 211 and 193.

136. Interview Wilkinson/Sir Rodric Braithwaite, 6 February 2007.

137. News Chronology, *Chemical Weapons Convention Bulletin* (Journal of the Harvard Sussex Program on CBW Armament and Arms Limitation), No. 17 (September 1992), p. 14.

138. Interview Wilkinson/Sir Rodric Braithwaite, 6 February 2007.

139. Donaldson and Nogee, *The Foreign Policy of Russia*, p. 11.

140. Heisbourg, *The Strategic Implications of Change in the Soviet Union*, p. 38; and Donaldson and Nogee, *The Foreign Policy of Russia*, p. 10.

141. Herrmann and Lebow, *Ending the Cold War*, p. 46.

142. Pavel Baev, *The Russian Army in a Time of Troubles* (London: Sage Publications, 1996), p. 31.

143. Donaldson and Nogee, *The Foreign Policy of Russia*, p. 15.

144. Mangold and Goldberg, *Plague Wars: The Terrifying Reality of Biological Warfare*, p. 159.

145. 'Decree of the President of the Russian Federation: On Ensuring Fulfilment of International Obligations in the Area of Biological Weapons dated 11 April 1992', US National Security Council Collection Files, document provided courtesy of Dr Ron Manley (formerly of the Organisation for the Prohibition of Chemical Weapons, The Hague).

146. 'Russian 1992 Confidence Building Measures Form F', Box E1352, Harvard Sussex Project Archive, University of Sussex.

147. Interview Wilkinson/Sir Rodric Braithwaite, 6 February 2007.

148. Breslauer, *Gorbachev and Yeltsin as Leaders*, p. 157.

149. Michael Dobbs, 'Yeltsin Appeals for American Aid', *Washington Post*, 18 June 1992, p. 1, cited in Breslauer, *Gorbachev and Yeltsin as Leaders*, p. 211.

150. Interview Wilkinson/Sir Rodric Braithwaite, 6 February 2007.

151. Baev, *The Russian Army in a Time of Troubles*, p. 28.

152. Letter from Douglas Hurd (UK Foreign Secretary) and Lawrence Eagleburger (US Secretary of State) to Andrei Kozyrev (Russian Foreign Minister) on 24 August 1992, English translation obtained from Mark Urban, Diplomatic Editor, BBC Newsnight, London on 14 February 2007.

153. Confidential Interview A.

154. Ibid.

155. Ibid.

156. Ibid.

157. Confidential email correspondence (Interview I).

6. STRANGER THAN FICTION: THE CURIOUS CASE OF SOUTH AFRICA

1. Helen E. Purkitt and Stephen S. Burgess, *South Africa's Weapons of Mass Destruction* (Bloomington, IN: Indiana University Press, 2005), p. 1.

2. T. V. Paul, *Power Versus Prudence: Why Nations Forgo Nuclear Weapons* (Montreal: McGill-Queen's University Press, 2000), p. 113.

3. Nicolas Isla, 'Transparency in Past Offensive Biological Weapons Programmes: An Analysis of Confidence Building Measure Form F 1992–2003' (Hamburg Centre for Biological Arms Control, Occasional Paper No. 1, June 2006), p. 3.

4. Ibid., p. 19.

5. Marlene Burger and Chandre Gould, *Secrets and Lies: Wouter Basson and South Africa's Chemical and Biological Warfare Programme* (Cape Town: Zebra Press, 2002), p. 13.

6. National Archive, Kew, Box AVIA 22/1735, Report to Chief of the (UK) General Staff, Future of the Chemical Defence Factories, dated 7 September 1945.

7. National Archive, Kew, Box WO 188/820, Liaison on Chemical Warfare Matters, Field Trials, dated 26 July 1944.

8. National Archive, Kew, Box WO 188/820, Minutes of the Fourteenth Meeting of the Board of Management C.D. Factories (UDF), Casualties, dated 15 December 1943.

9. National Archive, Kew, Box AVIA 22/1735, Summary of 'H' Accident Statistics for Six Months Ending 31 December 1942, dated 21 January 1943.

10. National Archive, Kew, Box AVIA 22/1739, Memo from Air Ministry, London, dated 11 October 1945.

11. National Archive, Kew, Box AVIA 22/1735, Letter from South African Consulate to Ministry of Supply, London, dated 17 December 1946.

12. National Archive, Kew, Box AVIA 22/1735, Letter from Chief of the General Staff (UK), to Chairman and Managing Director of the Industrial Development Corporation of South Africa, dated 4 February 1945.

13. National Archive, Kew, Box AVIA 22/1735, Report to Chief of the (UK) General Staff, Future of the Chemical Defence Factories, dated 7 September 1945.

14. Purkitt and Burgess, *South Africa's Weapons of Mass Destruction*, p. 87.

15. Chandre Gould and Alastair Hay, 'The South African Biological Weapons Programme', ch. 9 of Mark Wheelis, Lajos Rozsa and Malcolm Dando (eds), *Deadly Cultures: Biological Weapons Since 1945* (Cambridge, MA: Harvard University Press, 2006), p. 192.

16. Richard Van Der Walt, Hannes Steyn and Jan Van Loggerenberg, *Armament and Disarmament: South Africa's Nuclear Experience* (New York: iUniverse Inc., 2005), p. 30.

17. Ibid., p. 30.

18. Rodney Davenport and Christopher Saunders, *South Africa: A Modern History* (Basingstoke: Macmillan Press, 2000), p. 460.

19. Der Walt, Steyn and Loggerenberg, *Armament and Disarmament*, p. 32.

20. Purkitt and Burgess, *South Africa's Weapons of Mass Destruction*, p. 64.

21. Davenport and Saunders, *South Africa: A Modern History*, p. 547.

22. See ibid., pp. 547–56.

23. Robert Davies and Dan O'Meara, 'Total Strategy in Southern Africa: An Analysis of South African Regional Policy Since 1978', *Journal of Southern African Studies*, Vol. 11, No. 2 (April 1985), pp. 183–211, this p. 183.

24. Gavin Cawthra, *Brutal Force: The Apartheid War Machine* (London: IDAF, 1986), pp. 24–5, cited in Chandre Gould and Peter Folb, *Project Coast: Apartheid's Chemical and Biological Warfare Programme* (United Nations Publication, 2002), p. 11.

25. Joseph Hanlon, *Beggar Your Neighbours* (London: Catholic Institute for International Relations, 1986), p. 7, cited in Gould and Folb, *Project Coast*, p. 11.

26. Der Walt, Steyn and Loggerenberg, *Armament and Disarmament*, pp. 13–15.

27. Purkitt and Burgess, *South Africa's Weapons of Mass Destruction*, p. 60.

28. Ibid., p. 59.

29. Davies and O'Meara, 'Total Strategy in Southern Africa', p. 184.

30. Ibid., p. 12.

31. Burger and Gould, *Secrets and Lies*, p. 13.

32. Gould and Folb, *Project Coast*, p. v.

33. Burger and Gould, *Secrets and Lies*, p. 13.

34. Gould and Folb, *Project Coast*, p. 2.

35. Ibid., pp. 89–90.

36. Reduced Defence Command Council, Minutes of meeting held at 07h30 on 25 October 1990 at Samik, Appendix A: Proposed philosophy for chemical warfare for the South African Defence Principles and feedback about the current status in the SA Defence Force, SADF document handed to TRC by Gen. Knobel during the TRC hearings into chemical and biological warfare in June and July 1998, cited in Gould and Folb, *Project Coast*, p. 2.

37. Tom Mangold and Jeff Goldberg, *Plague Wars* (London: Macmillan, 1999), p. 214.

38. Colonel Eugene de Koek, interview with Phillip van Niekerk, Pretoria Central Prison, 3 March 1996, cited in Stephen Ellis, 'The Historical Significance of South Africa's Third Force', *Journal of Southern African Studies*, Vol. 24, No. 2 (June 1998), pp. 261–99, this p. 268.

39. Mangold and Goldberg, *Plague Wars*, p. 218.

40. Purkitt and Burgess, *South Africa's Weapons of Mass Destruction*, p. 87.

41. Ibid., p. 89.

42. Confidential Interview D.

43. Purkitt and Burgess, *South Africa's Weapons of Mass Destruction*, p. 96.

44. Burger and Gould, *Secrets and Lies*, p. 17.

45. Purkitt and Burgess, *South Africa's Weapons of Mass Destruction*, p. 85.

46. Gould and Folb, *Project Coast*, p. 1.

47. Wouter Basson, *Projek Coast: Moontlikhede vir privatisering* (Project Coast: Possibilities for privatisation), SADF Document GG/UG/302/6/COAST/BFW, 28 November 1989, pp. 2–4, cited in Chandre Gould and Peter Folb, 'The South African Chemical and Biological Warfare Program: An Overview', *Non-Proliferation Review* (Fall/Winter 2000), pp. 10–23, this p. 12.

48. Ibid., p. 19.

49. 'Briefing to President Mandela on the Defensive Chemical and Biological Warfare Programme of the SADF and the RSA's Position WRT the CWC and BWC', Top Secret document TRC 20, dated 18 August 1994, made available to TRC. Document held in Harvard Sussex Program Archive, University of Sussex, unfiled and unreferenced by archive.

50. Purkitt and Burgess, *South Africa's Weapons of Mass Destruction*, p. 97.

51. Burger and Gould, *Secrets and Lies*, p. 1.

52. Ibid., p. 20.

53. Purkitt and Burgess, *South Africa's Weapons of Mass Destruction*, p. 103.

54. Gould and Folb, *Project Coast*, p. 8.

55. Confidential Interview D.

56. Ibid.

57. Translation of 'Wouter Basson's report (in Africaans) of his trip to the USA re C & B; in 1981'. Document held in Harvard Sussex Program Archive, University of Sussex, unfiled and unreferenced by archive.

58. Mangold and Goldberg, *Plague Wars*, p. 242.

59. Confidential Interview D.

60. Burger and Gould, *Secrets and Lies*, p. 91.

61. Confidential Interview D.

62. Confidential Interview E with Foreign Office Official, 18 October 2007.

63. Confidential Interview D.

64. 'Testing of Racial Weapons Alleged', *Washington Times*, 13 August 1984, p. 6. It is likely that the term 'ethnic chemical weapons' refers to genetically engineered biological agents.

65. 'Israel, South Africa said to create ethnic weapon', *Baltimore Sun*, 3 April 1985.

66. Gordon Thomas, *Gideon's Spies* (London: JR Books, 2008), pp. 493–4.

67. Confidential Interview D.

68. Honore M. Catudal, Jr, *Israel's Nuclear Weaponry* (London: Grey Seal Books, 1991), p. 71.

69. 'Brothers in Arms—Israel's secret pact with South Africa', *Guardian*, 7 February 2006.

70. Confidential Interview D.

71. Confidential Interview D.

72. Chemical and Biological Defence Establishment, 'Report on an Investigation into the Alleged use of Chemical Weapons in Mozambique, January 1992', Doc-

ument labelled TRC 85 and stamped 'Pretoria, S.A. Army Headquarters 10 March 1992'. Obtained from the Archive of the Harvard Sussex Project, University of Sussex, unreferenced and unfiled. It does seem unlikely that a single shell exploding would deliver sufficient agent to cause these casualties—some reports referred to a drone aircraft being used to deliver agent. This would seem to be a more likely means to cause the level of casualties detailed.

73. Dr B. J. Davey, 'An Account of Attempts to Initiate a Joint South African/United Kingdom Investigation into Alleged Use of Chemical Warfare in Mozambique', Document labelled TRC 90, stamped SECRET, and dated 17 March 1992. Obtained from the Archive of the Harvard Sussex Project, University of Sussex, unreferenced and unfiled.

74. Ibid.

75. Ibid.

76. Report of the mission dispatched by the Secretary General to investigate an alleged use of chemical weapons in Mozambique, dated 12 June 1992, from http:// unbisnet.un.org on 13 August 2008.

77. Chemical and Biological Defence Establishment, 'Report on an Investigation into the Alleged use of Chemical Weapons in Mozambique, January 1992', Document labelled TRC 85 and stamped 'Pretoria, S.A. Army Headquarters 10 March 1992'. Obtained from the Archive of the Harvard Sussex Project, University of Sussex, unreferenced and unfiled.

78. Ibid.

79. From www.fwdklerk.org.za/download_docs/06_05_07_Steyn_Investigation_ A.doc on 13 August 2008.

80. Ibid.

81. Staff Paper Prepared for the Steyn Commission on Alleged Dangerous Activities of SADF Components, Top Secret, document not labelled. Obtained from the Archive of the Harvard Sussex Project, University of Sussex, unreferenced and unfiled.

82. Lt. Gen. D. Knobel, 'Briefing to President Mandela on the Defensive Chemical and Biological Warfare Programme of the SADF and the RSA's Position WRT the CWC and BWC', Top Secret, document labelled TRC 20, dated 18 August 1994. Obtained from the Archive of the Harvard Sussex Project, University of Sussex, unreferenced and unfiled.

83. Confidential Interview D.

84. From www.fwdklerk.org.za/download_docs/06_05_07_Steyn_Investigation_ A.doc on 13 August 2008.

85. Hilton Hamann, *Days of the Generals* (Cape Town: Zebra Press, 2001), p. 191.

86. Confidential Interview D.

87. Confidential Interview D. The use of the word 'offshoots' here is interesting, perhaps suggesting that this information was obtained off the back of other operations, or indeed from agents deeply immersed in the programmes themselves.

88. Burger and Gould, *Secrets and Lies*, p. 174.

89. 'British Arms Dealers Linked to Apartheid's Brigadier Death', *Observer*, 7 June 1998, p. 8.

90. Burger and Gould, *Secrets and Lies*, p. 95.

91. Confidential Interview D.

92. In particular, see James Sanders, *Apartheid's Friends: The Rise and Fall of South Africa's Secret Service* (London: John Murray, 2006), p. 328.

93. Confidential Interview D.

94. Confidential Interview F.

95. South African Chemical and Biological Warfare Programme, Trial Report Number 48, covering 23–26 July 2001, from section headed Monday 23 July. Taken from http://ccrweb.ccr.uct.ac.za on 2 July 2008.

96. Confidential Interview D.

97. Burger and Gould, *Secrets and Lies*, p. 114.

98. Confidential Interview D.

99. Ibid.

100. Mangold and Goldberg, *Plague Wars*, p. 241.

101. Purkitt and Burgess, *South Africa's Weapons of Mass Destruction*, p. 104.

102. Mangold and Goldberg, *Plague Wars*, p. 280.

103. Purkitt and Burgess, *South Africa's Weapons of Mass Destruction*, p. 70

104. Mangold and Goldberg, *Plague Wars*, p. 262.

105. From 'Plague Wars: South Africa, the Secret Killings', Paladin Pictures, 1998. Author's own collection.

106. Purkitt and Burgess, *South Africa's Weapons of Mass Destruction*, p. 170.

107. For the full details of this incident, see 'Jailed "go-between" on UK–Iran arms deals is freed to keep MI6 secrets out of court', *Guardian*, Saturday 6 February 1999, taken from www.guardian.co.uk on 2 July 2008.

108. See Burger and Gould, *Secrets and Lies*, p. 158.

109. Hamann, *Days of the Generals*, p. 209.

110. Confidential Interview D.

111. Ibid.

112. Robin Renwick, *Unconventional Diplomacy in Southern Africa* (London: Macmillan, 1997), p. 149.

113. Confidential Interview, cited in Mangold and Goldberg, *Plague Wars*, p. 270.

114. T. J. Byron, *Elimination Theory: The Secret Covert Networks of Project Coast* (Baltimore, MD: PublishAmerica, 2004), p. 164.

115. Confidential Interview D.

116. Sanders, *Apartheid's Friends*, p. 333.

117. Confidential Interviews and Dr Wouter Basson Interview, June 1998, cited in Mangold and Goldberg, *Plague Wars*, p. 274.

118. Sanders, *Apartheid's Friends*, p. 332.

119. Lt. Gen. D. Knobel, 'Briefing to President Mandela on the Defensive Chemical and Biological Warfare Programme of the SADF and the RSA's Position WRT the CWC and BWC', Top Secret, document labelled TRC 20, dated 18 August 1994. Obtained from the Archive of the Harvard Sussex Project, University of Sussex, unreferenced and unfiled.

120. Interview with F. W. de Klerk, taken from http://www.pbs.org/wgbh/pages/frontline/shows/plague/sa/deklerk.html on 16 August 2006.

121. Interview with Ronnie Kasrils, Deputy Defence Minister, taken from http://www.pbs.org/wgbh/pages/frontline/shows/plague/sa/deklerk.html on 12 August 2008.

122. Sanders, *Apartheid's Friends*, p. 333.

123. Confidential Interview D.

124. Ibid.

125. Ibid.

126. Lt. Gen. D. Knobel, 'Briefing to President Mandela on the Defensive Chemical and Biological Warfare Programme of the SADF and the RSA's Position WRT the CWC and BWC', Top Secret, document labelled TRC 20, dated 18 August 1994. Obtained from the Archive of the Harvard Sussex Project, University of Sussex, unreferenced and unfiled.

127. Ibid.

128. Ibid.

129. Purkitt and Burgess, *South Africa's Weapons of Mass Destruction*, p. 189.

130. South African Council for the Non-Proliferation of Weapons of Mass Destruction, 'National Policy on Non-Proliferation, Disarmament and Arms Control', taken from www.thedti.gov.za on 4 February 2008.

131. Ibid.

132. Ibid.

133. South Africa in fact signed the BTWC on 10 April 1972, ratifying it on 3 November 1975. South Africa signed the CWC on 14 January 1993, with it entering into force on 29 April 1997.

134. Isla, 'Transparency in Past Offensive Biological Weapons Programmes: An Analysis of Confidence Building Measure Form F 1992–2003', p. 19.

135. Ibid.

136. Ibid.

137. Mangold and Goldberg, *Plague Wars*, p. 282.

138. Chandre Gould, telephone interview with former US ambassador Priceman Lyman, 14 June 2001, cited in Gould and Hay, 'The South African Biological Weapons Programme', ch. 9 of Wheelis, Rozsa and Dando (eds), *Deadly Cultures*, p. 202.

139. Wheelis, Rozsa and Dando (eds.), *Deadly Cultures*, p. 203.

140. Confidential Interview E with Foreign Office Official, 18 October 2007.

141. Email correspondence, Wilkinson/Dr Graham Pearson, 31 October 2007.

142. Ibid.

143. Confidential Interview D.

144. Daniel P. Knobel, in the transcript of the TRC hearing on Chemical and Biological Warfare, Cape Town, 12 June 1998, cited in Gould and Folb, 'The South African Chemical and Biological Warfare Program: An Overview', p. 13.

145. Confidential Interview D.

146. Email correspondence, Wilkinson/Dr Graham Pearson, 31 October 2007.

147. Confidential Interview D.

148. Ibid.

149. Email correspondence, Wilkinson/Dr Graham Pearson, 31 October 2007.

150. Confidential Interview D.

151. Confidential Interview D.

152. For an overview of the downfall of Basson, see Mangold and Goldberg, *Plague Wars*, pp. 276–82.

153. See Hansard, 7 April 2005, Column 1755W; 11 January 2006, Column 658W; 16 January 2006, Column 986W; 18 January 2006, Column 1327W; 28 June 2006, Column 440W; 27 February 2008, Column 1708W; 2 May 2008, Column 430.

154. Confidential Interview D.

155. Truth and Reconciliation Commission of South Africa Report, *Special Investigation: Chemical and Biological Warfare*, Vol. 2, Ch. 6, p. 522.

156. Burger and Gould, *Secrets and Lies*, p. 9.

157. Confidential Interview D.

7. GAS AND GADDAFI: LIBYAN CHEMICAL WEAPONS DEVELOPMENT

1. Taken from www.whitehouse.gov/news/releases/2003/12/20031219–14.html on 30 September 2008. This web page contains further information on the entire content of the Libyan statement.

2. From http://new.bbc.co.uk/1/hi/world/africa/3336627.stm on 30 September 2008.

3. Ibid.

4. It is important to stress here that the research carried out for the purposes of this chapter does not consider issues associated with Libyan nuclear research and development programmes. Whilst the activities of the A. Q. Khan network in particular are widely reported in terms of their relationship with the Libyan nuclear programme, especially in the context of intelligence (as discussed by Lord Butler in the *Review of Intelligence on Weapons of Mass Destruction* in the wake of the Iraq war in 2004), it did not seemingly impact on or relate to Libyan attempts to acquire chemical or biological weapons.

5. Taken from www.whitehouse.gov/news/releases/2003/12/20031219-14.html on 1 October 2008.

6. *Review of Intelligence on Weapons of Mass Destruction* (London: The Stationery Office, 2004), p. 22.

7. Dafna Hochman, 'Rehabilitating a Rogue: Libya's WMD Reversal and Lessons for US Policy', *Parameters* (Spring 2006), pp. 63–78, this p. 64.

8. Malfrid Braut-Hegghammer, 'Libya's Nuclear Turnaround: What Lies Beneath?' *RUSI Journal* (December 2006), pp. 52–4, this p. 53.

9. Dirk Vandewalle, *A History of Modern Libya* (Cambridge: Cambridge University Press, 2006), p. 175.

10. Hochman, 'Rehabilitating a Rogue', p. 74.

11. *Review of Intelligence on Weapons of Mass Destruction*, p. 20.

12. Tim Niblock, *Pariah States and Sanctions in the Middle East* (Boulder, CO: Lynne Rienner Publishers, 2001), p. 12.

13. Peter Wilson, 'The Contribution of Intelligence Services to Security Sector Reform', *Conflict, Security and Development*, Vol. 5, No. 1 (April 2005), pp. 87–107, this p. 89.

14. Richard Aldrich, *The Hidden Hand: Britain, America and Cold War Secret Intelligence* (London: John Murray, 2001), p. 5.

15. Len Scott, 'Secret Intelligence, Covert Action and Clandestine Diplomacy', *Intelligence and National Security*, Vol. 19, No. 2 (Summer 2004), pp. 322–41, this p. 331.

16. Ibid.

17. Shlomo Shpiro, 'The CIA as Middle East Peace Broker?' *Survival*, Vol. 45, No. 2 (Summer 2003), pp. 91–112, this p. 91.

18. William E. Odom, *Fixing Intelligence: For a More Secure America* (New Haven, CT: Yale University Press), p. 186, cited in John D. Stempel, 'Covert Action and Diplomacy', *International Journal of Intelligence and Counterintelligence*, Vol. 20, No. 1 (2007), pp. 122–35, this p. 133.

19. Robert Waller, 'Case Study 2: Libya', *The Deterrence Series* (Alexandria, VA: Chemical and Biological Arms Control Institute, 1998), p. 3.

20. Ibid., p. 3.

21. For one of the earliest media reports concerning Libyan CW found during the research for this book, see Simon Russel, 'Libya obtained Soviet nerve gas warheads and passed some of them to Syria and Iran', *Sunday Telegraph*, 24 November 1986.

22. Daniel Byman, *Deadly Connections: States that Sponsor Terrorism* (Cambridge: Cambridge University Press, 2007), p. 291.

23. Ibid.

24. Ibid.

25. Timothy Naftali, *Blind Spot: The Secret History of American Counterterrorism* (New York: Basic Books, 2005), p. 127.

26. 'Libya gives nerve gas warheads to Syria and Iran, paper says', *Baltimore Sun*, 11 November 1986, p. 2.

27. See, for example, Ronald Bruce St John, *Libya: From Colony to Independence* (Oxford: One World, 2008), p. 187.

28. Elaine Sciolino, 'US Sends 2,000 Gas Masks to the Chadians', *New York Times*, 25 September 1987, p. 6.

29. International Defence Digest, *International Defence Review*, Vol. 20 (November 1987), p. 1455, University of Sussex, Harvard Sussex Project archive, file C3 (Libya).

30. Michael R. Gordon, 'US Suspects Libyans of Chemical Arms Site', *New York Times*, 17 December 1987, p. 5.

31. Transcript AAS-1/89, Milavnews, Vol. 28 (327), January 1988, p. 17, University of Sussex, Harvard Sussex Project archive, file C3 (Libya).

32. See Vandewalle, *A History of Modern Libya*, in particular pp. 77–82.

33. Nicholas Laham, *The American Bombing of Libya* (London: McFarland and Company, 2008), p. 203.

34. 'Gaddafi says Arabs have right to germ warfare', Reuters, Tunis, 30 March 1996.

35. Laham, *The American Bombing of Libya*, p. 203.

36. Ibid., p. 204.

37. David Shayler, 'Don't Shoot the Messenger', *Observer*, Sunday 27 August 2000, from www.guardian.co.uk/uk/2000/aug/27/davidshayler.comment1 accessed on 22 June 2009.

38. R. A. Davidson, *Reagan vs. Qaddafi: Response to International Terrorism?* (R. A. Davidson, 2002), p. 113, cited in Laham, *The American Bombing of Libya*, p. 204.

39. Niblock, *Pariah States and Sanctions in the Middle East*, p. 12.

40. Chronology, *Chemical Weapons: Conference on Disarmament* (Brookline, MA: Institute for Defense and Disarmament Studies, 1988).

41. Harvey Morris, 'Libya ships nerve gas consignment to the Somalians', *The Independent*, 23 November 1988, p. 11.

42. 'Libya Denies US Charge on Chemical Weapons', *International Affairs*, TASS (Moscow), 22 November 1988, p. 27.

43. 'Al-Qaddafi Interviewed on Chemical Plant', transcript, JANA (Tripoli), 25 December 1988, University of Sussex, Harvard Sussex Project Archive, file C3 (Libya).

44. Bill Gertz, 'Libya producing chemical weapons at full capacity', *Washington Times*, 21 May 1990.

45. Bill Gertz, '2nd chemical arms plant spied in Libya', *Washington Times*, 21 May 1990, pp. A1 and A6.

46. Vandewalle, *A History of Modern Libya*, p. 116.

47. Christopher Walker, 'Another gesture as Gaddafi alters his image', *The Times*, 7 June 1991, p. 3.

48. 'British firm helped Gaddafi make poison gas missiles', *Sunday Times*, 5 April 1992, p. 1.

49. CIA report to US Senate Hearing before the Committee on Governmental Affairs, *Proliferation Threats of the 1990s*, 27 August 1993, University of Sussex, Harvard Sussex Project Archive, file C3 (Libya) 1993–5.

50. W. Andrew Terrill, 'Libya and the Quest for Chemical Weapons', *Conflict Quarterly*, Vol. XIV, No. 1 (Winter 1994), pp. 47–61.

51. Tim Weiner, 'Huge Chemical Arms Plant Near Completion in Libya, US Says', *New York Times*, 25 February 1996, p. 8.

52. 'Tarhunah Tunnels Part of Great Man-Made River Project', *Weekly Economic Report*, MENA (Cairo), 13 April 1996.

53. Joshua Sinai, 'Libya's pursuit of Weapons of Mass Destruction', *Non-Proliferation Review*, Vol. 4, No. 3 (Spring/Summer 1997), pp. 92–100, this p. 98.

54. Confidential Interview G.

55. Ibid.

56. Ibid.

57. Ibid.

58. Alan George and Shyam Bhatia, 'Londoner built plant for Qaddafi', *Observer*, 8 January 1989, p. 1.

59. Jesse Birnbaum, 'The Mysterious Doctor B', *Time*, 27 February 1989, pp. 16–17.

60. Ibid.

61. Confidential Interview G.

62. Confidential Interview H with Foreign Office official, 15 April 2008.

63. Confidential Interview G.

64. Birnbaum, 'The Mysterious Doctor B'.

65. George and Bhatia, 'Londoner built plant for Qaddafi', p. 1.

66. Jean Pascal Zanders, 'Chemical Weapons Proliferation: Mechanisms Behind the Imhausen/Rabta Affair', *Vredesonderzoek Interdisciplinaire Periodiek*, Interfacultair Overlegorgaan Voor Vredesonderzoek Van De Vrue, Universiteit Brussel, 1990, p. 29.

67. Whilst the role of Barbouti will not be considered further here, it is interesting to note that in 1994 it was reported that he had faked his own death, including a burial, in 1990. For further details, see Peter Koenig and Tim Kelsey, 'Afterlife of an arms fixer', *Independent on Sunday*, 17 July 1994, p. 6.

68. 'Published Information on the Rabta Plant', *Arms Control Reporter*, September 1989, University of Sussex, Harvard Sussex Project Archive, file C3 (Libya).

69. Ibid.

70. Confidential Interview G.

71. Zanders, 'Chemical Weapons Proliferation', p. 30.

72. Ibid., p. 31.

73. 'Britain "has proof" of gas plant', *Daily Telegraph*, 5 January 1989, p. 1.

74. Joe Connell, Marie Colvin and Brian Moynahan, 'British Spies found Libyan Poison Plant', *Sunday Times*, 6 January 1989, p. 1.

75. Confidential Interview G.

76. Maurice Weaver, 'Does Libya have anything to hide?' *Daily Telegraph*, 5 January 1989, p. 15.

77. Confidential Interview G.

78. Kenneth Timmerman, *The Poison Gas Connection: Western Suppliers of Unconventional Weapons and Technologies to Iraq and Libya* (Los Angeles, CA: Simon Wiesenthal Centre, 1990), pp. 31–2.

79. Confidential Interview G.

80. Chronology, *Arms Control Reporter*, September 1988, University of Sussex, HSP Archive, file C3 (Libya).

81. Chronology, *Arms Control Reporter*, December 1989, University of Sussex, HSP Archive, file C3 (Libya).

82. Confidential Interview G.

83. Ibid.

84. Ibid.

85. Michael R. Gordon, 'Plant Said to Make Poison Gas in Libya is Reported on Fire', *New York Times*, 15 March 1990, p. A1.

86. Confidential Interview G.

87. Adel Darwish, 'Libya fire "almost certainly a hoax"', *Independent*, 10 April 1990, p. 12.

88. Confidential Interview G.

89. Michael Evans, 'Spy agencies join forces to combat secret arms trade', *The Times*, 20 September 1993, p. 13.

90. John Sweeney and Denis Staunton, 'Heathrow tunneller built Gaddafi weapons chamber', *Observer*, 22 March 1998, p. 1.

91. Evans, 'Spy agencies join forces to combat secret arms trade', p. 13.

92. Confidential Interview G.

93. An excellent account of Libya's attempts to procure nuclear technologies is given in Gordon Corera, *Shopping for Bombs* (London: Hurst & Co., 2006).

94. BBC 2 *Newsnight*, interview with William Waldegrave (Minister of State, Foreign and Commonwealth Office), 5 January 1989.

95. Ibid.

96. Waller, 'Case Study 2: Libya', p. 6.

97. Confidential Interview G.

98. Ibid.

99. See Con Coughlin, 'S Africa agrees weapons deal with Gaddafi', *Sunday Telegraph*, 21 June 1998.

100. Michael Theodoulou, 'Saddam sends scientists to Libya for safety', *The Times*, 13 February 1998, p. 18.

101. Confidential Interview G.

102. Ronald Bruce St John, *Libya: From Colony to Independence* (Oxford: One World, 2008), p. 254.

103. Waller, 'Case Study 2: Libya', p. 17.

104. Vandewalle, *A History of Modern Libya*, p. 89.

105. Niblock, *Pariah States and Sanctions in the Middle East*, p. 64.

106. Ray Takeyh, 'The Rogue Who Came in from the Cold', *Foreign Affairs*, Vol. 80, No. 3 (May–June 2001), pp. 62–72.

107. Ibid.

108. Ibid.

109. Ibid.

110. Ibid.

111. Braut-Hegghammer, 'Libya's Nuclear Turnaround', p. 53.

112. Judith Miller, 'How Gaddafi Lost his Groove: The complex surrender of Libya's WMD', dated 16 May 2006, University of Sussex, Harvard Sussex Programme Archive, file C3 (Libya), unpublished work.

113. Braut-Hegghammer, 'Libya's Nuclear Turnaround', p. 53.

114. Confidential Interview G.

115. Ibid.

116. Ibid.

117. Miller, 'How Gaddafi Lost his Groove'.

118. Ibid.

119. Martin Indyk, 'The Iraq war did not force Gaddafi's hand', *Financial Times*, 9 March 2004, p. 21.

120. Michael Evans, 'Libya knew game was up before Iraq war', *The Times*, 13 March 2004, p. 8.

121. Miller, 'How Gaddafi Lost his Groove'.

122. Sanders, *Apartheid's Friends*, p. 370.

123. Ian Black, 'Terror talks: would contacting al-Qaida be a step too far?' *Observer*, 15 March 2008, p. 20 (UK News section). See also http://www.guardian.co.uk/politics/2008/mar/18/northernireland.northernireland

124. Wyn Bowen, *Libya and Nuclear Proliferation*, Adelphi Paper (Oxford: Routledge, International Institute for Strategic Studies, 2006), p. 65.

125. Confidential Interview H with Foreign Office official, London, 15 April 2008.

126. Confidential Interview G.

127. Confidential Interview H.

128. In particular, see Corera, *Shopping for Bombs*, ch. 8 which details the negotiations referred to here.

129. Ibid., p. 183.

130. Confidential Interview H.

131. Bowen, *Libya and Nuclear Proliferation*, p. 71.

132. *Libya coming in from the Cold*, Jane's Islamic Affairs Analyst, March 2005, p. 7.
133. See, for example, Rupert Cornwell, 'White House claims about Tripoli's WMD "were exaggerated"', *Independent*, 26 March 2006, p. 5; and William J. Broad, 'US Wrong on Libya, group says: Nuclear capabilities "distorted" in briefing', *International Herald Tribune*, 26 March 2004, p. 3.
134. As stated in *Review of Intelligence on Weapons of Mass Destruction*, p. 20.

8. BEFORE INTELLIGENCE FAILED: WAS IRAQ A WATERSHED?

1. As has been discussed elsewhere in this book, the inquiries with published reports are: *Review of Intelligence on Weapons of Mass Destruction* (London: The Stationery Office, 2004) [Butler Report]; *Report of the Inquiry into the Circumstances Surrounding the Death of Dr David Kelly C.M.G* (London: The Stationery Office, 2004) [Hutton Report]; *The Decision to Go to War with Iraq* (London: The Stationery Office, 2003) [Foreign Affairs Select Committee, FASC Report]; *Iraq Weapons of Mass Destruction—Intelligence and Assessments* (London: The Stationery Office, 2003) [Intelligence and Security Committee, ISC Report].
2. *Review of Intelligence on Weapons of Mass Destruction*, p. 150.
3. Ibid.
4. Ibid.
5. *The Report of the Iraq Inquiry: Executive Summary* (London: The Stationery Office, 2016), para. 574.
6. Ian Davis and Andreas Persbo, 'After the Butler Report: Time to Take on the Group Think in Washington and London', *BASIC Papers: Occasional Papers on International Security Policy*, No. 46 (July 2004), accessed at www.basicint.org/pubs/Papers/BP46.htm on 6 February 2009.
7. *Review of Intelligence on Weapons of Mass Destruction*, p. 151.
8. Ibid., p. 153.
9. Ibid.
10. *National Intelligence Machinery* (London: The Stationery Office, 2006), pp. 37 and 20.
11. Central Intelligence Agency (Office of Public Affairs), *A Consumer's Guide to Intelligence* (Washington, DC: CIA, 1999), p. vii.
12. *National Intelligence Machinery*, p. 37.
13. Ibid., p. 37.
14. BASIC (British American Security Information Council) Biological Weapons Update, taken from www.basicint.org/update/BWU040713.htm on 6 February 2010.
15. *Review of Intelligence on Weapons of Mass Destruction*, p. 114.
16. Comments made by Professor Conor Gearty in the Introduction to W. Runciman (ed.), *Hutton and Butler: Lifting the Lid on the Workings of Power* (Oxford: Oxford University Press, 2005).

17. Interview with Lord Butler, 7 February 2007, cited in Anthony Seldon, *Blair Unbound* (London: Simon & Schuster, 2007), p. 138.

18. Ibid., p. 137.

19. Taken from http://news.bbc.co.uk/1/hi/uk_politics/8471091.stm on 23 January 2010.

20. Gordon Thomas, *Inside British Intelligence* (London: JR Books, 2009), p. 365.

21. Michael Herman, 'Intelligence and the Iraqi threat: British joint intelligence after Butler', *Journal of the Royal United Services Institute*, Vol. 149, No. 4 (2004), pp. 18–24.

22. For further development of this argument, see Stephen Kettell, *Dirty Politics: New Labour, British Democracy and the Invasion of Iraq* (London: Zed Books, 2006).

23. *Report of the Iraq Inquiry: Executive Summary* (London: The Stationery Office, 2016), para. 838.

24. For information relating to SIS BW intelligence gathering in Russia in the 1920s, see, for example, National Archive, Kew, Box WO 188/784, *Soviet Russia, Bacteriological Warfare*, page CX 9767, dated 17 January 1927. For details on UK intelligence involvement in CBW through ALSOS, see, for example, John D. Hart, 'The ALSOS Mission, 1943–1945: A Secret U.S. Scientific Intelligence Unit', *International Journal of Intelligence and Counterintelligence*, Vol. 18 (2005), pp. 508–37.

25. The type of detail relating to German and Soviet CBW obtained via Project ALSOS can be seen, for example, in National Archive, Kew, Box WO 208/4277, *Report on the Interrogation of Professor H. Kliewe May 7ᵗʰ –11ᵗʰ 1945*, by Major H. M. B. Adam, Major J. M. Barnes, Captain W. J. Cromartie, Captain Carlo Henze and Lieutenant J. W. Hofer, Reference A-B-C-H-H/149, page 5, dated 13 May 1945. From this date up until the early 1970s, information relating to UK intelligence involvement in countering CBW is notable only by its absence from the public record.

26. According to Professor Richard Aldrich of the University of Warwick, in the 1990s the UK was spending upwards of £2.5 billion on intelligence, of which 89 per cent was spent on SIGINT, as developed later in this chapter.

27. Interview Wilkinson/Sir Rodric Braithwaite, London, 6 February 2007.

28. Robert Jervis, 'Reports, Politics, and Intelligence Failures: The Case of Iraq', *Journal of Strategic Studies*, Vol. 29, No. 1 (2006), pp. 3–52, this p. 29.

29. Ibid., p. 27.

30. Jonathan Aitken, *Pride and Perjury* (London: HarperCollins, 2000), pp. 4–7.

31. For a useful discussion on the differences between information and intelligence, see Christopher Andrew, Richard J. Aldrich and Wesley K. Wark (eds), *Secret Intelligence: A Reader* (Abingdon: Routledge, 2009), especially pp. 5–7.

32. Ibid., p. 114.

33. Philip Davies, 'A Critical Look at Britain's Spy Machinery: Collection and Analysis on Iraq' (New York: CIA, Studies in Intelligence, 2007).

34. *Review of Intelligence on Weapons of Mass Destruction*, p. 103.

35. Michael, S. Goodman, 'The Dog That Didn't Bark: The Joint Intelligence Committee and Warning of Aggression', *Cold War History*, Vol. 7, No. 4 (2007), pp. 529–51. The full text of the Nicoll Report is reproduced here.

36. See the interview with Lord Butler, 7 February 2007, cited in Seldon, *Blair Unbound*, pp. 137–8.

37. *Review of Intelligence on Weapons of Mass Destruction*, p. 160.

38. Jervis, 'Politics and Intelligence Failures: The Case of Iraq', p. 28.

39. See, for example, Christopher Hill, *The Changing Politics of Foreign Policy* (Basingstoke: Palgrave Macmillan, 2003), p. 66.

40. Ibid.

41. Jervis, 'Politics and Intelligence Failures: The Case of Iraq', p. 36.

42. Ibid., p. 35.

43. Ibid., p. 10.

44. See Paul Williams, 'Who's Making UK Foreign Policy?' *International Affairs*, Vol. 80, No. 5 (2004), pp. 909–29, especially pp. 921–4.

45. Lawrence Freedman, 'War in Iraq: Selling the Threat', *Survival*, Vol. 46, No. 2 (Summer 2004), pp. 7–50, this p. 39.

46. Ibid.

INDEX

INDEX

INDEX

INDEX

INDEX

INDEX